Clinical Interpretation of the Wechsler Adult Intelligence Scale

Clinical Interpretation of the Wechsler Adult Intelligence Scale

Irla Lee Zimmerman, Ph.D.

and

James M. Woo-Sam, Ph.D.

with Alan J. Glasser, Ph.D.

GRUNE & STRATTON New York and London

Library of Congress Cataloging in Publication Data

Zimmerman, Irla Lee.

Clinical interpretation of the Wechsler Adult Intelligence Scale (WAIS).

Includes bibliographies.

1. Wechsler adult intelligence scale. I. Woo-Sam, James M., 1932- joint author. II. Title. [DNLM: 1. Intelligence tests. BF 431 Z73c 1973]
BF431.Z53 153.9'32 72-11825
ISBN 0-8089-0780-8

Grune & Stratton, Inc.
111 Fifth Avenue, New York, New York 10003

Library of Congress Catalog Card Number 72-11825
International Standard Book Number: 0-8089-0780-8

Printed in the United States of America

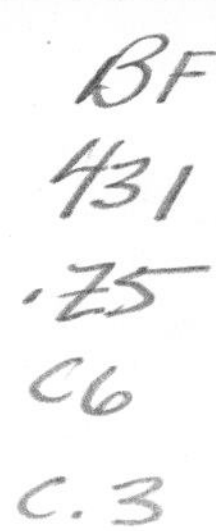

Irla Lee Zimmerman, Ph.D., is a clinical psychologist in private practice in Whittier, California. Dr. Zimmerman, a diplomate in clinical psychology, is co-author of *Clinical Interpretation of the Wechsler Intelligence Scale for Children.*

James M. Woo-Sam, Ph.D., is a Psychologist at Rancho Los Amigos Hospital in Downey, California.

Alan J. Glasser, Ph.D., is co-author, with Dr. Zimmerman, of *Clinical Interpretation of the Wechsler Intelligence Scale for Children.*

The results of our examination have no value if separated from all comment; they must be interpreted.

—A. Binet, 1908

Contents

NOMENCLATURE

The abbreviation WAIS will be used throughout this book to indicate the Wechsler Adult Intelligence Scale. The names of the subtests also appear in abbreviated form throughout the book. The single letters I, C, A, S, D, and V stand for the Verbal subtests Information, Comprehension, Arithmetic, Similarities, Digits, and Vocabulary, respectively. The two-letter combinations DS, PC, BD, PA, OA correspond to the Performance subtests Digit Symbol, Picture Completion, Block Design, Picture Arrangement, and Object Assembly respectively. FIQ, VIQ, and PIQ stand for Full scale IQ, Verbal IQ, and Performance IQ respectively. DQ stands for Deterioration Quotient.

CHAPTER 1

THE WAIS AS A TEST INSTRUMENT

HISTORY

The original Wechsler Bellevue was developed by David Wechsler in 1939 in the course of his work at the Department of Psychiatry at New York City's Bellevue Hospital. The scale was designed to evaluate the intellectual functioning of the older child and adult and was offered as an alternative to the Stanford-Binet forms L and M which clinical evidence had demonstrated to be unsuitable for use with adults.

Two versions of the Wechsler Bellevue were offered, form I and form II, although form II was not developed until approximately five years later with the purpose of providing an alternate in test-retest situations. Form II did not receive the acceptance accorded to form I, and in 1949 Wechsler adapted and modified items from this scale in constructing the Wechsler Intelligence Scale for Children (WISC). In so doing the original goal of providing an alternate the Binet for the measurement of adult intelligence was changed since the WISC covered the ages five through fifteen.

The ready acceptance of the WISC was accompanied by problems regarding the use of the Wechsler Bellevue I. The two scales overlapped over half of the age range covered by the WISC. Consequently when in 1955 a revision of the Wechsler Bellevue I was completed, the overlap was eliminated, the new scale being designed specially for older adolescents and adults (16 years and above). As if to reflect the new emphasis, the revised scale was renamed the Wechsler Adult Intelligence Scale (WAIS).

Generally the WAIS is an expanded version of the older Wechsler Bellevue I with items added to increase reliability.

The original format relative to item specifications and their modes of presentation was retained, modified to reflect the desirable alterations experience and improvement in scaling techniques over the previous sixteen years had indicated as necessary. Perhaps the most important technical innovation was the use of better sampling procedures. In contrast to the original standardization sample which was drawn almost wholly from an eastern all-white population, the WAIS was standardized on a sample size almost 70 percent greater (1081 to 1700), and drawn from a wide array of urban and rural areas and representing non-whites in direct proportion to their incidence in the general population.

Within five years of its introduction the WAIS was one of the most frequently used psychological tests. Sundberg (1961) reported that it ranked sixth in use in clinical services in the United States. Silverstein (1963a) noted a similar rank at institutions for the mentally retarded. The scale continues to retain its popularity. Lubin, Wallis, and Paine (1971) found in their survey of institutions, community mental health centers, counseling agencies, and Veteran Administration settings that it was second only to the Bender Gestalt in use. They also noted that in many agencies the WAIS forms part of a no-deviation accepted quartet of WAIS, Bender Gestalt, Rorschach, and Draw a Person.

In view of such popularity it might be helpful to consider briefly situations when the WAIS should not be used. One such situation arises in the evaluation of the severely retarded adult. Standard tables in the manual do not provide full scale IQ scores under 40. A "gray area" of testing is that involving the borderline retarded. As will be shown in the other tests chapter (Chapter 2), the WAIS may be overestimating the intellectual levels of such individuals. Higher up the range, in the evaluation of the gifted, the ceiling is too low, thereby leading to an underestimating of the intellectual level. That this theoretical possibility does indeed occur is supported by the study of Kennedy, Willcutt, and Smith (1963). Mathematically gifted adolescents obtained a mean Performance IQ of only 125.

Table 1–1

EXTRAPOLATED WAIS FULL-SCALE IQS

	Age Group									
Scaled Score	*16–17*	*18–19*	*20–24*	*25–34*	*35–44*	*45–54*	*55–64*	*65–69*	*70–74*	*75 up*
10	44	42	40	40	43	47	51	54	60	65
9	44	42	40	40	42	46	50	53	59	64
8	43	41	39	39	42	46	50	52	59	64
7	43	41	39	39	41	45	49	52	58	63
6	42	40	38	38	40	45	48	51	58	63
5	42	40	38	37	40	44	48	51	57	62
4	41	39	37	37	39	43	47	50	56	62
3	40	38	36	36	39	43	47	49	56	61
2	40	38	36	36	38	42	46	49	55	60
1	39	37	35	35	37	42	45	48	55	60

Source: From A. B. Silverstein, WISC and WAIS IQs for the mentally retarded, *American Journal of Mental Deficiency*, 1963, 67, 617–618.

Silverstein (1963) has attempted to extent the usefulness of the WAIS in the evaluation of the retarded by providing extrapolated full scale IQ score equivalents for scaled scores of 10 and below. This is only a partial solution, for even if the equivalents are accurate, a scaled score of ten can be obtained with zero scores on several of the eleven subtests in which case it would be difficult to determine the subject's range of abilities. See Table 1-1.

As yet no solution has been offered relative to the problem of overestimation at the borderline level of intelligence, and the underestimation of the gifted. For this latter group, the WAIS may be of use in estimating suspected loss in intellectual function due to either functional or organic deterioration.

In conclusion, the authors advocate that the use of the WAIS be based on a thorough understanding of the strengths and weaknesses of the scale. This understanding will enable the user to determine the situations and conditions where the WAIS will be the choice over several available alternates. The WAIS is a valuable instrument but there are occasions when it may have little to offer when the time required for administration, scoring, and interpretation is contrasted with the actual needs of the patient. The skilled clinician will make the decisions as the situations arise.

WHERE IN THE BATTERY

If a decision has been made to administer the WAIS, consideration should be given to its placement in the test battery. In some cases, however, as in the evaluation of intellectual skills for educational, vocational, and rehabilitation purposes, the WAIS is often the only major test used. When a battery of tests is administered, as in the evaluation of the emotionally disturbed subjects, the question of placement within the battery is an important issue.

Meyer (1961) suggests that the value of the Wechsler in such circumstances is the provision of a measure of reality testing. Projective measures can be likened to x-rays used to detect as yet unobservable pathology, while the WAIS serves as a measure of how the subject copes with the here and now. Invasion of pathology into WAIS responses, therefore, is far more ominous than examples found in such tests as the Rorschach. This view corroborates the findings by Stone and Dellis (1960), who reported less pathology in the WAIS records of schizophrenics than in their projective test responses. Piotwroski (1958) recommends that the Rorschach precede the WAIS so that the reality-oriented response set needed to respond to a test of intelligence does not carry over to limit the measure of personality. In contrast, L'Abate (1964) suggests, following Rappaport et al. (1945), that a test of intelligence should be given before a projective test such as the Rorschach. Grisso and Meadow (1967) specifically explored the effects of test interference when the Rorschach preceeded the WAIS. They noted impairment on certain subtests (discussed in the subtest chapters to follow).

The present authors find the WAIS an ideal beginning for most test batteries. In content, as well as in purpose, it is less threatening, compared to projective tests, to the emotionally disturbed and serves to foster testing rapport.

MAJOR DIMENSIONS OF THE WAIS

Since the WAIS subtests can be treated by sections as well as independently, and since any number of combinations are possible, in subsequent chapters each of the subtests will be discussed individually and as they are combined to form brief tests. Focus here centers on combinations constituting specific indexes and factorial entities.

Verbal Versus Performance IQ (VIQ=PIQ)

All Wechsler scales supply independent verbal and performance IQ scores. Clinicians consider that the differences between the two scores provide diagnostic clues. Discussing the WAIS, Wechsler (1958, p. 160) himself advised that "in most instances a difference of 15 or more IQ points may be interpreted as diagnostically significant." Blatt and Allison (1968) state their view of verbal-performance discrepancy more explicitly, perhaps with some exaggeration: "It allows the clinician to describe the individual's unique organization of psychological function and from this to infer the defenses, the nature and quality of drives and impulses, the degree of pathology, as well as his assets and capacities for adaptation and coping" (p. 437).

Newland and Smith (1967) summarized differences between verbal and performance IQs necessary to satisfy the 0.05 and 0.01 confidence levels, as computed from standardization data. For three age levels, 18–19, 25–34, and 45–54, a difference of 10 points between the two IQs was sufficient to reach the 0.05 level. For the two younger age levels, a difference of 13 points was sufficient to reach the 0.01 level, but for subjects 45 to 54 years of age, this dropped to 12 points.

Often overlooked by those concerned with verbal-performance differences is the fact that a discrepancy of as much as 25 points occurred once in every 100 subjects of the standarization population. While a discrepancy of 13 or more points might be statistically significant, Guertin, Rabin, Frank, and Ladd (1962) estimate that such differences are not unusual in the general population until they reach a magnitude of 25 points or more. Postulated significances based solely on the magnitude of the differences, ignoring clinical observations, therefore, are of limited diagnostic value.

Recognition of this fact has led to hypotheses specifying the direction of differences and the associated clinical implications.

Verbal IQ Superior to Performance IQ

Verbal IQ greater than performance IQ appears to be a characteristic of right-hemisphere or diffuse brain damage. In their review of the WAIS, Guertin, Ladd, Frank, Rabin, and Hiester (1966) conclude, "For the present, it is relatively safe to assume that a VIQ > PIQ pattern is not just characteristic of cerebral pathology sui generis, but may be indicative of pathology in the right hemisphere or of a more diffuse kind" (p. 401). Their 1971 review offers additional support. "Individuals with right-hemisphere damage show greater performance impairment than verbal. However right hemisphere dominance for non-verbal perceptual organization is not clearly deducible" (p. 325).

Verbal IQ higher than performance IQ has also been reported for adolescent girls with ovarian dysgenesis (Cohen, 1962), for subjects of low intelligence with "infection" or "other" central nervous system pathology (Fisher, 1960), murderers pleading insanity and given a psychotic diagnosis (Kahn, 1968), for older black delinquents (Henning & Levy, 1967), black homeless men (Levinson, 1964), and first-time applicants for shelter care (Levinson, 1965). Additionally, Blatt and Allison (1968) consider a higher verbal score to be the characteristic pattern in the bright normal and superior IQ ranges, supported by Kennedy et al. (1963) and general college samples (Plant, 1958). Blatt and Allison further mention this pattern as diagnostic of depression since the condition "often involves psychomotor retardation on tasks with time limits, and those subtests which require active manipulation tend to reflect this retardation" (p. 436).

Verbal IQ Below Performance IQ

A verbal IQ below the performance IQ appears also to be characteristic of organicity. With one exception (Smith, 1966), all the studies reviewed by Guertin et al. (1971) indicate this pattern in left-hemisphere damaged persons. In the Duke, Bloor, Nugent, and Majzoub study (1968) patients with left-sided lesions gained significantly on performance IQ postoperatively, but they did not make equivalent gains on verbal IQ.

One large diagnostic group consistently demonstrating this pattern appears to be juvenile delinquents. Gorotto (1961) noted VIQ < PIQ for runaways and truants and those charged with drinking, theft, or murder. Kahn (1968) confirmed the pattern for sociopaths, although not for murderers pleading insanity and given a psychotic diagnosis, previously mentioned. Additionally, Blatt and Allison (1968) observe that the verbal IQ tends to be lower than its performance counterpart in the lower intelligence ranges and that in the diagnostic entities this also holds true for hysteric and narcissistic personalities. However, as Frank (1970) points out, narcissistic neurosis has been used interchangeably with such terms as latent schizophrenia, psychotic character, ambulatory schizophrenia, schizoid personality, and preschizophrenic personality.

Conclusion

The question is not whether VIQ-PIQ differences are significant, but rather what such differences signify. The situation is analogous to elevation in body temperature. Fever is clearly an abnormal condition. However, fever per se cannot be regarded as diagnostic of any specific disease since it is associated with any number of disease conditions. Likewise, VIQ-PIQ differences should be regarded as one of the more common clues in which the subject tested deviates from normal expectancy. The significance of the deviation can be established only by other clues more specific and differentiating.

THE DETERIORATION QUOTIENT (DQ)

Wechsler's original deterioration quotient was derived from the basic observations that the full-scale IQ (FIQ) decreases with increasing age and that the decreases are largely a result of impaired performances on certain subtests. The deterioration quotient, or DQ, is the ratio between those subtests in which performance remains fairly constant and those in which impaired performance is evident. Originally intended as a measure of mental deterioration due to aging, the index was soon expanded to include any deterioration attributable to psychosis, brain damage, or the normal aging process. Payne (1960) specifically criticized this expansion as unwarranted.

The index devised for the Wechsler Bellevue was later modified for the WAIS. Wechsler's current formula groups I, V, PC, and OA as subtests that remain constant and are designated "Hold" (H); S, D, DS, and BD are grouped as subtests on which performance deteriorates, and are designated "Don't Hold" (DH). Pictorially, the formula is represented as:

$$\text{WAIS DQ} = \frac{H - DH}{H}$$

$$\frac{DH}{H} = \frac{S + D + DS + BD}{I + V + PC + OA}$$

Norman (1966) analyzed this formula for sex differences and pointed out that, as presently computed, males will show greater deterioration than females. To correct for this bias, he proposed separate formulas, one for males and one for females. The male ratio is expressed:

$$\text{male } \frac{DH}{H} = \frac{S + D + DS + BD}{I + A + PC + OA}$$

The female ratio varies slightly:

$$\text{female } \frac{DH}{H} = \frac{S + D + DS + PA}{I + V + BD + OA}$$

Norman then allowed that it was more pragmatic to use Wechsler's formula for males and his own revised version for females.

Nevertheless, Bersoff (1970) tested Norman's male version on organics, psychotics, and controls. Despite statistically significant differences between the organics and control group, the Norman DQ did not provide a reliable indication of deterioration.

Kraus (1966) proposed another modification. Using hospitalized undifferentiated depressives, undifferentiated schizophrenics, and undifferentiated psychoneurotics and personality disorders, he empirically derived the following Hold–Don't Hold ratios:

$$\text{Depressive} = \frac{DH}{H} = \frac{DS + PC + PA + OA}{I + C + A + V}$$

$$\text{Schizophrenic} = \frac{DH}{H} = \frac{D + DS + PA + BD + OA}{I + C + S + V + PC}$$

$$\text{Neurotic and personality disorder} = \frac{DH}{H} = \frac{A + DS + BD + OA}{C + S + V + PC}$$

It is evident that deterioration of intellectual functioning is not constant within diagnostic groups or for both sexes. Wechsler's original formulation had tended to ignore the complexity that is involved. While the modifications could be a step in the right direction, Wechsler's statement that "published studies have not given too much support to the claims . . . regarding the validity of the Hold–Don't Hold Index" (1958, p. 213) remains the last word.

FACTOR ANALYTIC DIMENSIONS

As applied to the WAIS, factor analysis ideally should identify the major dimensional components inherent in the scale. This method can provide a rigorous criterion for constructing brief forms and allow the user to select specific dimensions for special application.

Unfortunately, theory and practice are not always congruent. In the first place, different types of analysis tend to produce different results. For example, while Cohen (1957) was able to compress all the variables involved in the eleven WAIS subtests into five factors, Saunders (1960) needed five factors to account for the Information subtest alone. In the second place, sample composition affects obtainable factors. Age, education, socio-economic status, and diagnositic categories are sample variables that have been shown to influence resulting factorial composition. Thirdly, different approaches to the same sample can result in the extraction of different factors. The outcome is that there have been several analytic studies of the WAIS, each designed to reflect specific conditions. The purpose of this section is to review some of the more important ones.

Cohen's study (1957) is a good starting point since the data analyzed is based on the WAIS standardization sample for the age groups 18 to 19, 25 to 34, 45 to 54, and 60 to over 75. The following five factors were identified:

Factor A. Termed Verbal Comprehension, this factor seems to reflect the richness of a person's vocabulary, his ability to comprehend and express thoughts and ideas verbally. The content of the thoughts and ideas will vary with the subject matter considered.

Factor B. Termed Perceptual Organization, this factor relates to the ability to perceive spatial and sequential relationships and the skill with which an individual is able to organize manually related elements into composite wholes. It appears to be the nonverbal or performance counterpart to verbal comprehension.

Factor C. Termed Memory, this factor has also been labeled Freedom from Distractability and Stimulus Trace. It seems to involve immediate memory as well as the ability to concentrate and recall previously learned material as necessary to meet new conditions.

Factors D and E. These factors were regarded as too specific for interpretation and not named by Cohen. They have no analogue in previous factor analytic studies of the Wechsler series.

In addition to the above, a second-order factor was found and described by Cohen as G. All subtests correlated appreciably with this factor, and it seemed to correspond to general intellectual functioning. We can describe it here as the composite of skills, intellectual or otherwise, used singly, additively, and substantively as man seeks to cope with his environment. Problems encountered in life will vary both in terms of complexity and variety, and these facets will determine which skill or set of skills assumes prominence. Also, since there is seldom only one correct solution or only one process involved in the solution of a problem, G indicates the degree of flexibility with which a person is able to consider alternatives. Certainly, G is related to Wechsler's definition of intelligence (Wechsler, 1958).

A number of studies consider special populations. For example, Shaw (1967) used college students in his factor analysis. Three factors emerged: Factor I corresponded to Cohen's verbal comprehension, factor II to Cohen's perceptual organization. Factor III was considered artifactual, reflecting "feminine superiority in perceptual speed" (principally on DS).

Berger, Bernstein, Klein, Cohen, and Lucas (1964) factor analyzed the WAIS protocols of chronic schizophrenics. Again, factors conforming to verbal comprehension, perceptual organization, and memory emerged. A fourth factor corresponding to Factor E (undefined) in Cohen's original analysis was also reported.

Maxwell (1960) identified the first three factors for the aged, as did Dennerll, Den Broeder, and Sokolov (1964) for epileptics. Sprague and Quay (1966) and Taylor (1964) analyzed the protocols of mental defective and dull normal adults. Sprague and Quay, with their lower level sample, noted that only seven of the eleven subtests loaded on the general factor (G) and that a verbal, a performance, and a trace factor (somewhat similar to Cohen's memory factor) could account for obtained variance. Taylor used "verbal-numerical-educational," "Gestalt perception," and "mechanical assembly" to describe his derived factors.

Of an organic sample, Russell (1972) noted that "while the factor structure of the WAIS is not affected to any extent, the brain-damaged *S*'s performance on the WAIS is impaired and reduced" (p. 138). On the other hand, Zimmerman, Whitmyre, and Fields (1970), reporting on differentiated brain-damaged samples, suggest that "there may be meaningful distinctions between pathological groups" (p. 465).

Apart from a factor of general intelligence, two factors—one verbal and one performance—seem to emerge from all factor analytic studies reviewed, regardless of age, diagnostic label, intellectual level, and education. A third factor variously described as memory, trace, and freedom from distractability appears in most of the studies. However, other factors are unstable and appear related to specific samples or general test conditions. Major differences are not with the factors themselves, but rather how each of the eleven subtests load on each of the factors. In the chapters dealing with the subtests individually, it will be seen that subtest loadings do vary across such variables as age, education, and diagnostic categories.

SEX DIFFERENCES ON THE WAIS

Wechsler (1958) had found small, systematic, but for the most part negligible sex differences favoring males on the verbal, performance, and full scale of the WAIS. When the standardization data for the individual subtests were analyzed, the differences were found to exist in eight of the subtests, five favoring males and three, females. Wechsler assumed this to mean that men both behave and "think" differently from women. To heighten this difference for the purpose of analysis, he employed a selective combination of subtests favoring men and women respectively. Three subtests—Information (I), Arithmetic (A), and Picture Completion (PC)—were designated as masculine (M) and three others—Similarities (S), Vocabulary (V), and Digit Symbol (DS)—as feminine (F). The sum of the weighted scores of the one minus the other was expressed algebraically so that a plus difference signified a masculine and a minus a feminine trend. These results could be expressed as percentile equivalents (p. 150). Wechsler speculated that this MF score was comparable to standard masculinity-femininity tests like the MMPI or Miles-Terman.

The MF index was soon examined in a variety of studies. Levinson (1963), who found that the MF scores of superior males and females were similar, questioned the possibility of devising an MF intellectual discriminator. However, Krippner (1964) detected some relationship between the WAIS MF and the MMPI Mf scale scores for college males seeking counseling. Shaw (1965) found his college sample revealed male superiority on I and A and female superiority on DS. Other differences did not confirm Wechsler's subtests as sexually differentiating.

In a clinical approach Coslett (1965) confirmed significant sex differences on MF for psychiatric patients. However, scores of paranoid schizophrenics did not show the expected sexual confusion on MF. McCarthy, Anthony, and Domino (1970) compared MF indexes on a number of standard measures, using college students as subjects. All four measures (CPI, Franck, MMPI, and WAIS MF) differentiated significantly between the sexes. However, both males and females were more "female" on the Wechsler percentile equivalents (34 percent male, 73 percent female). None of the correlations between the four measures were significantly different from zero. The authors conclude that this indicates that the WAIS MF is "in no way a personality measure" (p. 416) and no indication of sexual inversion or homosexuality.

Nevertheless, the WAIS MF is measuring something. As Wechsler says, "there exist significant sexual differences in at least certain aspects of intelligence" (1958, p. 149).

WAIS RELIABILITY

The reported reliability of the WAIS was based on the split-half correlations of three age groups, 18 to 19, 25 to 34, and 35 to 54, from the standardization sample. Correlations for the verbal, performance, and full-scale IQs were 0.96, 0.93 to 0.94, and 0.97, respectively, or as Cronbach (1960) noted admiringly, spectacularly high and, of course, above that to be expected for test-retest correlations. Studies of test stability have corroborated Cronbach regarding lower reliability coefficients. However, in all the test-retest studies examined, correlations are generally high enough to suggest that the WAIS is a reliable instrument. For example, in a study of 24 psychiatric patients Coons and Peacock (1959) found test-retest correlations for verbal, performance, and full-scale IQs of 0.98, 0.96, and 0.98. In a similar study of 30 psychiatric cases Mogel and Satz (1963) noted correlations of 0.90, 0.84, and 0.93 for the same scales, with a mean full IQ increase of only one point.

A nonpatient sample of above average ability (IQ 118) retested after 13 years (Kangas & Bradway, 1971) showed much lower results: verbal IQ 0.70, performance IQ 0.57, full-scale IQ 0.73, plus an eight-point mean increase in IQ.

Several studies covered the retarded. Silverstein (1968) reported correlations of 0.79 VIQ, 0.71 PIQ, and 0.78 FIQ after four years, while Rosen, Stallings, Floor, and Nowakiwska (1968), retesting after two and a half years, found correlations of 0.87 VIQ, 0.92 PIQ, and 0.88 FIQ and a two-point mean increase in IQ.

When the subtests were analyzed, results were much less reliable. For example, the verbal subtests were analyzed by Quershi (1968) for a 17-year-old normal sample. Using both split-half and test-retest analysis, he found results roughly comparable, ranging from a test-retest correlation low of 0.54 for Digit Span (D) to a high of 0.89 for Vocabulary. Coons and Peacock (1959) reported test-retest correlations ranging from 0.84 for Digit

Span to 0.95 for Vocabulary for their psychiatric sample. Rosen et al. (1968) for their mentally retarded sample revealed a range of test-retest correlations from 0.60 on Comprehension to 0.88 on Digit Symbol.

In summary, Wechsler's efforts in improving the reliability of adult measurement with the WAIS has been more than justified for the test as a whole. Data show that reliability based on test stability, the absence of which had been noted by early reviewers, is in general comparable to split-half findings. However, the results of the test as a whole cannot be assumed to apply when the test is considered in terms of major breakdowns or individual subtests. The current evidence is that the verbal and performance scale breakdown can be used, since reliability of both is generally good. For the individual subtests some, such as Vocabulary, Similarities, and Information, have good reliability while others, such as Digits and Picture Completion, are generally less reliable. Interpretations based on differential performances on these subtests should be made with caution.

VALIDITY

Three kinds of independent criteria are used in validating tests. The first is ratings by selected judges. Of course, since intelligence testing was introduced because of the unreliability of judges (such as teachers), the use of such a criterion is questionable.

A second criterion is the degree of conformity to normal growth curves, a concept not particularly relevant at the adult level.

A third type of criterion is a comparison with some sort of independent measure of achievement.

Research has been conducted on the prediction of grades by the WAIS, with mixed results. Haugen (1967) found the WAIS unable to predict grades in college math. But Plant and Lynd (1959) reported that the WAIS predicted grades as well as the college-oriented American Council on Education Psychological Examination (ACE).

In contrast, levels of academic achievement are acceptably measured. Average high school WAIS scores are consistently below those of college students (Conry & Plant, 1965), which are, in turn, below those of adolescents identified as gifted in mathematics (Kennedy, Willcutt, & Smith, 1963).

Other studies cover psychiatric patients. Differences between patients judged competent or incompetent to handle their own affairs were not detected by the WAIS but did relate to MMPI psychotic scales (Cooke, 1969) Yet Geiser (1961) reported that the WAIS and Rorschach could classify with 92 percent accuracy the degree of pathology in a psychiatric sample.

It is clear that the relationship between intelligence and behavioral correlates that are supposedly related to intellectual functioning depend on the adequacy of the behavioral criteria.

WAIS PROFILE ANALYSIS

By not confining a subject to a specific mode of response, the omnibus nature of the Wechsler scales with their many subtests is no doubt related to their effectiveness as measures of intelligence. However, the subtest profile on the WAIS test blank has proved irresistible for those interested in the analysis of the specific differences from one section or one subtest to another. Wechsler himself (1958), while warning of the unreliability of the individual subtests (a point basic to profile analysis), notes that the qualitative data to be obtained, even though largely inferential, is actually the essence of a good test.

Perhaps the basic problem is to establish at what point differences between subtests or between verbal and performance IQs should be considered abnormal and/or meaningful. With growing experience, the examiner can draw upon his own background to judge such differences. However, for those relatively new to the task, there are a series of studies that draw upon the standardization data to distinguish between abnormality and reliability of various subtest and verbal versus performance IQ discrepancies.

Field (1960) points out two ways to judge differences, suggesting that the use to be made of the results will determine which is used. The first is to

Table 1–2
THE ABNORMALITY OF VERBAL-PERFORMANCE DISCREPANCIES IN IQ

% in Population Obtaining Given or Greater Discrepancy	*Age (yrs) WAIS* 18–19 25–34	*45–54*	*60–64*	*65–69*	*70–74*	*75+*
50	6.8	6.2	6.3	7.4	7.8	8.5
25	11.7	10.6	10.9	12.7	13.4	14.6
20	13.0	11.8	12.1	14.1	14.9	16.3
10	16.7	15.2	15.6	18.1	19.1	20.8
5	19.9	18.1	18.6	21.6	22.8	24.9
2	23.7	21.5	22.1	25.7	27.1	29.6
1	26.2	23.8	24.5	28.4	30.0	32.8
0.1	33.5	30.4	31.2	36.3	38.2	41.8

Source: J. G. Field, Two types of tables for use with Wechsler's Intelligence Scales. *Journal of Clinical Psychology,* 1960, **16**, 4.

Table 1–3
THE RELIABILITY
OF VERBAL-PERFORMANCE
DISCREPANCIES IN IQ

Probability of Obtaining Given or Greater Discrepancy by chance	*Age (yrs)* *WAIS* *18–19* *25–34* *45–54*
.50	3.3
.25	5.7
.20	6.4
:10	8.2
.05	9.8
.02	11.6
.01	12.8
.001	16.4

Source: J. G. Field, Two types of tables for use with Wechsler's Intelligence Scales. *Journal of Clinical Psychology*, 1960, 16, 4.

assess any such differences in terms of the proportion of the normative population upon whom the same or larger difference was observed. This has been described as the Abnormality of a Discrepancy. The second is by comparing found differences to the range of differences attributable to the errors of measurement. This approach, called the Reliability of Discrepancies or Differences, lists differences reliable at or beyond a certain level of probability. For the various age levels Field presents Tables 1-2–1-5 (see pages16–19) comparing differences between verbal and performance IQs, any two subtest scale scores, and, using the same approach, any two, three, four, or five subtests to the remaining subtests. In the subtest chapters to follow similar data is presented in detail for specific subtests.

A particular advantage of Field's approach is that it allows the examiner to compare such aspects as timed tests versus untimed tests or verbal comprehension tests versus perceptual organization tests.

In this chapter we have given a historical review of the WAIS as a whole, its current standing in terms of use and reliability, and the major breakdowns to which it has been subjected.

In the following chapters we shall discuss the relationships of the WAIS to other standard tests with which it might be compared, examine each of the subtests in turn, focus on the use of brief forms, and integrate results in writing reports.

Table 1–4

RELIABILITY OF DIFFERENCES BETWEEN ANY TWO SUBTEST SCALED SCORES FOR DIFFERENT VALUES OF THE RANGE (WAIS)

Range	*2*		*3*		*4*		*5*		*6*		*7*		*8*		*9*		*10*	
Significance Level	5%	1%	5%	1%	5%	1%	5%	1%	5%	1%	5%	1%	5%	1%	5%	1%	5%	1%
Age (yrs)																		
18–19	3.5	4.7	3.7	4.9	3.9	5.0	4.0	5.1	4.0	5.2	4.1	5.2	4.1	5.3	4.2	5.3	4.2	5.4
25–34	3.6	4.8	3.8	5.0	4.0	5.1	4.0	5.2	4.1	5.3	4.2	5.4	4.2	5.4	4.3	5.5	4.3	5.5
45–54	3.5	4.6	3.7	4.8	3.8	4.9	3.9	5.0	4.0	5.1	4.0	5.2	4.1	5.2	4.1	5.2	4.1	5.3

Source: J. G. Field, Two types of tables for use with Wechsler's Intelligence Scales. *Journal of Clinical Psychology*, 1960, **16**, 4.

Table 1—5
RELIABILITY OF DIFFERENCES BETWEEN THE MEANS OF ANY TWO GROUPS OF SUBTESTS (WAIS)

Significance Level		*Age (yrs) 18–19*		*Age (yrs) 25–34*		*Age (yrs) 45–54*	
		5%	*1%*	*5%*	*1%*	*5%*	*1%*
Any 1 Subtest Compared with the Mean of:	2	6.71	7.56	6.86	7.73	6.60	7.44
	3	6.32	7.12	6.47	7.29	6.22	7.01
	4	6.12	6.90	6.27	7.06	6.03	6.79
	5	6.00	6.76	6.14	6.92	5.91	6.65
	6	5.92	6.66	6.06	6.82	5.82	6.56
	7	5.85	6.59	5.99	6.74	5.76	6.49
	8	5.80	6.53	5.93	6.68	5.70	6.42
	9	5.77	6.50	5.91	6.66	5.68	6.40
	10	5.75	6.47	5.88	6.62	5.66	6.37
The Mean of Any 2 Subtests Compared with the Mean of:	2	5.48	6.17	5.61	6.31	5.39	6.07
	3	5.00	5.63	5.12	5.76	4.92	5.54
	4	4.74	5.34	4.86	5.47	4.68	5.26
	5	4.58	5.16	4.69	5.28	4.51	5.08
	6	4.47	5.04	4.58	5.16	4.40	4.96
	7	4.39	4.95	4.50	5.06	4.32	4.87
	8	4.33	4.88	4.43	4.99	4.26	4.80
	9	4.28	4.82	4.38	4.94	4.22	4.75
The Mean of Any 3 Subtests Compared with the Mean of:	3	4.47	5.04	4.58	5.12	4.40	4.96
	4	4.18	4.71	4.28	4.82	4.12	4.64
	5	4.00	4.51	4.10	4.61	4.94	4.44
	6	3.87	4.36	3.96	4.46	3.81	4.30
	7	3.78	4.26	3.87	4.36	3.72	4.19
	8	3.28	3.69	3.35	3.78	3.23	3.63
The Mean of Any 4 Subtests Compared with the Mean of:	4	3.87	5.36	3.96	4.46	3.81	4.29
	5	3.66	4.14	3.76	4.24	3.62	4.07
	6	3.54	3.98	3.62	4.08	3.48	3.92
	7	3.43	3.87	3.51	3.96	3.38	3.81
The Mean of Any 5 Subtests Compared with the Mean of:	5	3.46	3.90	3.55	3.99	3.41	3.84
	6	3.31	3.74	3.40	3.82	3.27	3.68

Source: Field, J. G. Two types of tables for use with Wechsler's Intelligence Scales. *Journal of Clinical Psychology*, 1960, **16**, 6.

REFERENCES

Berger, L., Bernstein, A., Klein, E., Cohen, J., & Lucas, G. Effects of aging and pathology on the factorial structure of intelligence. *Journal of Consulting Psychology,* 1964, **28**, 199–207.

Bersoff, D. N. The revised deterioration quotient for the WAIS: a test of validity. *Journal of Clinical Psychology*, 1970, **26**, 71–73.

Blatt, S. J. & Allison, J. The intelligence test in personality assessment. In A. I. Rabin (Ed.). *Projective techniques in personality assessment*, New York; Springer, 1968.

Cohen, H. Psychological test findings in adolescents having ovarian dysgenesis. *Psychosomatic Medicine*, 1962, **24**, 249–256.

Cohen, J. The factorial structure of the WAIS between early adulthood and old age. *Journal of Consulting Psychology*, 1957, **21**, 283–290.

Conry, R., & Plant, W. T. WAIS and group test prediction of an academic success criterion: high school and college. *Educational and Psychological Measurement*, 1965, **25**, 493–500.

Cooke, G. The court study unit: patient characteristics and differences between patients judged competent and incompetent. *Journal of Clinical Psychology*, 1969, **25**, 140–143.

Coons, W. H., & Peacock, E. P. Inter-examiner reliability of the WAIS with mental hospital patients. *Ontario Psychological Association Quarterly*, 1959, **12**, 33–37.

Corotto, L. V. The relation of Performance to Verbal IQ in acting out juveniles. *Journal of Psychological Studies*, 1961, **12**, 162–166.

Coslett, S. B. The WAIS Masculinity-Femininity Index in a paranoid schizophrenic population. *Journal of Clinical Psychology*, 1965, **21**, 62.

Cronbach, L. J. *Essentials of psychological testing.* New York: Harper & Row, 1960.

Dennerll, R. D., Den Broeder, J., & Sokolov, S. L. WISC and WAIS factors in children and adults with epilepsy. *Journal of Clinical Psychology*, 1964, **20**, 236–240.

Duke, R. B., Bloor, B. M., Nugent, G. R., & Majzoub, H. S. Changes in performance on WAIS, Trail Making Test, and Finger Tapping Test associated with carotid artery surgery. *Perceptual and Motor Skills*, 1968, **26** 399–404.

Field, J. G. Two types of tables for use with Wechsler's Intelligence Scales. *Journal of Clinical Psychology*, 1960, **16**, 3–6.

Fisher, G. M. Differences in WAIS V and P IQs in various diagnostic groups of mental retardates. *American Journal of Mental Deficiency*, 1960, **65**, 256–260.

Frank, G. H. On the nature of borderline psychopathology: a review. *Journal of General Psychology*, 1970, **83**, 61–77.

Geiser, R. L. The psychodiagnostic efficiency of WAIS and Rorschach scores: a discriminant function study. *Dissertation Abstracts*, 1961, **22**, 915.

Grisso, J. T., & Meadow, A. Test interference in a Rorschach-WAIS administration sequence. *Journal of Consulting Psychology*, 1967, **31**, 382–386.

Guertin, W. H., Ladd, C. E., Frank, G. H., Rabin, A. I., & Hiester, D. S. Research with the WAIS; 1960–1965. *Psychological Bulletin*, 1966, **66**, 385–409.

Guertin, W. H., Ladd, C. E., Frank, G. H., Rabin, A. I., & Hiester, D. S. Research with the WAIS: 1965–1970. *Psychological Record*, 1971, **21**, 289–339.

Guertin, W. H., Rabin, A. I., Frank, G. H., & Ladd, C. E. Research with the WAIS: 1955–1960. *Psychological Bulletin*, 1962, **59**, 1–26.

Haugen, E. S. A study of the validity of the WAIS, SCAT, and STEP as predictors of success in college mathematics. *Dissertation Abstracts*, 1967, **28**, 124–125.

Henning, J. J., & Levy, R. H. Verbal-Performance IQ differences of white and Negro delinquents on the WISC and WAIS. *Journal of Clinical Psychology*, 1967, **23**, 164–168.

Kahn, M. W. Superior performance IQ for murderers as a function of overt act or diagnosis. *Journal of Social Psychology*, 1968, **76**, 113–116.

Kangas, J., & Bradway, K. Intelligence at middle age. *Developmental Psychology*, 1971, **5**, 333–337.

Kennedy, W. A., Willcutt, H., & Smith, A. Wechsler profiles of mathematically gifted adolescents. *Psychological Reports*, 1963, **12**, 259–262.

Kraus, J. On the method of indirect assessment of intellectual impairment: a modified WAIS index. *Journal of Clinical Psychology*, 1966, **23**, 66–69.

Krippner, S. The relationship between MMPI and WAIS masculinity-femininity scores. *Personnel and Guidance Journal*, 1964, **42**, 695–698.

L'Abate, L. *Principles of clinical psychology.* New York: Grune & Stratton, 1964.

Levinson, B. M. The WAIS quotient of subcultural deviation. *Journal of Genetic Psychology*, 1963, **103**, 123–131.

Levinson, B. M. A comparative study of the WAIS performance of native-born Negro and white homeless. *Journal of Genetic Psychology*, 1964, **105**, 211–218.

Levinson, B. M. Note on the intelligence and WAIS pattern of white first-time applicants for shelter care. *Psychological Reports*, 1965, **16**, 524.

Lubin, B., Wallis, R. R., & Paine, C. Patterns of psychological test usage in the United States: 1935–1969. *Professional Psychology*, 1971, **2**, 70–74.

Maxwell, A. E. Obtaining factor scores on the WAIS. *Journal of Mental Science*, 1960, **106**, 1060–1062.

McCarthy, D., Anthony, R. J. & Domino, G. A comparison of the CPI, Franck, MMPI, and WAIS masculinity-femininity indexes. *Journal of Consulting and Clinical Psychology*, 1970, **35**, 414–416.

Meyer, M. M. The case of El: blind analysis of the tests of an unknown patient. *Journal of Projective Techniques*, 1961, **24**, 375–382.

Mogel, S., & Satz, P. Abbreviation of the WAIS for clinical use: an attempt at validation. *Journal of Clinical Psychology*, 1963, **19**, 298–300.

Newland, T. E., & Smith, P. A. Statistically significant differences between subtest scaled scores on the WISC and the WAIS. *Journal of School Psychology*, 1967, **5**, 122–127.

Norman, R. D. A revised deterioration formula for the WAIS. *Journal of Clinical Psychology*, 1966, **22**, 287–294.

Payne, R. B. Cognitive abnormalities. In H. J. Eysenck (Ed.), *Handbook of abnormal psychology.* London: Pitman, 1960.

Piotrowski, I. *Perceptanalysis.* New York: Macmillan, 1958.

Plant, W. T. Mental ability scores for freshmen in a California state college. *California Journal of Educational Research*, 1958, **9**, 72–73.

Plant, W. T., & Lynd, C. A validity study and a college freshman norm group for the WAIS. *Personnel and Guidance Journal*, 1959, **37**, 578–580.

Quershi, M. Y. The optimum limits of testing on the Wechsler Intelligence Scales. *Genetic Psychology Monograph*, 1968, **78**, 141–190.

Rappaport, D., Gill, M. M., & Schafer, R. *Diagnostic psychological testing.* Chicago: Year Book Publishers, 1945.

Rosen, M., Stallings, L, Floor, L., & Nowakiwska, M. Reliability and stability of WAIS IQs for institutionalized mentally subnormal subjects. *American Journal of Mental Deficiency*, 1968, **73**, 218–225.

Russell, E. W. A WAIS factor analysis with brain-damaged subjects using criterion measures. *Journal of Consulting and Clinical Psychology*, 1972, **39**, 133–139.

Saunders, D. R. A factor analysis of the Information and Arithmetic items of the WAIS. *Psychological Reports*, 1960, **6**, 367–383.

Shaw, D. J. Sexual bias in the WAIS. *Journal of Consulting Psychology*, 1965, **29**, 590–591.

Shaw, D. J. Factor analysis of the collegiate WAIS. *Journal of Consulting Psychology*, 1967, **31**, 217.

Silverstein, A. B. Psychological testing practices in state institutions for the mentally retarded. *American Journal of Mental Deficiency*, 1963, **67**, 443. (a)

Silverstein, A. B. WISC and WAIS IQs for the mentally retarded. *American Journal of Mental Deficiency*, 1963, **67**, 617–618. (b)

Silverstein, A. B. Evaluation of a split-half short form of the WAIS. *American Journal of Mental Deficiency*, 1968, **72** 839–840.

Smith, A. Verbal and nonverbal test performances of patients with "acute" lateralized brain lesions (tumors). *Journal of Nervous and Mental Diseases,* 1966, **141**, 517–600.

Sprague, R. L., & Quay, H. C. A factor analytic study of the responses of mental retardates on the WAIS. *American Journal of Mental Deficiency*, 1966, **70**, 595–600.

Stone, H. K., & Dellis, N. P. An exploratory investigation into the levels hypothesis. *Journal of Projective Techniques*, 1960, **24**, 333–340.

Sundberg, N. D. The practice of psychological testing in clinical services in the United States. *American Psychologist*, 1961, **16**, 79–83.

Taylor, J. B. The structure of ability in the lower intellectual range. *American Journal of Mental Deficiency*, 1964, **68**, 766–774.

Wechsler, D. *The measurement and appraisal of adult intelligence*. Baltimore: Williams & Wilkins, 1958.

Zimmerman, S. F., Whitmyre, J. W., & Fields, F. R. J. Factor analytic structure of the WAIS in patients with diffuse and lateralized cerebral dysfunction. *Journal of Clinical Psychology*, 1970, **26**, 462–465.

CHAPTER 2

OTHER TESTS COMPARED TO THE WAIS

Chapter 1 has reviewed evidence concerning the WAIS as a reliable and valid test. This chapter presents information regarding the comparability of the WAIS to other measures of intelligence. Several points must be considered.

When the WAIS is given as a retest, differences between it and the original measure must be interpreted. When the WAIS is not particularly applicable (severe motor handicap or aphasia, for example), another test might be chosen. Finally, when time or trained personnel are not available, a screening test may be substituted.

The examiner concerned about any of the above points can utilize this section in several ways. First, he can note if a certain test has been used with the type of subject that he has in mind. Second, he can estimate the reliability of the results, as based on other studies. Third, he can find out if a correction factor should be considered to improve comparability of results.

WECHSLER BELLEVUE

After the replacement of the Wechsler Bellevue I (WB I) with the revised and better standardized WAIS, attempts to compare the two scales were

Table 2–1
COMPARISON OF THE WECHSLER BELLEVUE I WITH THE WAIS – ADULT

	N	Subjects	CA	Design	WB I V M	WB I V SD	WB I P M	WB I P SD	WB I F M	WB I F SD	WAIS V M	WAIS V SD	WAIS P M	WAIS P SD	WAIS F M	WAIS F SD	Correlations rV	rP	rF
Cole & Weleba, 1956	46	college students	19–29	CB*	125		123		127		127		130		130		0.87	0.52	0.82
Dana, 1957	105	college students	21	CB I, C, S only	(124)						(121)						(0.87)		
	103	college students	21	V only	(11 subtest mean)						(12 subtest mean)						(0.67)		
Neuringer, 1963	51	college students	19	CB	120	9	118	12	121	10	120	9	124	11	124	10	0.77	0.34	0.64
Duncan & Barrett, 1961	28	college students	31	WB 10 yr earlier	118	8	116	10	119	8	121	9	115	8	119	9	0.83	0.45	0.82
Rabourn, 1957	50	college counseling cases	20	CB	115	9	117	10	118	9	116	9	112	10	115	8			
Karson et al., 1957	52	Air Force psychiatric patients	33	CB	121	6	126	9	125	6	120	7	121	9	122	6	0.76	0.56	0.69
Fitzhugh & Fitzhugh, 1964	179	brain-damaged patients	40	WB 23 mo earlier	75	16	80	17	75	17	74	15	74	15	72	14	0.95	0.84	0.87
Goolishian & Ramsay, 1956	395	psychiatric patients		WB only	103	16	102	18	103	18									
	154			WAIS only							101	19	95	14	99	15			

*counterbalanced

frequent (see Table 2–1). Lubin, Wallis, and Paine (1971) report that between 1955 and 1969 the Wechsler Bellevue had fallen to 26 in weighted-score rank for usage; therefore, comparisons between the two are of more academic than practical value.

Generally, results have been based on college student samples, with the corresponding restriction of range. Added to this is the retention of material (60 percent) from one test to the other. The range of correlations was from 0.64 to 0.87 for the full-scale IQ, with a median of 0.82. This dropped considerably lower for the performance scale, where more changes had been incorporated (range, 0.34 to 0.84; median, 0.52). The IQs were not always equivalent by any means. Performance IQs differed by six points, and this could be in either direction. Verbal IQs were more apt to be similar. There are not enough studies to generalize about the effects of level of intelligence on these findings.

The differences noted between the original Wechsler scale and its metamorphosized WAIS represent no criticism of either, but only the effects of the changes deliberately introduced.

Two studies (see Table 2–2) compared the poorly standardized Wechsler Bellevue II (later developed into the WISC) with the WAIS. Correlations were in the high 0.70s for small samples that were quite homogeneous. The verbal IQs were higher and the performance IQs lower for the WAIS.

WECHSLER INTELLIGENCE SCALE FOR CHILDREN (WISC)

WAIS-WISC comparisons are inevitable since at age 16 the WAIS replaces the WISC as the standard measure of intelligence. Initial studies noted the increase in IQ scores of mentally retarded subjects when the WAIS was introduced. Such findings could have serious implications. Thus, an individual labeled as retarded for many years would suddenly be considered misclassified on the basis of the new WAIS scores. Students in special classes for the retarded would be thoughtlessly removed. Aside from the possibly serious effects of accusations against those who had done the original testing, and the general weakening of faith in measurement, this has already frequently meant the loss of an adequate special class placement, leaving the subject nominally no longer mentally retarded, but actually unchanged.

The studies examined below compare the WISC-WAIS results and allow some conclusions to be drawn as to the meaning of test differences. See Table 2-3.

Fisher (1962) who had originally raised the entire question of WAIS validity in a comparison of Binet-WAIS results for institutionalized retardates,

Table 2–2

COMPARISON OF THE WECHSLER BELLEVUE II WITH THE WAIS

	N	Subjects	CA	Design	WB II						WAIS								
					V		P		F		V		P		F				
					M	*SD*	*M*	*SD*	*M*	*SD*	*M*	*SD*	*M*	*SD*	*M*	*SD*	r*V*	r*P*	r*F*
Quereshi & Miller, 1970	72	normal students	17	CB 3 wk	104	10	115	13	112	12	109	8	112	12	111	9	0.80	0.66	0.78
Light & Chambers, 1958	72	MR	20	CB 2 mo	69	6	76	14	70	9	73	5	74	10	73	6	0.62	0.83	0.77

Table 2–3

SUMMARY OF STUDIES COMPARING WISC AND WAIS

	N	Subjects	CA	Design	WISC						WAIS						Correlations		
					V		P		F		V		P		F				
					M	SD	M	SD	M	SD	M	SD	M	SD	M	SD	rV	rP	rF
Fisher, 1962	127	institutionalized MR	13→19	6 yr					57	9					67	10			0.70
Green, 1966	50	school children	15→16	4 mo							+(2)*		+(4)*		+(3)*		0.86	0.88	0.92
Hannon & Kicklighter, 1970	120	school boys—total	16	CB 2 wk					104	24					103	19	0.96	0.87	0.95
		(low group)							(69)	11					(76)	9			(0.70)
		(average group)							(106)	13					(105)	9			(0.80)
		(high group)							(132)	6					(125)	7			(0.70)
Quereshi, 1968	124	school children	15	CB 3 mo	109	11	111	13	111	11	108	9	105	10	107	8	0.76	0.68	0.78
Quereshi, 1970	72	school children	17	CB 1 mo	109	8	112	12	111	9	107	10	119	18	114	13	0.84	0.70	0.84
Ross & Morledge, 1967	30	school children	15→16	1 mo	97	19	103	18	100	19	100	16	104	14	102	16	0.95	0.92	0.96
Simpson, 1968	120	slow learners	16	CB ½ day	80	10	88	14	82	11	88	10	91	10	89	9	0.76	0.73	0.80
Walker & Gross, 1970	15	MR	13→16	3 yr					64	8					74	10			0.94
Webb, 1963	20	black MR	15→17	2 yr	68	4	74	12	68	7	77	6	84	8	79	7	0.80	0.91	0.94
Webb, 1964	16	black MR	14→17	3 yr	68	5	71	11	67	7	76	4	80	6	76	4	0.87	0.83	0.91
	16	white MR	14→17	3 yr	69	6	77	10	70	8	79	8	86	12	81	9	0.87	0.81	0.83

*WAIS surpasses WISC; means and standard deviations not reported.

noted a ten-point increase from WISC to WAIS for a similar population retested after 5½ years.

Webb (1963), comparing WISCs obtained at age 15 with WAIS scores at age 16 for black retardates in public school, noted the high correlation (0.84 FIQ) between the two. Nevertheless, the WAIS IQs were significantly above those on the WISC by six to eight points. In a second study of both black and white retardates given the WISC at age 14 and retested with the WAIS at age 17, the full-scale IQ differences rose to ten points, again favoring the WAIS (Webb, 1964).

Walker and Gross (1970) confirmed these results for a similar population tested at age 13 and retested at 16 with the WAIS. As before, the correlations were high, but the WAIS FIQ was ten points above the WISC, here attributable to an increase on the verbal scale.

In contrast, Barclay, Griedman, and Fidel (1969) compared matched subjects not given both tests. They reported no differences in IQs for institutionalized retardes, but some pattern differences.

The inevitable questions as to the comparability of Wechsler scales for normal subjects led to several studies focusing on the transfer from WISC to WAIS at the transitional age 15 to 16. Green (1966) tested 50 normal subjects age 15 with the WISC and administered the WAIS 4 months later when each subject had reached age 16. Correlations were high, and WAIS IQs were only two to four points above the WISC scores. However, Hannon and Kicklighter (1970) reexamined Green's original data. Of the eight subjects with the lowest IQs, all scored higher on the WAIS by an average of 11 points. Only three of the eight subjects with the highest WAIS scores had earned higher scores on the WAIS than on the WISC, and the average difference of one point favored the WISC. In the average group, 24 of the 34 scored higher on the WAIS, although mean difference was only two points.

Ross and Morledge (1967) repeated the Green design using only a month time span. The correlations were higher, and the WAIS IQs were only one to three points above those of the WISC.

Obviously, these studies involved, and in some cases maximized, practice effects. Therefore, Quereshi (1968) used a counterbalanced (CB) design for 124 above average adolescents, age 15, ignoring "minor" age discrepancies involved in using 16-year-old WAIS norms. The WISC IQs surpassed the WAIS IQs by four points. When a similar sample of 17-year-olds were tested (Quereshi & Miller, 1970), again with a counterbalanced design, the WAIS surpassed the WISC by three points. However, using 120 "slow learners" (high school students scoring below 90 on either a group or individual test of intelligence), Simpson (1970) reported WISC-WAIS differences of seven points, favoring the latter.

Only Hannon and Kicklighter (1970) were able to control for level of ability, using 120 16-year-olds and a counterbalanced design. Half of the subjects were within the average level of ability, defined as IQs of 81 to 119, with one-quarter of the sample above and one-quarter below this range. While the correlations were markedly high (0.96 VIQ, 0.86 PIQ, 0.95 FIQ), WAIS scores were significantly above the WISC means for those in the below average range by seven points, while differences reverse at the other two levels.

A review of all the WISC-WAIS studies indicate a range of correlations from 0.78 to 0.96, with a median of 0.91, which is encouragingly high. In other words, the IQs of these two tests retain their same rank from test to retest. However, the scales are equivalent only in the average range, while the differences between WISC and WAIS IQs for retarded subjects will give a spurious indication of "improvement" averaging as much as ten points. Unless examiners keep this increase in mind, test results will not be properly interpreted. It would appear that a correction of about ten points should be subtracted from the WAIS IQs of subjects with IQs below 85.

STANFORD BINET (SB)

Since the Stanford Binet preceeded all Wechsler scales and is still second only to these measures as a major test of intelligence, comparisons with the WAIS are essential. WAIS-Binet comparisons are generally of two kinds: comparison of scores under simultaneous administration and comparison of scores when the Binet was administered in early childhood followed by the WAIS administered in adolescence and adulthood. Correlations obtained under longitudinal conditions are generally low, reflecting normal age changes. These range from 0.39 (Kangas & Bradway, 1971) to 0.68 (Ross 1971) for periods as long as 40 years. However, if the low correlations can be attributable to time changes, the IQ differences are still to be considered. Here, the WAIS is much higher than the Binet for the retarded. Updating to current administrations, the WAIS IQ remains higher for below average subjects, with a seven- to ten-point differential for subjects with Binets above 50. However, the Fisher, Kilman, and Shotwell (1961) samples, separated by age and with Binet IQs below 50, show differences ranging from 13 to 23 points, again with the WAIS higher. The authors felt that age was an important factor. Generally, correlations for the retarded based on concurrent administrations ranged from 0.74 to 0.96, with a median of 0.77.

The correlations cited involved the 1937 Stanford Binet L (SB L). Studies comparing SB L and WAIS are detailed in Table 2–4. Surprisingly

Table 2–4

COMPARISON OF THE STANFORD BINET L WITH THE WAIS

	N	Subjects	CA	Design	SB L		WAIS V		WAIS P		WAIS F		Correlations rV	rP	rF
					M	*SD*	*M*	*SD*	*M*	*SD*	*M*	*SD*			
Bradway & Thompson, 1962	111	longitudinally studied normals	29	CA 4→29	113	16	110	13	105	12	109	11	0.60	0.54	0.64
				CA 13→29	112	16	110	13	105	12	109	11	0.81	0.51	0.80
				CA 29	124	15	110	13	105	12	109	11	0.89	0.46	0.83
Kangas & Bradway, 1971	48	same normals	42	CA 4→42	111	15	117	10	118	12	118	10	0.28	0.29	0.39
				CA 13→42	113	14	117	10	118	12	118	10	0.57	0.18	0.53
				CA 29→42	124	15	117	10	118	12	118	10	0.68	0.14	0.58
Ginalli & Freeburne, 1963	109	college students	18	CB	122	13	112	10	110	12	110	11			0.90
Wechsler, 1955	52	white reformatory males			100	17					95	12			
Klapper & Birch, 1967	45 total	cerebral palsied		retest	81		94		82		88				
	(28)	stable		after	(82	18)	(89	21)	(77	12)	(83	16)	(0.91)	(0.69)	(0.92)
	(14)	increase		14 yr	(76	12)	(106	12)	(92	14)	(100	13)	(0.78)	(0.55)	(0.77)
	(3)	decrease			(98	)	(78	)	(76	)	(76	)			
Ross, 1971	116 total	MR	47	CA 7→47	67	10	79	13	86	16	81	14	0.67	0.59	0.68
	(21)		47	CA 7→47	60	11	70	12	75	16	71	14	0.70	0.57	0.69
				current	61	18	70	12	75	16	71	14	0.91	0.85	0.96
	(90)	English-speaking childhood home		CA 7→47	66	10					79	14			
	(26)	non-English-speaking childhood home		CA 7→47	70	6					88	10			
Bregelman & Kenny, 1961	75	MR males	37	CB	51	11	60	8	62	14	58	11	0.79	0.78	

Table 2–5

COMPARISONS OF STANFORD BINET L-M WITH THE WAIS

	N	Subjects	CA	SB L·M		WAIS						Correlations		
						V		P		F				
				M	SD	M	SD	M	SD	M	SD	r_V	r_P	r_F
Kangas & Bradway, 1971	48	longitudinally studied normals	42	130	14	117	10	118	12	118	10	0.86	0.36	0.77
Kennedy et al., 1963	130	gifted math. students	16–18	139	8	138	8	125	11	135	8	0.60	0.09	0.45
McKerracher & Scott, 1966	31	British psychiatric patients	16–48	78	23					82	12	0.82	0.73	0.90
Fisher et al., 1961	180	institutionalized MR	18–34	44	9					58	8			0.74
			55–73	41	8					64	9			0.78
Cochran & Pedrini, 1969	72	institutionalized MR	21	48	12	63	10	64	13	61	11	0.89	0.79	0.90
Kroshe et al., 1965	23	institutionalized MR		4	4					56	6			

Table 2–6
COMPARISON OF THE PPVT WITH THE WAIS

				PPVT		WAIS						Correlations		
						V		P		F				
	N	*Subjects*	*CA*	*M*	*SD*	*M*	*SD*	*M*	*SD*	*M*	*SD*	r_V	r_P	r_F
Bonner, 1969	60	normal black students	16											0.61
Ernhart, 1970	118	psychiatric diagnostic problems	32	87	26					87	20	0.88	0.75	0.86
Shaw, 1961	–	psychiatric patients												0.84
Malerstein & Belden, 1968	10	Korsakoff syndrome patients		112						102	7			
	10	alcoholics		123						113	14			0.91
Tobias & Gorelick, 1961	107	sheltered workshop inmates	17	66	12					60	10			0.61
												0.66*	0.42*	0.64*
Cochran & Pedrini, 1969	72	MR males	21	64	14	63	10	64	13	61	11	0.60	0.69	0.72
Pool & Brown, 1970	150	psychiatric outpatients		81	23					79	17‡			0.81
Wells & Pedrini, 1971	92	institutionalized MR males	20–34	65	15	64	11	68	15	65	15	0.71	0.65	0.74
	58	institutionalized MR females	20–34	62	10	60	8	65	13	60	10	0.75	0.57	0.72

*based on PPVT raw score
‡short form of WAIS

few studies have explored the newer and presumably more comparable Stanford Binet L-M (SB L-M), introduced in 1960 (see Table 2–5). However, results are much the same. Correlations show a median of 0.78. The SB L-M is higher for the two well above average samples, but for the below average, the WAIS surpasses the SB L-M by 4 to 23 IQ points.

For those who must use the Binet and WAIS interchangeably, caution is obviously the watchword. However undependable the Binet might be considered, the WAIS is undoubtedly "overpredicting" IQs for the retarded.

PEABODY PICTURE VOCABULARY TEST (PPVT)

The format of the Peabody Picture Vocabulary Test (PPVT) allows the examiner to evaluate word recognition or "hearing" vocabulary without actual verbalization on the part of the subject. It can be rapidly and easily administered by personnel of limited psychological sophistication, or even by trained clerks (Ernhart, 1970). Since vocabulary is traditionally considered a good measure of general intelligence, the PPVT appears to be an attractive substitute for the WAIS, especially so for the severely physically handicapped where the WAIS is considered inappropriate because of the need for motor and speech skills on the part of the subject.

Unfortunately, studies thus far have not capitalized on the applicability to the physically handicapped. Most of the relatively limited research with the WAIS deal with psychiatric or retarded samples. Correlations range from 0.61 to 0.91, with a median in the high 0.70's. The PPVT mean IQs are generally higher than the WAIS scores by a few points, partly a result of the greater variability encountered on this test with nonnormal samples. Tobias and Gorelick (1961) feel that the PPVT overestimates the WAIS IQs of retarded adults because vocabulary skills may continue to mature beyond other intellectual factors. The one study using normal subjects (black high school students—Bonner, 1969) had the lowest correlation (0.61) and did not report the IQ scores.

AMMONS FULL RANGE PICTURE VOCABULARY TEST (AFRPVT)

The Ammons Full Range Picture Vocabulary Test, forms A and B, has been suggested as a rapid alternative to the WAIS, taking 5 or 10 minutes to administer. There are a few studies available comparing the two tests for a range of samples, including psychiatric patients, the aged, retarded, and vocational rehabilitation cases. Correlations between the WAIS FIQ and

Table 2–7
COMPARISON OF AFRPVT WITH WAIS

	N	Subjects	CA	AVRPVT*		WAIS						Correlations		
						V		P		F				
				M	SD	M	SD	M	SD	M	SD	rV	rP	rF
Dickinson et al., 1968 1968	38	vocational rehabilitation	17–55	85	20	95	19	87	15	90	16	0.89	0.82	0.87
Sterne, 1960	54	VA chronically ill	36–86	98		103		96		100		0.85	0.68	0.84
Granick, 1971	50	aged adults	76	(MA	12½)	91	14	87	14	89	14	0.86	0.81	0.92
Sydiaha, 1967	40	psychiatric patients	16–69	(MA	13½)					85	18			0.49
				B(MA	14½)									B 0.88
Hogan, 1969	52	male psychiatric patients										0.83	0.50	0.76
												B 0.84	0.41	0.73
Vellutino & Hogan, 1966	35	psychiatric patients	28–59									0.85	0.39	0.78
Fisher et al., 1960	31	younger MR	18–34	60	11	64	9	62	11	61	10	0.58	0.36	0.50
				B 58	13							B 0.52	0.37	0.45
	35	older MR	35–50	50	14	59	8	58	11	56	8	0.50	0.64	0.70
				B 49	14							B 0.60	0.62	0.74

*Form A unless marked.

Form A range from 0.49 to 0.92 with a median of 0.77. However, the IQs are not equivalent; the WAIS IQs are uniformly higher, by as much as ten points. The Ammons alternate Form B was reported on by several authors. Generally, results seemed comparable, although Sydiaha (1967) found a marked superiority of Form B for his psychiatric cases, which were closer both in scores and in correlations, the latter an 0.88 compared to 0.49 for Form A.

QUICK TEST (QT)

Perhaps the most rapid of the vocabulary tests suggested as alternatives to the WAIS is the Ammons' Quick Test. Available in three forms, it can be administered in 3 to 10 minutes and requires only a pointing response. A relatively large number of studies compare the various forms or all three summed with the WAIS for college students, the elderly, psychiatric patients, the retarded, and physically handicapped (see Table 2–8).

Correlations with the FIQ range from 0.34 to 0.98, with a median of 0.75. Like the PPVT, the Quick Test means tend to underestimate the WAIS by about three or four points, with a slightly greater discrepancy, surprisingly, between the Quick Test and the WAIS verbal scale.

However, for a retarded sample, Methwin (1964) noted that the WAIS surpassed the QT when the IQ was below 58, while the reverse was true at a higher level. He suggested caution in using the QT but did find that the three forms were equivalent. Davis and Dizzonne (1970) specifically noted that the QT was highly resistant to the reduction in performance often associated with pathology.

Cull and Colvin (1970) found the QT satisfactory for quick assessment of verbal ability in a rehabilitation setting. However, Stewart, Cole, and Williams (1967) found that for their black psychiatric sample the QT might run seven to eight points higher than the WAIS, even though the correlations were relatively high. Abindin and Byrne (1967), reporting on subjects referred as suffering from organic versus functional disorders, felt that nothing was to be gained in giving all three forms.

In summary, for the time involved, the Quick Test does appear to be an appealing little screening test.

RAVEN PROGRESSIVE MATRICES (RPM)

This nonverbal scale originated in England, and there are now several forms of it in use. Administration and scoring are simple; perhaps these

Table 2–8

COMPARISON OF THE QUICK TEST WITH WAIS

	N	Subjects	CA		QT		WAIS						Correlations			
							V		P		F					
					M	SD	M	SD	M	SD	M	SD	rV	rP	rF	
Feldman, 1968	56	college students	21		107	8	123	7	115	10	121	6	0.36	*	0.34	
Joesting & Joesting, 1972	45	welfare	19		59	22	70	21	70	21	68	22	0.84	0.83	0.86	
Levine, 1971	50	elderly volunteers	60–100		114	20	113	17	105	14	110	16	0.88	0.78	0.88	
Libb & Coleman, 1971	30	rehabilitation	16–56		78	19					82	15	0.83	0.74	0.84	
Cull & Colvin, 1970	30	physically handicapped	over 50		89	16	92	16					0.80			
Abidin & Byrne, 1967	30	air force patients: organic disorders	33		102	13	106	14	97	15	102	14	0.65	0.61	0.70	
	32	functional disorders	32		102	13	108	12	105	13	107	11	0.80	0.53	0.76	
Ogilvie, 1965	30	VA psychiatric patients	42		95	11	100	12	97	10	99	10	0.82	0.38	0.75	V only 0.83
Borgatta & Corsini, 1960	75	psychiatric patients	26								94	12		0.60–0.98		
Davis & Dizzonne, 1970	43	neuropsychiatric patients	39		99	14	100	15	91	12	95	14	0.84	0.58	0.77	
Quattlebaum & White, 1969		psychiatric patients													0.86†	
Stewart et al., 1967	52	psychiatric black patients	31	I‡	82	15	76	13	75	14	74	13	0.73	0.74	0.82	
				II‡	83	14							0.75	0.65	0.78	
				III‡	84	14							0.71	0.61	0.74	
Carlisle, 1965	106	MR	28		62	11	65	10	72	13	6	10	0.68	0.40	0.64	
Methwin, 1964	82	MR	30		48	16					57	9	0.61	0.58	0.63	

*not significant †short form WAIS ‡Forms I, II, III

factors are the key consideration in the several attempts to use the RPM as a brief alternate to the WAIS. Applications have run the gamut from psychiatric patients (Hall, 1957; McLeod & Rubin, 1962; Sydiaha, 1967) to the retarded (Anderson, Kern, & Cook, 1967; Orme, 1961) and the aged (Granick, 1971). There are three main deficiencies that limit its potential usefulness: (1) no adequate standardization for American samples; (2) a format not providing IQ scores; and (3) a low test ceiling, thus eliminating evaluation of above average adults.

Thus far only the problem of IQ scores has been researched. Shaw (1967) provided a table of equivalent IQ scores for raw scores. However, Orme (1968) criticized the table because no provision was made for the aging factor. For example, the fiftieth percentile is represented by a raw score of 44 at age 40 to 45. Shaw's conversion table gives an equivalent IQ of 102. However, for older patients there is no allowance for age changes. At age 65 the fiftieth percentile is obtained from a raw score of only 24 according to the PM norms. Orme has provided a table of equivalent IQ scores for five groups of English retarded subjects stratified from age 16 through 65, that allows for this.

Table 2–9 presents a comparison of RPM-WAIS studies. Correlations with the WAIS FIQ range from 0.43 to 0.93 with a median of 0.67. The RPM tends to correlate somewhat higher with the performance than the verbal section of the WAIS. Since most scores for the RPM are given as raw scores, a comparison of these is difficult, as noted above.

SHIPLEY HARTFORD SCALE (SH)

Originally called the Shipley Institute of Living Scale, the Shipley Hartford Scale was designed to measure intellectual impairment by comparing a measure of vocabulary with one of abstracting ability. Over the years, the Shipley Hartford has been used increasingly in psychiatric settings as a rapid screening test of curren intellectual functioning. Unlike most of the other measures in this section, it is practically self-administering. Simplified instructions and a table to convert raw scores to WAIS IQ estimates allow the test to be administered and scored by nonprofessionals (Bartz & Loy, 1970).

Most studies involve psychiatric cases (see Table 2–10). Prado and Taub (1966) found that an average or better SH score indicated an average or better WAIS score. Correlations range from 0.73 to 0.90, with a median of 0.79. However, level of intelligence is a variable influencing correlation size. In their study Watson and Klett (1968) note that Shipley Hartford IQ scores of 93 and below correlate at a very low level with the WAIS (0.23),

Table 2–9

COMPARISON OF RAVEN PROGRESSIVE MATRICES WITH WAIS

				RPM raw score		WAIS V		WAIS P		WAIS F		Correlations		
	N	*Subjects*	*CA*	*M*	*SD*	*M*	*SD*	*M*	*SD*	*M*	*SD*	r*V*	r*P*	r*F*
Granick, 1971	50	aged	76	17	6	91	14	87	14	89	14	0.60	0.49	0.60
Hall, 1957	82	VA psychiatric patients	32	21	5(1938)	111	13	102	13	109	13	0.58	0.70	0.72
Jurjevich, 1967	131	military psychiatric patients	23	IQ 105	18	110	9	107	10	110	13	(0.38 to 0.68)		
McLeod & Rubin, 1962	81	psychiatric patients	30	31						96	16	0.58*	0.68*	0.67*
Sydiaha, 1967	40	psychiatric patients	49	25	11					85	18			0.53
Anderson et al., 1968	83	possible MR	27	27		90		87		88				0.43
	44	organic	26	24		85		79		81				
Anderson et al., 1967	107	MR	26	27	6	88	14	85	14	86	13	0.47	0.52	0.55
Orme, 1961	203	English MR	16–65					(40 to 80)						0.93
Shaw, 1967	87	psychiatric patients												0.83
Pringle & Haanstad, 1971	89	psychiatric patients	16–63											0.77

*Rho

Table 2–10

COMPARISON OF THE SHIPLEY HARTFORD SCALE WITH THE WAIS

	N	Subjects	CA	SH		WAIS V		WAIS P		WAIS F		Correlations		
				M	SD	M	SD	M	SD	M	SD	rV	rP	rF
Watson & Klett, 1968	96	VA psychiatric patients	39	106	10	102	15	96	12	100	13	0.74	0.59	0.78
Paulson & Lin, 1970	290	psychiatric patients	35	107	19					104	14			0.78
Weins & Banaka, 1960	140	psychiatric patients		99						100	13			0.80
Suinn, 1960	29	VA psychiatric patients		104	16					102	16	0.83	0.58	0.76
Monroe, 1966	30	female psychiatric patients		93 (98 (91	13* 11)† 19)‡					91	15			0.86* (0.86)† (0.83)‡
Sines & Simmons, 1959	30	psychiatric patients	40	91						96	14			0.90
Wahler & Watson, 1962	105	mental health patients										0.88		
		vocational rehab patients										0.87		
Bartz, 1968	91	psychiatric patients												0.73
Pringle & Haanstad, 1971	49	psychiatric patients	16–63											0.83
Stone & Ramer, 1965	51	psychiatric patients	29	88						87^{xx}	16			0.79^{xx}
Mack, 1970	54+	psychiatric patients		97	14	100	16	95	15	97	16	0.74	0.70	0.76

*Modesto scoring †Caldwell scoring ‡Grayson scoring ^{xx}short form compared to scores above this point with a correlation of 0.73. While several conversion tables are available (Monroe, 1966; Bartz & Loy, 1970), the SH IQs tend to be slightly (sometimes significantly) higher than the WAIS. The questions of the effects of age, education, and sex on scores were not sufficiently considered at first. Paulson and Lin (1970) present detailed comparison tables that allow for age correction.

The Shipley Hartford is one more of the screening tests available to those unable to give a full WAIS. With the above reservations in mind, it appears a valuable supplemental tool.

MISCELLANEOUS TESTS

The following represent less frequently utilized or studied measures that might be considered for screening purposes.

Kent EGY

An unusually brief test for screening purposes is the Kent EGY, which consists of ten items but is limited by having an IQ ceiling of only 100. For the few samples reported, the correlations range from 0.68 to 0.77. The lack of age correction for the Kent may artificially lower the correlations. However, Gynther and Mayer (1960) note that the Kent does not overestimate the WAIS and that it can be used successfully to select the nondefectives in a psychiatric population. Of the non-defectives, 95 percent were correctly identified as compared to 46 percent of the defectives, resulting in an overall accuracy of 66 percent.

Otis Test

The Otis test, which can be group administered, has been reported for relatively few samples. WAIS means surpass the Otis for a delinquency sample. For samples of college students and prisoners, correlations are in the high 0.70s.

Revised Beta

The Revised Beta has been utilized as a screening test compared to the WAIS for retarded, psychiatric, and prisoner groups. The correlations vary widely, from 0.37 to 0.83 for the full-scale IQ, with the performance surpassing the verbal correlation rather markedly. The median correlation is

Table 2–11
COMPARISON OF THE KENT EGY WITH THE WAIS

	N	*Subjects*	*CA*	*Kent*	*WAIS*			*Correlations*		
					V	*P*	*F*	r*V*	r*P*	r*F*
Templer & Hartlage, 1969	72	psychiatric patients	33	84			80			0.77
Clore, 1963	30	VA psychiatric patients		raw score 27 ambiguous				0.69	0.61	0.68
				or 24 strict scoring				0.69	0.63	0.70

Table 2–12
COMPARISON OF THE OTIS WITH THE WAIS

	N	*Subjects*	*Otis*	*WAIS*			*Correlations*		
				V	*P*	*F*	r*P*	r*F*	r*V*
Darbes, 1960	99	college students							0.75
Siebert, 1963	40F	delinquents	89			94			
	59M		80			86			
Cowden et al., 1971	209M	prisoners					0.73	0.74	0.78
	60F								

Table 2–13

COMPARISON OF THE REVISED BETA WITH THE WAIS

	N	*Subjects*	*CA*	*Beta*		*WAIS*						Correlations		
						V		*P*		*F*				
				M	*SD*	*M*	*SD*	*M*	*SD*	*M*	*SD*	r*V*	r*P*	r*F*
Panton, 1960	100	white prisoners		94		91		92		91		0.76	0.84	0.83
	100	black prisoners		79		77		79		76		0.67	0.75	0.81
Watson & Klett, 1968	96	VA psychiatric patients	39	93	12	102	15	96	12	100	13	0.46	0.71	0.37
Patrick & Overall, 1968	74	female psychiatric patients	34									0.74	0.84	0.83
Bartz, 1968	43	psychiatric patients												0.69
Funkhouser, 1968	47	female MR	25	60	14	60	9	59	12	58	10	0.48	0.79	0.73
Libb & Coleman, 1971	30	rehabilitation cases	16–56	86	16					82	15	0.74	0.83	0.83
Rochester & Bodwell, 1970	50	indigent black males	32	80	12	74	9	77	10	75	9	0.59	0.79	0.78
	50	indigent black females	33	82	10	76	6	80	9	76	6	0.29	0.73	0.73

Table 2–14
COMPARISON OF THE AGCT WITH THE WAIS

						WAIS						Correlations		
			CA	AGCT		V		P		F				
	N		M	M	SD	M	SD	M	SD	M	SD	rV	rP	rF
Brodsky, 1966	612	military prisoners	23	78	8					90	7			0.32
Watson & Klett, 1968	96	VA psychiatric patients	39	101	23	102	15	96	12	100	12	0.68	0.63	0.73
Hollender & Broman, 1969	98	black disadvantaged (pred. females)	25							80	10	0.68	0.41	0.63

.78. Generally the Beta IQ surpasses the full scale IQ for the below average, but this is reversed for the average.

Originally, the Beta was standardized on men. However, this is apparently not a limitation, since the three studies utilizing women report correlations of 0.73 to 0.83, (Patrick & Overall, 1968, Funkhouser, 1968, Rochester & Bodwell, 1970).

Army General Classification Test (AGCT)

The Army General Classification Test (AGCT), also known as the Army Classification Battery, may have outlived its usefulness, but clinicians seem to find it difficult to abandon. Inevitably, comparisons have been made with the WAIS. Conclusions are difficult to draw at this point. In Brodsky's study (1966) of military prisoners, not only is the correlation low (0.32), but IQs are not comparable. The WAIS IQ was approximately 12 points higher. On the other hand, Watson and Klett (1968) report almost identical WAIS and AGCT IQs for psychiatric patients, with correlations reaching a fairly respectable 0.74. Hollender and Bromon (1969) studied black disadvantaged adults. No AGCT IQs were given, but the correlation with the WAIS was 0.63.

REFERENCES

Wechsler Bellevue

Cole, D., & Weleba, L. Comparison data on the Wechsler Bellevue and the WAIS. *Journal of Clinical Psychology*, 1956, 12, 198–199.

Cook, R. A., & Hirt, M. L. Verbal and performance IQ discrepancies on the WAIS and Wechsler Bellevue Form I. *Journal of Clinical Psychology*, 1961, 17, 382–383.

Dana, R. H. A comparison of four verbal subtests of the WB-I and the WAIS. *Journal of Clinical Psychology*, 1957, 13, 70–71.

Duncan, D. R., & Barrett, A. M. A longitudinal comparison of intelligence involving the Wechsler Bellevue I and the WAIS. *Journal of Clinical Psychology*, 1961, 17, 318–319.

Fitzhugh, L. C. & Fitzhugh, K. B. Relationship between Wechsler Bellevue Form I and WAIS performance of subjects with long-standing cerebral dysfunction. *Perceptual and Motor Skills*, 1964, 19, 539–543.

Goolishian, H. A., & Ramsay, R. The Wechsler Bellevue Form I and the WAIS: a comparison. *Journal of Clinical Psychology*, 1956, 12, 147–151.

Karson, S., Pool, K. B., & Freud, S. L. The effects of scale and practice on WAIS and WB I test scores. *Journal of Consulting Psychology*, 1957, 21, 241–245.

Light, M. L., & Chambers, W. R. A comparison of the WAIS and WB II with mental defectives. *American Journal of Mental Deficiency*, 1958, 62, 878–881.

Lubin, B., Wallis, R. R., & Paine, C. Patterns of psychological test usage in the United States: 1935–1969. *Professional Psychology*, 1971, 2, 70–74.

Neuringer, C. The form equivalence between the WB IQ scale, Form I and the WAIS. *Educational and Psychological Measurement*, 1963, **23**, 755–764.

Prado, W. M., & Schnadt, F. Differences in WAIS-WB function with three psychiatric groups. *Journal of Clinical Psychology*, 1965, **21**, 184–186.

Rabourn, R. E. A comparison of WAIS and WB Intelligence Scale. Unpublished doctoral dissertation, University of Southern California, 1957.

Quereshi, M. Y., & Miller, J. M. The comparability of the WAIS, WISC, and WB II. *Journal of Educational Measurement*, 1970, **7**, 105–111.

WISC

Barclay, A., Griedman, E C., & Fidel, Y. A comparative study of WISC and WAIS performance scores and score patterns among institutionalized retardates. *Journal of Mental Deficiency Research*, 1969, **13**, 99–105.

Fisher, G. M. Further evidence of the invalidity of the WAIS for the assessmen of intelligence of mental retardates. *Journal of Mental Deficiency Research*, 1962, **6**, 41–43.

Green, H. B. A statistical comparison of the WISC and the WAIS, *Dissertation Abstracts*, 1966, **26**, 5866.

Hannon, J. E., & Kicklighter, R. WAIS versus WISC in adolescents. *Journal of Consulting and Clinical Psychology*, 1970, **35**, 179–182.

Quereshi, M. Y. The comparability of WAIS and WISC subtest scores and IQ estimates. *Journal of Psychology*, 1968, **68**, 73–82.

Quereshi, M. Y., & Miller, J. M. The comparability of the WAIS, WISC, and WB II *Journal of Educational Measurement*, 1970, **7**, 105–111.

Ross, R. T., & Morledge, J. A comparison of the WISC and WAIS at chronological age 16. *Journal of Consulting and Clinical Psychology*, 1967, **31**, 331–332.

Simpson, R. L. A study of the comparability of the WISC and WAIS. *Journal of Consulting and Clinical Psychology*, 1970. **34**, 156–158.

Walker, K. P., & Gross, F. L. IQ stability among educable mentally retarded children. *Training School Bulletin*, 1970. **66**, 181–187.

Webb, A. P. A longitudinal comparison of the WISC and WAIS with educable mentally retarded negroes. *Journal of Clinical Psychology*, 1963, **19**, 101–102.

Webb, A. P. Some issues relating to the validity of the WAIS in assessing mental retardation. *California Journal of Educational Research*, 1964, **15**, 130–135.

Stanford Binet

Benson, R. R. The Binet Vocabulary score as an estimate of intellectual functioning. *Journal of Clinical Psychology*, 1963, **19**, 134–135.

Bradway, K. P., & Robinson, N. M., Significant IQ changes in 25 years, a follow up. *Journal of Educational Psychology*, 1961, **52**, 72–74.

Bradway, K. P., & Thompson, C. W. Intelligence at adulthood: a 25-year follow up. *Journal of Educational Psychology*, 1962, **53**, 1–14.

Bradway, K. P., Thompson, C. W., & Cravens, R. B. Preschool IQs after 25 years. *Journal of Educational Psychology*, 1958, **49**, 278–281.

Brengelman, J. C., & Kenny, J. T. Comparison of Leiter, WAIS, and Stanford Binet in retardates. *Journal of Clinical Psychology*, 1961, **17**, 237–238.

Burnett, A. A comparison of the PPVT, WB and Stanford Binet of educable retardates. *American Journal of Mental Deficiency*, 1965, **69**, 712–715.

Cochran, M. L., & Pedrini, D. T. The concurrent validity of the 1965 WRAT with adult retardates. *American Journal of Mental Deficiency*, 1969, **73**, 654–656.

Fisher, G. M., Kilman, B. A., & Shotwell, A. M. Comparability of intelligence quotients of mental defectives on the WAIS and the 1960 revision of the Stanford Binet. *Journal of Consulting Psychology*, 1961, **25**, 192–195.

Giannell, A. S. & Freeburne, C. M. The comparative validity of the Wechsler and Stanford Binet with college freshmen. *Educational and Psychological Measurement*, 1963, **23**, 557–567.

Himelstein, P. Research with the Stanford Binet Form LM. The first five years. *Psychological Bulletin*, 1966, **65**, 156–164.

Himelstein, P. Use of the Stanford Binet Form LM with retardates, a review of recent research. *American Journal of Mental Deficiency*, 1968, **72**, 691–699.

Kangas, J. A. & Bradway, K. P. Intelligence at middle age. *Developmental Psychology*, 1971, **5**, 333–337.

Kennedy, W. A., Willcutt, H., & Smith, A. Wechsler profiles of mathematically gifted adolescents. *Psychological Reports*, 1963, **12**, 259–262.

Klapper, Z. A. & Birch, H. G. A 14-year follow-up study of cerebral palsy: intellectual changes and stability. *American Journal of Orthopsychiatry*, 1967, **37**, 540–547.

Kroske, W. H., Fretwell, L. N., & Cupp, M. E. Comparison of the Kahn Intelligence Tests, Experimental Form, Stanford Binet, and the WAIS for familial retardates. *Perceptual and Motor Skills*, 1965, **21**, 428.

McKerracher, D. W., & Scott, J. IQ scores and the problem of classification. *British Journal of Psychiatry*, 1966, **112**, 537–541.

Ross, R. A 40-year follow-up of mental retardates: changes in intelligence test scores. Paper presented at California State Psychological Association Convention, 1971.

Peabody Picture Vocabulary Test

Bonner, L. W. Comparative study of the performance of Negro seniors of Oklahoma City High Schools on the WAIS and the PPVT. *Dissertation Abstracts*, 1969, **30**, 921A.

Cochran, M. L., & Pedrini, D. T. The concurrent validity of the 1965 WRAT with adult retardates. *American Journal of Mental Retardation*, 1969, **73**, 654–656.

Ernhart, C. B. The correlation of PPVT and WAIS scores for adult psychiatric patients. *Journal of Clinical Psychology*, 1970, **26**, 470–471.

Malerstein, A. J., & Belden, E. WAIS, Shipley Hartford Institute of Living Scale, and PPVT in Korsakoff's syndrome. *Archives of General Psychiatry*, 1968, **19**, 743–750.

Pool, D. A., & Brown, R. The PPVT as a measure of general adult intelligence. *Journal of Consulting and Clinical Psychology*, 1970, **34**, 8–11.

Shaw, J. H. Comparability of PPVT and WAIS scores with schizophrenics without brain damage. Unpublished study, Nampa State School, Nampa, Iowa, 1961, quoted in C. B. Ernhart, The correlation of PPVT and WAIS scores for adult psychiatric patients. *Journal of Clinical Psychology*, 1970, **26**, 470–471.

Tobias, J., & Gorelick, J. The validity of the PPVT as a measure of intelligence of retarded adults. *Training School Bulletin*, 1961, **58**, 92–98.

Wells, D. G. & Pedrini, D. T. Relationships among WAIS, Goodenough-Herris and PPVT with institutionalized retarded adults. *Perceptual and Motor Skills*, 1971, **33**, 227–232.

Ammons Full Range Picture Vocabulary Test

Dickinson, T. C., Neubert, J., & McDermott, D. Reliability of scores on FRPVT and WAIS in a vocational rehabilitation setting. *Psychological Reports*, 1968, **23**, 1263–1266.

Fisher, G. M., Shotwell, A. M., & York, D. H. Comparability of the Ammons FRPVT with the WAIS in the assessment of intelligence of mental retardates. *American Journal of Mental Deficiency*, 1960, **64**, 995–999.

Granick, S. Brief tests and their interrelationships as intellectual measures of aged subjects. American Psychological Association, *Proceedings*, 1971, **79**, 599–600.

Hogan, T. P. Relationship between the Ammons IQ norms and WAIS test performances of psychiatric subjects. *Journal of Clinical Psychology*, 1969, **25**, 275–276.

Sterne, D. M. Use of the Ammons FRPV with the long-term chronically ill. *Journal of Clinical Psychology*, 1960, **16**, 192–193.

Sydiaha, D. Prediction of WAIS IQ for psychiatric patients using the Ammons Full Range Picture Vocabulary and Raven Progressive Matrices. *Psychological Reports*, 1967, **20**, 823–826.

Vellutino, F. R., & Hogan, T. H. The relation between the Ammons and WAIS test performance of unselected psychiatric subjects. *Journal of Clinical Psychology*, 1966, **22**, 69–71.

Quick Test

Abidin, R. R. & Byrne, A. V. Quick Test validity study and examination of form equivalence. *Psychological Reports*, 1967, **20**, 735–739.

Borgatta, E. F., & Corsini, R. T. The Quick Word Test and the WAIS. *Psychological Reports*, 1960, **6**, 201.

Carlisle, A. I. Quick Test performance by institutionalized retardates. *Psychological Reports*, 1965, **17**, 489–490.

Cull, J. G., & Colvin, C. R. Correlations between the Quick Test and the WAIS verbal scale in the rehabilitation setting. *Psychological Reports*, 1970, **27**, 105–106.

Davis, W. E., & Dizzone, M. F. Relationship between the Quick Test and the WAIS. *Psychological Reports*, 1970, **26**, 457–458.

Feldman, S. E. Utility of some rapid estimations of intelligence in a college population. *Psychological Reports*, 1968, **22**, 23–26.

Joesting, J. & Joesting, R. Quick test validation: scores of adults in a welfare setting. *Psychological Reports*, 1972, **30**, 537–538.

Levine, R. Validation of the Quick Test for intelligence screening of the elderly. *Psychological Reports*, 1971, **29**, 167–172.

Libb, J. W. & Coleman, J. M. Correlations between the WAIS and Revised Beta, Wechsler Memory Scale, and Quick Test in a vocational rehabilitation center. *Psychological Reports*, 1971, **29**, 863–865.

Methwin, M. Quick Test performance of mentally retarded individuals. *American Journal of Mental Deficiency*, 1964, **68**, 540–542.

Ogilvie, R. D. Correlation between the Quick Test and the WAIS as used in a clinical setting. *Psychological Reports*, 1965, **16**, 497–498.

Quattlebaum, L. F., & White, W. F. Relationship between two quick screening measures of intelligence for neuropsychiatric patients. *Psychological Reports*, 1969, **24**, 691–693.

Stewart, H., Cole, S., & Williams, R. Relation between the Quick Test and WAIS in a restricted clinical sample. *Psychological Reports*, 1967, **20**, 383–386.

Raven Progressive Matrices

Anderson, H. E., Jr., Kern F. E., & Cook, C. Correlational and normative data for the Progressive Matrices with retarded populations. *Journal of Psychology*, 1967, **67**, 221–225.

Anderson, H. E., Jr., Kern, F. E., & Cook, C. Sex, brain damage, and race effects in the Progressive Matrices with retarded populations. *Journal of Social Psychology*, 1968, **78**, 207–211.

Granick, S. Brief tests and their interrelationships as intellectual measures of aged subjects. American Psychological Association, *Proceedings*, 1971, **79**, 599–600.

Hall, J. C. Correlation of a modified form of Raven's Progressive Matrices (1938) with the WAIS. *Journal of Consulting Psychology*, 1957, **21**, 23–26.

Jurjevich, R. M. Intellectual assessment with Gorham's Proverbs Test, Raven's Progressive Matrices and WAIS. *Psychological Reports*, 1967, **20**, 1285–1286.

Levinson, B. M. A comparison of the Coloured Progressive Matrices with the WAIS in a normal-aged white male population. *Journal of Clinical Psychology, 1959,* **15**, 288–291.

McLeod, H. N., & Rubin, J. Correlation between Raven Progressive Matrices (1956) and the WAIS. *Journal of Consulting Psychology*, 1962, **62**, 190–191.

Orme, J. E. The Coloured Progressive Matrices as a measure of intellectual subnormality. *British Journal of Medical Psychology*, 1961, **34**, 291–297.

Orme, J. E. A comment on estimating WAIS IQ from Progressive Matrices scores. *Journal of Clinical Psychology*, 1968, **24**, 94–95.

Pringle, R. K., & Haanstad, M. Estimating WAIS IQs from Progressive Matrices and Shipley Hartford scores. *Journal of Clinical Psychology*, 1971, **27**, 479–481.

Shaw, D. J. Estimating WAIS IQs from Progressive Matrices scores. *Journal of Clinical Psychology*, 1967, **23**, 184–185.

Sydiaha, D. Prediction of WAIS IQ for psychiatric patients using the Ammons Full Range Picture Vocabulary and Raven Progressive Matrices. *Psychological Reports*, 1967, **20**, 823–826.

Shipley Hartford Scale

Bartz, W. R. Relationship between Wechsler, Beta, and Shipley Hartford scores. *Psychological Reports*, 1968, **22**, 676.

Bartz, W. R., & Loy, D. L. The Shipley Hartford as a brief IQ screening device. *Journal of Clinical Psychology*, 1970, **26**, 74–75.

Mack, J. L. A comparative study of group test estimates of WAIS verbal, performance, and full scale IQs. *Journal of Clinical Psychology*, 1970, **26**, 177–179.

Monroe, K. L. Note on the estimate of the WAIS full-scale IQ. *Journal of Clinical Psychology*, 1966, **22**, 79–81.

Paulson, M. J., & Lin, T. Predicting WAIS IQ from Shipley Hartford scores. *Journal of Clinical Psychology*, 1970, **26**, 453–461.

Prado, W. M., & Taub, D. V. Accurate prediction of individual intellectual functioning by the Shipley Hartford. *Journal of Clinical Psychology*, 1966, **22**, 294–296.

Pringle, R. K., & Haanstad, M. Estimating WAIS IQs from Progressive Matrices and Shipley Hartford scores. *Journal of Clinical Psychology*, 1971, **27**, 479–481.

Sines, L. K., & Simmons, H. The Shipley Hartford Scale and the Doppelt Short Form as estimators of WAIS IQs in a state hospital population. *Journal of Clinical Psychology*, 1959, **15**, 452–453.

Stone, L. R. A., & Ramer, J. C. Estimating WAIS IQs from Shipley Scale scores: another cross validation. *Journal of Clinical Psychology*, 1965, **21**, 297–298.

Suinn, R. M. The Shipley Hartford Retreat Scale as a screening test of intelligence. *Journal of Clinical Psychology*, 1960, **16**, 419.

Wahler, H. J., & Watson, L. S. A comparison of the Shipley Hartford as a power test with the WAIS verbal scale. *Journal of Consulting Psychology*, 1962, **26**, 105.

Watson, C. G., & Klett, W. B. Prediction of WAIS IQs from the Shipley Hartford, the AGCT, and the revised Beta examination. *Journal of Clinical Psychology*, 1968, **24**, 338–341.

Weins, A. H., & Banaka, W. H. Estimating WAIS IQ from Shipley Hartford scores, a cross validation. *Journal of Clinical Psychology*, 1960, **16**, 452.

Miscellaneous Bibliography

Kent EGY

Clore, G. L. Kent EGY: differential scoring and correlation with the WAIS. *Journal of Consulting Psychology*, 1963, **27**, 372.

Gynther, M. D., & Mayer, A. D. The prediction of mental deficiency by means of the Kent EGY. *American Journal of Mental Deficiency*, 1960, **64**, 988–990.

Templer, D. I., & Hartlage, L. C. Physicians' IQ estimates and Kent IQ compared with WAIS IQ. *Journal of Clinical Psychology*, 1969, **25**, 74–75.

Otis Test

Cowden, J. E., Peterson, W. M., & Pacht, A. R. The validation of a brief screening test for verbal intelligence at several correctional institutions in Wisconsin. *Journal of Clinical Psychology*, 1971, **27**, 216–218.

Darbes, A. Relationships among college students' scores on ACE, Otis, and WAIS tests. West Virginia Academy of Science, *Proceedings*, 1960, **32**, 214–216.

Siebert, L. A. Matched Otis and Wechsler IQ scores of delinquents. *Journal of Clinical Psychology*, 1963, **19**, 215–1216.

Revised Beta

Bartz, W. R. Relationship between Wechsler, Beta, and Shipley Hartford scores. *Psychological Reports*, 1968, **22**, 676.

Funkhouser, T. R. Correlation study of the Revised Beta Examination in a feminine retarded population. *American Journal of Mental Deficiency*, 1968, **72**, 875–878.

Libb, J. W. & Coleman J. M. Correlations between the WAIS and Revised Beta, Wechsler Memory Scale and Quick Test in a vocational rehabilitation center. *Psychological Reports*, 1971, **29**, 863–865.

Mack, J. L. A comparative study of group test estimates of WAIS verbal, performance, and full scale IQs. *Journal of Clinical Psychology*, 1970, **26**, 177–179.

Panton, J. H. Beta-WAIS comparisons and WAIS subtest configuration within a state prison population. *Journal of Clinical Psychology*, 1960, **16**, 312–317.

Patrick, J. H., & Overall, J. E. Validity of Beta IQs for white female patients in a state psychiatric hospital. *Journal of Clinical Psychology*, 1968, **24**, 343–345.

Rochester, D. E., & Bodwell, A. Beta-WAIS comparisons for illiterate and indigent male and female negroes. *Measurement and Evaluation in Guidance*, 1970, **3**, 164–168.

Watson, C. G., & Klett, W. G. Prediction of WAIS IQs from the SH, AGCT, and Revised Beta Examination. *Journal of Clinical Psychology*, 1968, **24**, 338–341.

Army General Classification Test

Brodsky, S. L. The Army Classification Battery General Test score as a measure of intelligence in a military prisoner population. *Journal of Clinical Psychology*, 1966, **22**, 81–84.

Hollender, J. W., & Broman, H. J. Intellectual assessment in a disadvantaged population. *Measurement in Evaluation and Guidance*, 1969, **2**, 19–24.

Watson, C. G. & Klett, W. G. Prediction of WAIS IQs from the SH, the AGCT, and the Revised Beta Examination. *Journal of Clinical Psychology*, 1968, **24**, 334–341.

CHAPTER 3

INFORMATION

Since the erudite person is by definition one characterized by his wide grasp of knowledge, the common practice of assessing one's intellectual ability by measuring his fund of general knowledge and information possesses strong face validity. In recognition of this fact, information has been the subject of mental examinations for years—although items of this nature were generally omitted from initial intelligence scales. The Army Alpha Scale of World War I was the first test to demonstrate the utility of information items. Since then, they have been widely used as integral parts in measures of intelligence.

The objection was, and has been raised, that the range of information is a biased measure of intelligence because it necessarily depends, in large degree, upon education and cultural opportunities. Wechsler in answer to this objection provided items that the average individual with average educational opportunity might be able to acquire for himself.

In the Information (I) subtest of the WAIS assessment items cover a wide spectrum of data—from basic overlearned facts, such as colors in the flag, to such knowledge as would be attained only through studious application to learning, whether formal or informal. Curiosity and receptivity to mental stimulation appear to be important elements in the acquisition and retention of such general bits of information. Cultural factors may determine the direction of interests as well as the amount of exposure.

WHAT THE TEST MEASURES

The basic question answered in this subtest is the amount of so-called general information that the individual has absorbed from his environment rather than the way that he utilizes this knowledge.

Areas of interest as well as experiential and reading backgrounds of the subject are tapped. Memory, remote rather than immediate, is perhaps a basic requirement for what is being examined. For this reason Information is not greatly affected by age. However, it is dependent upon and is interrelated with such elusive factors as intellectual curiosity and motivation as well as with reading habits and auditory comprehension. Arrest or impairment of the storage of information items must set in early or the deterioration must be very severe to have any profound effect on this measure.

DESCRIPTION

In its present form the Information subtest of the WAIS consists of 29 items, 16, or 55 percent, of which are carried over from the earlier Wechsler Bellevue I. The inclusion of easier initial items extends the range of the test at the lower level and assures initial success to all but the lowest scoring portion of the population. Other new items extend the test at the bright average level, which had been insufficiently assessed on the previous Wechsler. The total range of items is adequate for all but the most gifted.

FACTOR ANALYSIS

Cohen (1957b) describes the Information subtest as one of the best measures of G or general intelligence. The correlation with G for the standardization group at ages 18 to 19, 25 to 34, and 45 to 54 is 0.83. For a supplementary standardization group, age 60 to 75 and over, the correlation is decreased to 0.73. In terms of the percentage of variance attributable to G, the drop is from 69 percent to 53 percent. In addition to G, Information is consistently associated with the specific factor of verbal comprehension. The degree of association with verbal comprehension depends upon the factor analytic method used, the populations sampled, and the conditions under which the samples were drawn. Cohen reported that aging lowered the correlation and that for the standardization group Information is more highly correlated with a memory factor. However, when Berger, Bernstein, Klein, Cohen, and Lucas (1964), using a different rotational technique, reanalyzed the same sample, loading on the memory factor was insignificant.

Actual correlations with verbal comprehension range from a low of 0.21 (Cohen, 1957a) for the ages 25 to 34 in the standardization group to a high of 0.81 for a stratified sample ages 20 to 74 (Birren, reported in Riegel & Riegel, 1962). Significant correlations with verbal comprehension are reported for chronic schizophrenics (Berger et al., 1964), the dull and mentally retarded (Sprague & Quay, 1966; Taylor, 1964), and epileptics (Dennerll, Den Broeder, & Sokolov, 1964). Shaw (1967) reported a moderate correlation between Information and the verbal comprehension factor with college students. Chronic organics in Russell's study (1972) also perform in such a manner as to allow for a significant correlation between Information and verbal comprehension, while Zimmerman, Whitmyre, and Fields (1970) offer evidence that, on the basis of the factor loading, patients with diffuse cerebral damage might be distinguished from those with either right side or left side involved. The correlation for the diffused involved (DI) was given as 0.89; for the left side involved (LI), 0.69; and for the right side involved (RI), 0.62.

The Information subtest may be considered a good indicator of those aspects of intelligence that stress the acquisition of general knowledge and information as necessary for effective behavior. Presumably, the process of acquisition is continuous, but the rate and efficiency of the acquisition process can be influenced by age, education, culture, socioeconomic factors, disease, and attitude. That the nature of the information acquired is primarily verbal is a reflection of the culture as much as of the subtest. Western civilization places heavy emphasis upon verbal communication.

ADMINISTRATION

The I subtest is the introduction to all the Wechsler scales, and clinical experience tends to confirm its value as beginning material since it is the kind of nonanxiety-arousing task to which subjects are accustomed.

The wide range of items, from easy to difficult, and the kinds of practical questions asked make it a palatable introduction for almost every subject. Particularly admirable is the absence of any "trick" aspect. Subjects rarely question the early items or find them threatening in the manner that some items (such as those in the Comprehension subtest) are considered in other subtests.

Administration of this subtest begins with item #5, and the earlier items are administered only if both items #5 and #6 are failed. Otherwise the earlier items are automatically credited. If the subject fails to pass items #2 through #4, the manual advises that the subtest be discontinued. Clinicians may also wish to consider the advisability of discontinuing the entire scale. Since a raw score of zero or 1 on this and other subtests would result in an IQ below 50, failure on this subtest might be considered a sign that the WAIS is a poor measure of ability for the subject being tested. A test with a wider range of lower scores, developed from easier items, such as the Stanford Binet L-M, might be considered. Under normal circumstances, the subtest is discontinued after five consecutive failures. Quershi's study (1968) suggests that if more than the recommended five failures are allowed, only a small percentage of the subjects substantially change their scores. Thus, the five-failure rule is usually sufficient. It also keeps the testee from being subjected to unnecessary failure.

In administering Information items the examiner may repeat questions or ask the subject to explain more fully if a response is either incomplete or not clear. However, he may not spell out words or alter the wording of an item. Therefore, the examiner must be careful to pronounce items accurately, a possible problem at the upper level.

Clinicians generally accept spontaneous corrections by the subject if given within the course of the test session. Worth noting in the protocol is a correction made later, or perhaps during a second testing session, if testing should continue through another sitting.

Guessing should be encouraged for several reasons: First, it establishes the test situation as less than a "life or death" proposition, a point which may be of increasing importance in further subtests. Second, bizarre responses may be elicited—the degree of reluctance to give such responses (that is, spontaneously uttered or only upon coaxing) can be important. Third, on questions having some latitude (height of women, population of the United States) the degree of under- or overestimation might be clinically relevant. For example, a very short man noted that the average woman was "6 feet tall."

All answers should be recorded verbatim; this applies to *all* verbal subtest answers.

TESTING THE LIMITS

Clinical judgment may suggest continuing the test beyond the five-failure level as a method of exploring the subject's ability, but IQs should, of course,

Table 3–1
ITEM PLACEMENT OF AVERAGE SCORES FOR FOUR AGE LEVELS

Age 16–17	(average raw score 13–14)	success through item #13 or #14
Age 25–34	(average raw score 15–16)	success through item #15 or #16
Age 45–54	(average raw score 15)	success through item #15
Age 65–69	(average raw score 13–14)	success through item #13 or #14

Source: D. Wechsler, *Manual, Wechsler Adult Intelligence Scale* (New York: The Psychological Corporation, 1955), p. 101–108.

be reported according to the rules in the manual, indicating in the body of the report the spread of successes. (Possible implications of such a spread will be discussed later.)

When easy items are failed or peculiar answers are given, further inquiry may establish the nature or reason for such responses. Addition of easier factual questions from the Binet or WISC can be useful.

SCORING

When the subject responds with an "either–or" answer and only one is correct, he must be urged to give his preference, which is then scored. However, on items where several answers are given that are not mutually exclusive, the best one may be scored.

Three items change in scoring according to changing norms and statehood in the United States. These are #11, #20, and #21. Otherwise, scoring is rarely a problem except on an item such as #19 where insufficient inquiry may be involved.

ITEM PLACEMENT

The Wechsler model of intellectual functioning posits a curve of growth and then decreasing ability with advancing age. A raw score that is average at an earlier age level tends, therefore, to be more difficult to achieve and thus merits a higher IQ at a later age. To assure comparable IQs, it was necessary to modify raw scores to allow for age changes. Wechsler (1955) covers this in his manual. Examination of Table 3–1 will indicate that the raw scores needed to yield an average weighted score do not vary much through the ages 16 to 69. The average raw score that is expected at age 16 and 17 is 13 or 14. For the young adult, age 25 to 34, this increases to 15 or 16. The raw score expected for the middle-age range (45 to 54) remains at 15, but this declines again to 13 or 14 for the older (65 to 69) age group.

While a scattering of successes is to be expected, thus taking the range of scores considerably higher, the average young subject should have gathered enough information in his lifetime from his environment to answer the questions through items #13 and #14. No doubt because item success reflects the widening experiences and interests which follow adolescence, average scores increase to item #15 in the middle-age levels. The decline in average raw scores with age is an interesting clue as to the influence of memory on scores, a topic covered in the Factor Analytic section.

The fact that average scores are midway in the subtest scale indicates the wide range and good selection of items for all age groups. The two easiest items were passed by 100 percent of the standardization sample, while the two most difficult were passed by 3 percent and 1 percent respectively (Wechsler, 1958).

SIGNIFICANT DIFFERENCES BETWEEN INFORMATION AND OTHER SUBTESTS

Basic to any attempt to analyze the profile is a question of the reliability of differences between subtest scores. The "psychograph" on the WAIS record form specifically warns of this. Nevertheless, differences among an individual's subtest scores are studied continuously in an attempt to understand or characterize the subject. Often such differences will be considered as strengths and weaknesses or "assets on which to capitalize and limitations that may suggest compensatory adjustments" (Newland & Smith, 1967, p. 122).

In Table 3–2 test score differences between the Information scale score and all other subtest scale scores necessary to satisfy the 0.05 and 0.01 confidence levels at three different age levels are presented. Depending on the subtest, wide differences in weighted scores must exist. For comparison at the 0.05 level of significance there must be a difference of two to four weighted score points, while at the 0.01 level the differences range from three to five points. The Vocabulary subtest requires only a two- or three-point difference at the younger and older age levels. Larger differences are seen for some performance subtests, and also for Digit Span in the verbal scale.

ITEM COMPOSITION AND DIFFICULTY

The Information subtest includes a number of items of a practical nature that almost all adults are able to pick up from their common everyday

Table 3–2
DIFFERENCES BETWEEN INFORMATION AND ALL OTHER SCALED SCORES NECESSARY TO SATISFY THE 0.05 AND 0.01 CONFIDENCE LEVELS

	Confidence	Subtests									
CA	*level*	*C*	*A*	*S*	*D*	*V*	*DS*	*PC*	*BD*	*PA*	*OA*
18–19	0.05	3	3	3	4	2	2	3	3	4	4
	0.01	4	4	4	5	3	3	4	4	5	5
25–34	0.05	3	3	3	4	3	a	3	3	4	4
	0.01	4	4	4	5	4		4	4	5	5
45–54	0.05	3	3	3	4	2	a	3	3	3	4
	0.01	4	4	4	5	3		4	4	4	5

[a]DS omitted.
Source: From T. E. Newland and P. A. Smith, Statistically significant differences between subtest scaled scores on the WISC and the WAIS, *Journal of School Psychology,* 1967, 5, 126.

experience—for example, items #6 and #8. Item difficulty is well dispersed, as we have noted, so that early items are passed by almost all and final items failed by almost all subjects. However, there are also some specific kinds of items that might penalize (or reward) certain subjects. For example, five items are based on a knowledge of geography and may be unexpectedly difficult for the individual who has had limited schooling (specifically, these are #9, #10, #12, #17, and #18). Half of these are above and half below the median level of item difficulty.

Other items are particularly difficult for foreigners. San Diego, Foley, and Walker (1970) noted three that were failed frequently by a Philippine college sample (these items were #14, #20, and #21). A literature emphasis involves the following five items: #7, #15, #24, #26, and #27. Those items involving possible changes over time include #11, #20, and #21, as well as #14 because of the shifting holiday recently instituted.

A particular concern is the general adequacy of item placement. Payne and Lehmann (1966), reporting on a large college population, found item placement agreed with Wechsler with few exceptions. One item assumed to be close to average (#17) actually proved to be much more difficult than placement suggests, while two of the upper level items (#22 and #24) in fact proved to be somewhat easier than expected. However, from #19 on item difficulty increased rapidly.

Both Wechsler (1958) and Shaw (1965) found this subtest to favor men over women. Payne and Lehmann (1966) noted six items to favor men over women (these were the following: #15, #18, #20, #21, #23, and #24), and four items to favor women over men (specifically, #11, #14, #22, and #27).

RESEARCH WITH THE INFORMATION SUBTEST

As noted, most factor analytic studies indicate that the Information (I) subtest is a consistent measure of verbal comprehension. Saunders (1960) proposes a fivefold breakdown of the subtest: (1) general information (regarded as a measure of total capacity); (2) current information; (3) cross-cultural information; (4) scientific information; and (5) role-oriented (intra-cultural) information. He further suggests that the I subtest—along with Comprehension (C) and Object Assembly (OA)—is indicative of the way the individual at adolescence strives to create a new and independent image of himself.

An examination of clinical groups considered by Wechsler (1958, pp 171–172) indicates that Information deviates 1.5 to 2.5 scale score points above the mean of the individual's other subtest scores for groups of subjects diagnosed as having organic brain disease and anxiety states and up to 3 or more units above the mean subtest score for schizophrenics. In contrast, Information tends to deviate from 1.5 to more than 3 units below the subject's mean for adolescent sociopaths. For mental defectives this subtest is either within the average range of the individual's performance or 1.5 to 2.5 units below the mean. Ladd (1964), utilizing samples of brain-damaged and neurotic patients somewhat similar to Wechsler's sample, reported no deviation from the mean of the other subtests. Apart from this, studies subjecting these hypotheses to experimental verification have often been lacking.

In a possible contradiction of Wechsler's hypothesis regarding organics in general, Rennick, Wilder, Sargeant, and Ashley (1968) reported that cases with mild chronic cerebral dysfunction showed no impairment on the Information subtest.

Norman and Wilensky (1961) compared a group of 100 schizophrenics to the WAIS standardization group, equating for education. The authors found that schizophrenics did more poorly on items calling for reasoning (#19, for example), as contrasted with those items requiring pure recall. Since the study lacked a proper control group, the results must be subjected to further validation. Characteristics of the standardization group might be different from that of a control group within the same geographic area from which the experimental sample was drawn.

Perhaps reflecting the above is the finding of San Diego, Foley, and Walker (1970) that Information was the lowest subtest for a sample of bilingual Phillipine college students. Using psychiatric samples, Bloom and Goldman (1962) also found a geographic differential—Connecticut patients surpassing Hawaiian patients on the subtest.

Dunn (1968) using college students tested the hypothesis that anxiety would be more disruptive of operationally simple but difficult tasks as compared to structurally complex but easy tasks. Information was used as an example of the former, and, as predicted, performance on this subtest was significantly affected by the presence of chronic anxiety, as measured by Sarason's Test of Anxiety Scale for Children. This finding appears to support the clinical observation that temporary, rather than chronic, anxiety does not affect performance on Information.

For clinicians who tend to attach diagnostic significance to particular item failures, the following two studies suggest caution in overinterpretation: Wolfson and Bachelis (1967) note that the time of year the test is administered affected success on the Washington's birthday item (#14), while Klett (1963) raises the possibility that the fifteenth item might be misplaced for the 18- to 19-year-olds. For this group it was the seventh most frequently passed item, although it appears as item #15 in the manual.

ADVANTAGES OF THE SUBTEST

As the initial subtest off the WAIS, Information has a number of advantages. First, it serves as a good introduction to the total task. The range of item difficulty is excellent; initial items are passed by almost all subjects, and yet even the brightest subject will be challenged by the terminal items. The format allows an introduction to the serial ordering of the subtests. Further, the items are emotionally neutral and nonthreatening, generally drawing on information readily available to the average person. Failures can be rationalized on the basis of limited experience, particularly as the items rely on specialized knowledge (geography, literature).

Information is a good measure of general intelligence and possesses good reliability. There is also the further advantage that the subtest can be relatively rapidly administered and scored, answers of one or two words being acceptable in most instances. The type of skills tapped by this subtest is generally resistant to the influence of pathological conditions, and thus may provide some indication of premorbid functioning in cases where deterioration is suspect.

LIMITATIONS OF THE SUBTEST

The educational and cultural loading of the items usually makes this subtest unduely hard for adults of foreign backgrounds, culturally deprived backgrounds, or limited education. Also, the subtest appears slightly easier for men than for women, a point to consider in choosing brief forms of the WAIS. Chronic anxiety can lower scores. Individuals who have been subjected to special education may succeed here beyond expectation due to coaching, "overlearning," or sheer memory without real understanding.

CONCLUSIONS

The Information subtest can provide interesting clues to the level of functioning and personality organization. The items do not usually elicit bizarre responses or personal references; thus, when these occur, they are profoundly significant.

Characteristically, college or gifted high school students achieve high score on the I subtest. The spread of successes provides a measure of alertness to the world around one, the breadth of information, and such specific aspects as current, scientific, role-oriented information, providing clues to endowment and to culture.

High scores suggest intellectual ambition, the degree of which might be assessed by a comparison of educational level with item success. Intellectualizing tendencies, striving, and ambition may be drawn upon. Specific successes might indicate the "overly enriched" (coached?) subject. Responses that continue into minute details far beyond the demands of the question suggest an obsessive orientation where "knowledge is security."

Relatively high scores have been noted in schizophrenics, the brain damaged, and anxiety state cases, as well.

A low score can represent a number of conditions. The cultural bias can result in significantly lowered scores for the foreign-born. For those familiar with the culture, a "nonachievement" orientation, such as that seen in the adolescent with delinquent tendencies or in the poor student with little affiliation to the school, may be indicated. An impoverished background is typically a problem, and the provincial subject may find Information difficult.

Failures are also common in those who rely on repressive defenses where "not knowing" is an advantage. Mental retardation tends to lower I scores below other skills.

Those who rely more on action than reflection may fail to store the scattered information necessary to succeed. Perfectionism too can lower scores for those who hesitate to present commonly accepted facts and struggle for an exactness that is not demanded.

Chronic anxiety at times may cause sudden memory gaps, and hence early failures. Memory loss will be reflected here only for extreme cases, where even overlearned material has been invaded.

REFERENCES

Berger, L., Bernstein, A., Klein, E., Cohen, J., & Lucas, G. Effect of aging and pathology on the factorial structure of intelligence. *Journal of Consulting Psychology*, 1964, **28**, 199–207.

Bloom, B. L., & Goldman, R. K. Sensitivity of the WAIS to language handicap in a psychotic population. *Journal of Clinical Psychology*, 1962, **18**, 161–162.

Cohen, J. A factor-analytically based rationale for the WAIS. *Journal of Consulting Psychology*, 1957, **21**, 451–457. (a)

Cohen, J. The factorial structure of the WAIS between early adulthood and old age. *Journal of Consulting Psychology*, 1957, **21**, 283–290. (b)

Dennerll, R. D., Den Broeder, J., & Sokolov, S. L. WISC and WAIS factors in children and adults with epilepsy. *Journal of Clinical Psychology*, 1964, **20**, 236–240.

Dunn, R. A. Anxiety, stress, and the performance of complex intellectual tasks: a new look at an old question. *Journal of Consulting and Clinical Psychology*, 1968, **32**, 669–673.

Klett, W. G. An analysis of item order in seven subtests of the WAIS. *Newsletter for Research in Psychology*, 1963, **5**, 30–32.

Ladd, C. E. WAIS performances of brain-damaged and neurotic patients. *Journal of Clinical Psychology*, 1964, **20**, 115–117.

Newland, T. E., & Smith, P. A. Statistically significant differences between subtest scaled scores on the WISC and the WAIS, *Journal of School Psychology*, 1967, **5**, 122–127.

Norman, R. P., & Wilensky, H. Item difficulty of the WAIS Information subtest for a chronic schizophrenic sample. *Journal of Clinical Psychology*, 1961, **17**, 56–57.

Payne, D. A., & Lehmann, I. J. A brief WAIS item analysis. *Journal of Clinical Psychology*, 1966, **22**, 296–297.

Quershi, M. Y. Optimum limits of testing on the Wechsler Intelligence Scales. *Genetic Psychology Monograph*, 1968, **78**, 141–190.

Rennick, P. M., Wilder, R. M., Sargent, J., & Ashley, B. J. Retinopathy as an indicator of cognitive-perceptual-motor impairment in diabetic adults. *Proceedings*, American Psychological Association, 1968, **3**, 473–474.

Riegel, K. F., & Riegel, R. M. A comparison and reinterpretation of factor structure of the W-B, the WAIS, and the HAWIE on aged persons. *Journal of Consulting Psychology*, 1962, **26**, 31–37.

Russell, E. W. A WAIS factor analysis with brain-damaged subjects using criterion measures. *Journal of Consulting and Clinical Psychology*, 1972, **39**, 133–139.

San Diego, E. A., Foley, J. M., & Walker, R. E. WAIS scores for highly educated young adults from the Phillipines and the U. S. *Psychological Reports*, 1970, **27**, 511–515.

Sarason, I. G., & Minard, J. Test anxiety, experimental instructions, and the WAIS. *Journal of Educational Psychology*, 1962, **53**, 299–302.

Saunders, D. R. A factor analysis of the Information and Arithmetic items of the WAIS. *Psychological Reports*, 1960, **6**, 367–383.

Shaw, D. J. Sexual bias in the WAIS. *Journal of Consulting Psychology*, 1965, **29**, 590–591.

Shaw, D. J. Factor analysis of the collegiate WAIS. *Journal of Consulting Psychology*, 1967, **31**, 217.

Sprague, R. L., & Quay, H. C. A factor analytic study of the responses of mental retardates on the WAIS. *American Journal of Mental Deficiency*, 1966, **70**, 595–600.

Taylor, J. B. The structure of ability in the lower intellectual range. *American Journal of Mental Deficiency*, 1964, **68**, 766–774.

Wechsler, D. *The measurement and appraisal of adult intelligence.* Baltimore: Williams & Wilkins, 1958.

Wolfson, W., & Bachelis, L. Time of year as a factor in success on WAIS items. *Psychological Reports*, 1967, **21**, 268.

Zimmerman, S. F., Whitmyre, J. W., & Fields, F. R. J. Factor analytic structure of the WAIS in patients with diffuse and lateralized cerebral dysfunction. *Journal of Clinical Psychology*, 1970, **26**, 462–465.

CHAPTER 4

COMPREHENSION

Questions designed to draw upon an examinee's awareness of bodily functions, the reasons behind certain customs, and the probable causes of behaviors in a variety of everyday social situations date to the original Binet. Such items have incorporated into all the Binet revisions, in group tests such as the Army Alpha, and in all the Wechsler scales. In the WAIS Comprehension subtest (C), emphasis is placed on the ability to verbalize probable or ideal behavioral reactions, and to justify behavior consistent with prevailing social values.

A basic assumption of this subtest is that one's ability to analyze and justify the reason for certain customs and, hopefully, one's ability to act in conformity are important elements of intelligent behavior. Since an act is considered the end result of both emotion and reason, everyday life experiences are as important as formal training in the propagating of socially desirable behaviors. In this sense, then, there is a built-in bias against the socially impoverished and the unassimilated foreign-born to the extent that their differing life experiences are not validly tapped by these measures.

WHAT THE TEST MEASURES

Comprehension measures the degree to which the subject has been able to evaluate accurately a sample of past experience (including the vicarious) and apply it to everyday social situations. It also assesses the degree of social acculturation, particularly in the sphere of moral or ethical judgments. Comprehension is less dependent on formal education than Information. However, ability to verbalize accurately and succinctly does play a role in the degree of success on the test. Thus, the test may penalize unduly those whose comprehension is adequate but whose verbalizations are not (sub-culture members, for instance).

This subtest is particularly vulnerable to the current emotional status (i.e., social withdrawal, negativism) of the testee and in numerous instances can suggest clues that highlight specific emotional problems. At times, bizarre or antisocial impulses may be clearly revealed. Inflexibility, indecisiveness as well as impulse-ridden or obsessional thinking may be shown. Examples of emotion-laden responses are listed in Table 4–1.

Table 4–1
CLINICAL SIGNS ELICITED BY COMPREHENSION ITEMS: EMOTIONALLY LADEN ANSWERS AND THEIR IMPLICATIONS

Item	*Response*	*Possible interpretations*
# 1 clothes	"germs kill you"	phobic
	"my mother says to"	personal reference, dependent
	"to wash them"	literal, retarded
# 2 engine	"run over you"	phobic
	"I never seen a train"	personal reference, concrete
# 3 envelope	"don't touch it, dirty"	phobic
	"open it up and take the money"	delinquent, provocative
	"give it to a policeman"	naive, retarded, moralistic
	"ignore it, none of your business"	reaction formation, delinquent
	"throw it away"	delinquent, hostile
	"read it"	paranoid

Table 4–1 (Continued)

Item	*Response*	*Possible interpretations*
# 4 bad company	"they hurt people"	phobic
	"I prefer bad company"	negative, provocative
	"they're bad!"	naive, retarded
	"I don't want to think about it"	hysterical, repressive
	"I don't think we necessarily should, some chance to straighten them out"	obsessive, righteous
	"who knows what bad company is?"	pseudo-sophisticated
# 5 movies	"yell fire"	unreflective
	"sing the Star Spangled Banner"	schizophrenic
	"show a scientist. *Q* Well you said the *first* to see"	alogical thinking
	"get a fire extinguisher and put it out" (*Q* re size of fire assumed)	foolhardy
	"save yourself" *Q*	asocial
	"get up and announce it"	unreflective
	"I shouldn't yell, but maybe I would, but (etc.)"	self-doubting
# 6 taxes	"to pay our relief checks"	personal reference
	"bad not to, it's the law"	naive, conforming
	"why should we, don't believe in them"	contentious, rebellious
	"but I don't pay taxes"	naive, literal
	"pay off politicians, graft!"	contentious, negative
	"to pay for wars, mainly"	social concern to point of loss of distance
	"if I didn't, I'd go to jail"	needs to verbalize external controls
# 7 iron	"hit somebody"	naive, literal
	"iron clothes"	retarded
	"burn yourself"	phobic
	"people strike for benefits"	alogical, concrete
	"strike when not going in accord with the boss"	alogical
	"it needs to be hot first"	literal

Table 4–1 (Continued)

Item	*Response*	*Possible interpretations*
# 8 child labor	"hurt children, rape them"	phobic, fears of exploitation
	"keep them from getting jobs and money"	personal reference, projection
	"I don't know, ain't married"	personal reference, denial, concrete
# 9 forest	"wait until found"	passive, dependent
	"probably die"	hysterical, phobic
	"by moss, sun, landmarks, climb a tree, etc."	obsessive compulsive
	"go back the same way"	unreflective
	"use a compass. *Q* then have to stay there"	unreflective
	*"you know people get so far out they can't get back, like me and my being nervous"	personal reference, traumatic neurosis
#10 deaf	"it's a disease, from sex"	phobic, hypochondriac, personal reference
	"your nerves, they're connected"	naive, retarded
	"no tongue"	alogical
	"can't hear to reason, no form of communication, crawl before walk" *Q*	decompensating obsessive
	"cause good Lord didn't mean for them to be born that way" (sic)	hysterical inattention
#11 city land	"not true!"	negative, argumentative, naive
	"country land is better, pretty"	naive
	"*I* prefer the country"	personal reference, contentious
	"I could say because the city concerned very much so in the community and urbanizing the city limit (etc.)"	decompensating obsessive
	*"was undeveloped like nature left it'	traumatic neurosis
	"city taxes, police to support, city officials to take care of"	naive, concrete

Table 4–1 (Continued)

Item	*Response*	*Possible interpretations*
#12 marriage	"men keep marrying women, take advantage of them"	phobic, fears of exploitation, personal referenc
	"so no adultery"	naive
	"sicknesses!"	hypochondrical concerns
	"law, don't know if I would agree"	contentious
	"people would be having children here and there"	naive, moralistic
	"you don't!"	argumentative
#13 brooks	"women talk a lot"	alogical
	"not much water running in quiet forest, not much going"	alogical
	"noise is made running over objects at a faster ratio"	decompensating obsessive
	"when you throw a rock into it, you can hear it hit"	literal, alogical
#14 swallow	"never heard, can't understand why, never heard"	concrete, personal reference
	"can't swallow your food"	literal, loose association
	"birds arrive together"	literal, naive
	"takes many types of different people together in unification of purpose working to build something, one person can't do by self!"	alogical, schizophrenic
	"a swallow bird! one act or one whole doesn't mean sum pleasures!"	alogical

*Responses and interpretations for Items 9 and 11 are taken from: Shafer, R., *Projective testing and psychoanalysis*, New York, International Universities Press, 1967.

DESCRIPTION

The Comprehension subtest, the second in the Verbal section, consists of 14 items, eight or 57 percent of which have been taken from the Wechsler

Bellevue I. The first two items, both new, are "buffers" to extend the lower range of the test. This assures initial success for almost all examinees. Otherwise, unlike Information, the additional new items are all at the top level (very superior), which extends considerably the difficulty of the subtest and thus its effective range.

FACTOR ANALYSIS

The subtest also measures general intelligence, or G, although to a lesser extent than Information does. Cohen (1957b) reports a correlation of 0.72 for the younger age group in the standardization sample, this correlation dropping to 0.60 for those over 60 years of age. In terms of percentage the drop is from 52 percent to 36 percent in variance attributable to G.

Similar to the Information subtest, Comprehension is also a measure of verbal comprehension at the younger age levels, and in Cohen's (1957b) analysis it is influenced by memory for the older age group. Berger, Bernstein, Klein, Cohen, and Lucas (1964), in their reanalysis of the standardization data, failed to confirm the memory factor. For a stratified sample, age 20 through 74, Birren (reported in Riegel & Riegel, 1962) indicated a high loading on verbal comprehension with a positive low loading on memory. Actual correlation with verbal comprehension ranges from Birren's 0.81, to 0.33 for the younger age levels of the standardization group (Cohen, 1957a).

Substantial correlation with verbal comprehension has also been reported for chronic schizophrenics (Berger, et al., 1964), chronic organics (Russell, 1972), epileptics (Dennerll, Den Broeder, & Sokolov, 1964), college students (Shaw, 1967), and the dull and mentally retarded (Spraque & Quay, 1966; Taylor, 1964). Unlike the Information subtest, factor loading in the Comprehension subtest is uniformly high on the verbal comprehension factor for all three groups (left, right, and diffuse) cerebral-damaged patients (Zimmerman, Whitmyre, & Fields, 1970).

The Comprehension subtest is a good measure of those aspects of general intelligence that probe into the individual's ability to verbalize the reasons for common practices and customs in his culture. Presumably, this skill is correlated with actual behavior. Clinicians generally associate high scores with social competency and the ability to hold impulsive behavior in check. The logic underlying customs and common practices are generally felt to become clearer with experience. At the level tested by the Wechsler scales, it is doubtful that age plays an important role since by late adolescence there should certainly be an awareness of the common expectations and society's reasons for these. It is also unlikely that customs so ingrained would be affected by old age. However, changes in attitudes, and certain disease processes can affect one's ability to verbalize statements consistent with expectations, or even to learn them in the first place.

ADMINISTRATION

As the second subtest in the WAIS, Comprehension represents a sudden change of pace. Although the early items are easy enough to have some components similar to the just administered Information, items soon present judgmental situations. This is particularly true for contentious subjects, who may, for example, wish to question why we *should* avoid bad company. Antagonism or quibbling is common in the responses. Halpern (1968) noted that item #6 (taxes) was associated with criticism of the Viet Nam war effort, although Martin (1968) on the basis of his clinical experience was unable to substantiate this finding. The conflict of these findings points to the obvious need to consider sampling differences and examiner variables.

The test is begun with item #3 (envelope). Any failure of items #3, #4, or #5 means that items #1 and #2 must be administered before proceeding further. Otherwise these are credited automatically. Four consecutive failures (zero scores) are necessary before discontinuing testing.

While questions may be repeated, no alteration or abbreviation of the question is permitted. Most difficulties with this subtest result from the examiner's accepting incomplete or vague responses.

Full inquiry is important throughout, particularly in view of the difficulty in scoring this subtest. The inquiry may be couched in such terms as a simple "Could you explain that more fully?" This can greatly improve the reliability and value of results.

Inquiry should also be made routinely of responses that seem to be stereotyped or overlearned to gauge the degree of actual comprehension. Underlying stereotypes or bizarre thinking may be present. For example, on the bad-company item (#4) a girl with a full-scale IQ of 55 responded promptly "Bad 'fluence. Bad 'flu-ence!" She did not know the correct word (influence) nor its implication.

One problem in administration arises from the placement of the WAIS in a test battery. Grisso and Meadow (1967) suggest that if the WAIS follows the Rorschach, there can be a deterioration of the C score.

TESTING THE LIMITS

As on the other subtests, testing the limits can be of value on Comprehension. For example it allows the examiner to be sure that the subject's failure to understand the specific wording of a question is not masking greater potential. Sometimes a slightly different wording can produce a dramatic difference in answers to certain questions. The importance of this point cannot be overstressed, as those engaged in polling will readily confirm.

Easier items from the Binet and WISC can be interjected in extreme cases. As noted for the Information subtest, these departures from standard administration do not provide scorable results.

SCORING

Comprehension is the most difficult and subjective of all the WAIS subtests to score. In a clinical sample (Walker, Hunt, & Schwartz, 1965) one-fourth of the responses to this subtest were scored differently from one examiner to another. Half of these unclear responses were considered "underinquired," so that scoring had to be done on the basis of insufficient data. The most difficult items to be scored were #7 (iron) and #14 (swallow), two of the three proverbs in the WAIS Comprehension. Sattler, Hillix, and Neher (1970) found ambiguous responses were particularly susceptible to a halo effect when the examiner was led to believe that the subject responding was either "bright" or "dull." (The harried young clinician should be comforted by the findings of Schwartz (1966), who reported that less experienced examiners score approximately the same as experienced ones.)

A particular problem for consideration is the three-level scoring (2, 1, 0), especially on item #8. Without prior warning, two or more reasons are necessary for a 2-point answer, whereas previously one sufficed. Further scoring guidelines suggested by Kitzinger and Blumberg (1951) for the Wechsler Bellevue I apply equally well to the WAIS. They suggest that if a response which is scored 2 in the manual is followed by or precedes a 1-point response, a score of 2 is given. When a good 2- or 1-point response is contaminated, that is, is followed by or follows an unacceptable answer, one should inquire into the subject's preference—for example, on #5 (movies), subject smiles broadly: "Go to the manager, that's what I should do (*laughing*). No, I yell 'Fire' if it's really there." If the subject deliberately tries to josh the examiner, the response should be scored with full credit, note being made of the behavior. On the other hand, if the subject defends the contradiction as a better choice, the response is not credited. A seemingly contradictory response must be scored according to the emphasis that the subject places on the contradiction. This frame of reference applies equally well to responses on the Similarities and Vocabulary subtests.

Table 4–2
ITEM PLACEMENT OF AVERAGE SCORES FOR FOUR AGE LEVELS

Age 16–17	(average raw score 16)	success through item #8 or above
Age 25–34	(average raw score 17–18)	success through item #9 or above
Age 45–54	(average raw score 17)	success through item #9 or above
Age 65–69	(average raw score 15)	success through item #8 or above

Source: D. Wechsler, Manual, *Wechsler Adult Intelligence Scale* (New York: The Psychological Corporation, 1955), p. 101–108.

ITEM PLACEMENT

The average raw scores on this subtest are relatively similar across the standardization age range (see Table 4–2).

The average adolescent (age 16 to 17) will reach a raw score of 16. Because of the 1- and 2-point scoring, typically this is achieved by successes considerably beyond item #8 (child labor), with scores of 2 on the first four to six items and scores of 1 from that point on. With advancing age, a one- to two-point increase is expected, but for the aged (65 to 69) there is a decline to a raw score of 15, or below that of the average adolescent.

The range of items is not as adequate as in Information. Wechsler (1958) points out that the last item was passed by 22 percent of the standardization cases.

SIGNIFICANT DIFFERENCES BETWEEN COMPREHENSION AND OTHER SUBTESTS

In an analysis of significant differences between Comprehension scale scores and the other WAIS subtest scale scores, Newland and Smith (1967)

Table 4–3
DIFFERENCES BETWEEN COMPREHENSION AND ALL OTHER SCALED SCORES NECESSARY TO SATISFY THE 0.05 AND 0.01 CONFIDENCE LEVELS

	Confidence	*Subtests*									
CA	*level*	*I*	*A*	*S*	*D*	*V*	*DS*	*PC*	*BD*	*PA*	*OA*
18–19	0.05	3	4	4	4	3	3	4	4	4	4
	0.01	4	5	5	5	4	4	5	5	6	6
25–34	0.05	3	4	4	4	3	a	4	4	4	4
	0.01	4	5	5	6	4		5	5	6	6
45–54	0.05	3	4	4	4	3	a	4	4	4	4
	0.01	4	5	5	6	4		5	5	5	6

[a]DS omitted.

Source: From T. E. Newland and P. A. Smith, Statistically significant differences between subtest scaled scores on the WISC and the WAIS, *Journal of School Psychology,* 1967, 5, 126.

report differences of three to four weighted score points necessary to reach the 0.05 level and four to six points to reach the 0.01 level. Vocabulary and Information required the least difference to reach significance. Otherwise required differences were approximately the same for both verbal and performance subtests at the 0.05 level, but rose sharply for Object Assembly at all three age levels, and Picture Arrangement and Digits for two of the three age levels, when the 0.01 level was required. (see Table 4–3).

ITEM COMPOSITION AND DIFFICULTY

The focus here is on practical problems. Dickstein and MacEvitt (1971) note that items #3, #4, #5, #6, #8, and #12 require social judgment, while the remainder of the items involve proverbs and nonsocial questions. Surprisingly, subjects high in need for approval tended to do less well on the social judgment items in their study.

Comprehension gives rise to emotionally laden themes for many individuals; a sampling of these are covered in Table 4–1 (see pp. 64–67).

An analysis of the adequacy of item placement is covered by Payne and Lehmann (1966) for a large college population. There are two item reversals: #8 (child labor) proved to be much harder than expected (twelfth in rank), while #10 (deaf) was considerably easier than expected (sixth in rank). Otherwise the range of items is not questioned, and the percentage passing each item decreased systematically as expected. Sex differences were seen for four items—#8, #9, #11, and #12, all favoring men.

RESEARCH WITH THE COMPREHENSION SUBTEST

Saunders (undated) regards performance on the Comprehension subtest as reflecting indirectly strength of identification as a civilized human. In the Wechsler (1958, pp. 171–172) analysis of clinical groups, Comprehension is expected to deviate from 1.5 to 2.5 units above the mean of the subject's other subtest scores for organic brain disease, anxiety states, and mental defectives. Depending on the type of schizophrenia, C scores vary from 1.5 to 2.5 units above the mean subtest scores to 1.5 to 2.5 units below the mean subtest scores. C either does not deviate or deviates from 1.5 to 2.5 units below the mean subtest scores for adolescent sociopath. Ladd (1964) utilized samples of brain-damaged and neurotic patients and found deviations from 1.5 to 2.5 units above the mean for the former, essentially agreeing with Wechsler's results, and 3 or more units above the mean for the latter, surpassing Wechsler's findings.

Hunt, Quay, and Walker (1966) offer some evidence that high scores on Comprehension serve as a measure of socialization. For 129 naval delinquents, clinicians' ratings of asociality based on Comprehension responses correlated positively with psychopathy scores based on three personality measures and correlated negatively with success on the Comprehension items. However, the clinical assumption that the "yell fire" response to the movies (#5) question is indicative of poor impulse control was not supported by Thomas (1962). Character and personality disorder patients did not significantly differ from schizophrenics or other psychotic disorders in the tendency to give the "yell fire" response.

Studies correlating performance on the Comprehension subtest for persons suffering from anxiety states, mental retardates and specific schizophrenic types are lacking. Fogel (1965) compared the discriminatory power of the C subtest among five others (PA, BD, A, D, and S) with the Gorham's Proverb Test for brain-damaged subjects. Of his sample, 64 percent were correctly identified by the Comprehension subtest.

Sarason and Minard (1962) indicated that for college students, low test-anxious *S*s were superior to high test-anxious *S*s on this scale. Whether or not situational stress affects results was not explored.

Finally, Dickstein and MacEvitt (1971) tested the Blatt and Allison (1968) hypothesis that this subtest reflects a subject's grasp of social conventionality and social judgment. Using the Marlowe-Crowne Social Desirability Scale, the authors identified 18 high need-approval and 21 low need-approval *S*s. In their study they found high need-approval *S*s to score significantly lower on those items of the Comprehension subtest involving social judgment.

Bloom and Goldman (1962) found that Comprehension did not differentiate between a Connecticut and Hawaiian psychotic population.

ADVANTAGES OF THE SUBTEST

The advantages offered by this subtest center around its being a fair and fairly reliable measure of general intelligence. It also is a good measure of the verbal comprehension factor for all age levels and pathological groups.

However, the clinical implications of responses to this subtest represent the chief advantage. Nowhere else does one gain such a rich sampling of a subject's coping ability. Active mastery versus passive dependency may be highlighted; the same applies to socialized versus antisocial behavior. Such aspects as the degree of "civilization" may be involved. In pathological conditions where the degree of pathology is masked, the first clue to the underlying disturbance is often demonstrated in an illogical or bizarre C response in an otherwise unremarkable protocol.

One final consideration is the relationship to the Information subtest in terms of the influence of formal training on obtained scores. The Comprehension subtest involves both judgment and facts, the Information subtest only the latter.

LIMITATIONS OF THE SUBTEST

A major difficulty with this subtest is the problem of scoring. Ambigious responses are particularly susceptible to a halo effect, depending on the examiner's impression of his subject. Further, the whole process is time consuming, ranking in the authors' experience as above that of any other subtest.

In addition, there can be unrealistic success for those who have been coached in social rules beyond the point of actual comprehension. Creative people who might seek for unusual responses will be penalized for their attempts at divergent thinking. The subtest is succeptible to placement in the battery and may be depressed if given after a projective test like the Rorschach. Items may have somewhat different meanings for people of different ages, populations, sophistication, and the like.

The inclusion of the three proverb items influences orientation or set to respond. This subtest is particularly vulnerable to negativism and hostility during the examination: contentiousness about the item rather than the response can be a problem.

CONCLUSIONS

The rich clinical clues elicited by this subtest more than compensate for its only moderate reliability in its present form as a measure of intelligence. Responses may reveal coping styles, such as passive, dependent, adequate, and self-mastering. Aggressive, negative, or hostile attitudes to questions involving social judgment may be elicted.

High scores are made by the college student or gifted high school youngster. The implication that impulses can be delayed and that proper behavior is to be expected may or may not be true, but, clearly, the ability to verbalize such rules of behavior is a help in deciding about a patient's ability to behave adequately.

Successes suggest a pragmatic, socially conventional individual. Canny practicality may be drawn upon, also wide experience and ability to think ahead. Suggestions of social maturity, social mindedness, and even overcompliance can be explored as well as the ability to organize practical knowledge. Successful individuals often verbalize well and are verbally productive.

Adequate judgment, common sense, social judgment, and competence are indicated by high scores. Among pathological groups, the brain damaged, the retarded, and subjects with anxiety states are noted to do relatively well on the C subtest.

Those who are unable to make adequate judgments about everyday situations are apt to score low on Comprehension. The overly concrete, those who reject the hypothetical premise of the question, or those who are contentious have difficulty. The nonverbal individual who does not develop his answer sufficiently will be penalized, especially if he presents himself in a way leading to negative bias on the part of the examiner.

Preoccupations with phobic themes, dependency, hostility, guilt, and the like, are apt to reduce scores. The intrusion of bizarre ideas or atypical affect can lower scores. Early psychotic processes may be reflected in selective failures. Sociopathic ideas may result in general failures. Social judgment can be impaired by high need-approval as well.

Doubt-laden individuals can find it difficult to select a response, while obsessive individuals may respond excessively, unable to recognize when they have said enough. Chronic anxiety states may be penalizing as well.

REFERENCES

Berger, L., Bernstein, A., Klein, E., Cohen, J., & Lucas, G. Effects of aging and pathology on the factorial structure of intelligence. *Journal of Consulting Psychology*, 1964, **28**, 199–207.

Blatt, S. J., & Allison, J. The intelligence test in personality assessment. In A. Rabin (Ed.). *Projective techniques in personality assessment.* New York: Springer, 1968. Pp 421–460.

Bloom, B. L., & Goldman, R. K. Sensitivity of the WAIS to language handicap in a psychotic population. *Journal of Clinical Psychology*, 1962, **18**, 161–162.

Cohen, J. A factor-analytically based rationale for the WAIS. *Journal of Consulting Psychology*, 1957, **21**, 451–457. (a)

Cohen, J. The factorial structure of the WAIS between early adulthood and old age. *Journal of Consulting Psychology*, 1957, **21**, 283–290. (b)

Dennerll, R. D., Den Broeder, J., & Sokolov, S. L. WISC and WAIS factors in children and adults with epilepsy. *Journal of Clinical Psychology*, 1964, **20**, 236–240.

Dickstein, L. S., & MacEvitt, M. Comprehension subtest on the WAIS and need for approval. *Psychological Reports*, 1971, **28**, 482.

Fogel, M. L. The Proverbs Test in the appraisal of cerebral disease. *Journal of General Psychology*, 1965, **72**, 269–275.

Grisso, J. T., & Meadow, A. Test interference in a Rorschach-WAIS administration technique. *Journal of Consulting Psychology*, 1967, **31**, 382–386.

Halpern, F. The trap. *Clinical Psychologist*, 1968, **21**, 59–61.

Hunt, W. A., Quay, H. C., & Walker, R. E. The validity of clinical judgments of asocial tendency. *Journal of Clinical Psychology*, 1966, **22**, 116–118.

Kitzinger, H., & Blumberg, E. S. Supplementary guide for administering and scoring the Wechsler Bellevue Intelligence Scale, Form I. *Psychological Monographs*, 1951, **65**, #319.

Ladd, C. E. WAIS performances of brain-damaged and neurotic patients. *Journal of Clinical Psychology*, 1964, **20**, 115–117.

Martin, H. J. Forum. *Clinical Psychologist*, 1968, **21**, 136–137.

Newland, T. E., & Smith, P. A. Statistically significant differences between subtest scaled scores on the WISC and the WAIS. *Journal of School Psychology*, 1967, **5**, 122–127.

Payne, D. A., & Lehmann, I. T. A brief WAIS item analysis. *Journal of Clinical Psychology*, 1966, **22**, 296–297.

Riegel, R. M., & Riegel, K. F. A comparison and reinterpretation of factor structure of the W-B, the WAIS, and the HAWIE on aged persons. *Journal of Consulting Psychology*, 1962, **26**, 31–37.

Roth, R. M. The Comprehension subtest of the WAIS as an indicator of social awareness. *Journal of Educational Psychology*, 1963, **56**, 387–388.

Russell, E. W. A WAIS factor analysis with brain-damaged subjects using criterion measures. *Journal of Consulting and Clinical Psychology,* 1972, **39**, 133–139.

Sarason, I. G., & Minard, J. Test anxiety, experimental instructions, and the WAIS. *Journal of Educational Psychology*, 1962, **53**, 299–302.

Sattler, J. M., Hillix, W. A., & Neher, L. A. Halo effect in examiner scoring of intelligence test responses. *Journal of Consulting and Clinical Psychology*, 1970, **34**, 172–176.

Saunders, D. R. Factor analysis of Comprehension and Similarities items from the WAIS. Unpublished paper quoted in: Saunders, D. R. & Gittinger, W. Patterns of intellectual functioning and their implications for the dynamics of behavior. Reprinted from: *The Role and methodology of classification and psychopathology.* Washington, D. C.: US Department of Health, Education, and Welfare, Public Health Service, undated.

Schafer, R. *Projective testing and psychoanalysis.* New York: International Universities Press, 1967.

Schwartz, M. L. The scoring of WAIS Comprehension responses by experienced and inexperienced judges. *Journal of Clinical Psychology*, 1966, **22**, 425.

Shaw, D. J. Factor analysis of the collegiate WAIS. *Journal of Consulting Psychology*, 1967, **31**, 217.

Sprague, R. L., & Quay, H. C. A factor analytic study of the responses of mental retardates on the WAIS. *American Journal of Mental Deficiency*, 1966, **70**, 595–600.

Taylor, J. B. The structure of ability in the lower intellectual range. *American Journal of Mental Deficiency*, 1964, **68**, 766–774.

Thomas, C. S. The "yell fire" response as an indicator of impaired impulse control. *Journal of Clinical Psychology*, 1966, **22**, 221–223.

Walker, R. E. Hunt, W. A., & Schwartz, M. L. The difficulty of WAIS C scoring. *Journal of Clinical Psychology*, 1965, **21**, 427–429.

Wechsler, D. *The measurement and appraisal of adult intelligence.* Baltimore: Williams & Wilkins, 1958.

Zimmerman, S. F., Whitmyre, J. W., & Fields, F. R. J. Factor analytic structure of the WAIS in patients with diffuse and lateralized cerebral dysfunction. *Journal of Clinical Psychology*, 1970, **26**, 462–465.

CHAPTER 5

ARITHMETIC

The developing child brings order to his world by becoming increasingly selective in his discriminations. He begins with gross differentiation, progresses through comparisons, and finally reaches quantification and numeration. Even before the advent of psychometrics, ability to manipulate numbers in solving problems was considered a rough and ready measure of intellectual functioning. Computational problems have been used in one form or another in most intelligence scales.

It is inconceivable to picture any western civilization in which a person can successfully adjust to the demands of society without some basic knowledge of number manipulations. Arithmetic is one of the "three Rs" taught to children. It is used in such diverse activities as purchasing grocery store items and calculating take-home pay.

Wechsler assumes that by adolescence mastery of these skills should be so complete that paper and pencil are not required for the items he utilized. In such a situation, then, attention and alertness assume greater importance. In fact, even on the easier Arithmetic items, subjects who perceive their performance as poor frequently attribute this to "nervousness" and resulting lapses in attention.

WHAT THE TEST MEASURES

As Piaget has demonstrated, the comprehension of the abstract concept of number is a measure of cognitive development. The Arithmetic subtest thus can illuminate this aspect of intellectual development and how it relates to the noncognitive (though not necessarily nonintellective) factors of attention and concentration.

Also involved in the test is the problem-solving "set" that allows the subject to abstract the number operation or operations—addition, subtraction, division, and multiplication from the matrix problem involving these operations.

Armchair philosophizing suggests that what is measured depends upon subject matter and situational context. For the illiterate, the concept of numbers and their manipulation may be of prime importance. For women in a Western culture, it is generally acceptable for them to be "poor at figures." Actual computational operations do not go beyond the seventh-grade level.

The timed element must certainly be considered as favoring certain vocational roles (for example, engineering and accountancy) while placing other occupations (for example, history and art) at a relative disadvantage. Arithmetic is also labeled a measure of concentration and freedom from distractability. A subject's erratic performance is suggestive of temporary inefficiency in this area.

DESCRIPTION

The Arithmetic subtest consists of 14 timed items, the only subtest in the verbal section with time limits. For items #1 through #4 the subject is allowed 15 seconds to reply verbally after the problem has been enunciated by the examiner. Through item #10 the time limit is increased to 30 seconds; from items #11 through #13, to 60 seconds; and for item #14, to 120 seconds. Bonuses can be obtained for speedy performance on the last four items.

As used in the WAIS, the Arithmetic subtest is four items longer than the Wechsler Bellevue I version, but shares seven of the original items.

FACTOR ANALYSIS

J. Cohen's (1957) analysis suggests that the Arithmetic subtest is on a par with Comprehension as a measure of G. It also follows the general trend in that the correlation decreases for the 60 and over age group. In terms of percentages, the drop is from 51 percent to 39 percent. Cohen reports Arithmetic as a weak measure of the memory factor for the younger ages, but it represents a substantial 26 percent of the variance for the older age group. In the Berger, Bernstein, Klein, Cohen, and Lucas (1964) reanalysis of the standardization sample, the correlation with the memory factor was insignificant for the 18 to 19 and above-60 age groups and slight (about 14 percent of the variance) for the 25 to 34 and 45 to 54 age groups. For the former groups, a moderate loading was found on the verbal comprehension factor. Birren's analysis (reported in Riegel & Riegel, 1962) of a stratified group 20 to 74 years old confirmed again the high loading on verbal comprehension and low positive loading on memory.

For college students, a medium loading (0.53) was reported by Shaw (1967) on perceptual organization. Chronic brain-damaged patients (Russell, 1972) appear similar to chronic schizophrenics (Berger, et al., 1964) in that the highest loading is on memory, but there are still significant loadings on verbal comprehension and perceptual organization. For the dull and mentally retarded, this subtest is a moderately good indicator of G and also of verbal comprehension (Sprague & Quay, 1966; Taylor, 1964). For epileptics, the highest loading occurs on the freedom-from-distraction factor (Dennerll, Den Broeder, & Sokolov, 1964). Results obtained for the left (LI), right (RI), and diffusely involved (DI) organic groups studied by Zimmerman, Whitmyre, and Fields (1970) are not easily explained. The highest correlation occurs on a highly specific factor, with significant loadings obtained on the Arithmetic and Picture Completion for the RI group, Arithmetic and Digit Span for the LI group, and Similarities for the DI group.

Thus, it appears that, apart from being a measure of G, the Arithmetic subtest measures different aspects for different populations. Current results suggest that in the majority of cases it measures an ability to conceptualize verbally and express numerical concepts. Secondarily, it measures the ability to concentrate and resist distraction, in the sense that the problem-solving process (unless there is sudden insight) demands concentration and application.

ADMINISTRATION

In a drastic change from the Wechsler Bellevue directions, Wechsler (1955) warns that this subtest should not be introduced as being composed of arithmetic problems, since such forewarning might adversely affect the performance of those with negative or defeatist attitudes in this area. Instead, the examiner simply says: "Let's try these."[1] Nevertheless, it is not unusual for subjects to complain that the subtest is unfair in asking them to concentrate or to claim that paper and pencil are essential. The manual prohibits the use of any such aid. A minor point might also be mentioned: at no time is the subject allowed to read any of the items, this practice being confined only to the WISC.

The subtest begins at item #3 (dollars), but if both this and the following item are failed, items #1 (blocks) and #2 (books)—simple counting and subtraction—are to be administered as well. Otherwise these are automatically credited. If both of these are failed, the subtest is discontinued. Items are ordinarily administered until four consecutive failures have occurred. Note should be made of correct answers if given after the time limit. Repetitions of questions are permitted if requested. However, time is counted from the end of the first presentation.

The Arithmetic subtest is the most school-oriented subtest in the WAIS. Individuals with little schooling are apt to be upset at the idea of being quizzed in this area. In our culture women particularly are apt to stress their dislike of and/or lack of ability in arithmetic.

Worth noting is how individuals react to this subtest. Are they distressed? Do they rally and do well? Do they reject the task as beyond their competence? How do they go about solving the problem? Were their approaches rational or bizarre?

TESTING THE LIMITS

In testing the limits Rappaport, Gill, and Schafer (1945) suggest that when subjects have given rapid but erroneous answers, they should be apprised of the errors; corrections can then be noted. Help might be given when necessary so that the stage at which failure occurs (simple arithmetic versus problem identification) can be explored. Under such circumstances credits are not allowed.

Other simple questions might be added for subjects who appear to be particularly limited: for example, adding up to five would be within the scope of the average 6-year-old, while the average 7-year-old can add up to ten (Gesell, 1940).

After testing is completed, one can also obtain some gross measure of the effects of anxiety, if such is suspected, either by repeating previously failed problems or by giving subjects paper and pencil to complete items rejected as

[1] This can cause some confusion. At times the "$4 and $5" item has given rise to a puzzled "400 pennies and 500 pennies?" only to be followed readily by the correct answer when the subject was told that this was an arithmetic problem.

too difficult without such aids. Such strategy allows for gross estimation as to whether the subject is familiar with the operations but unable to concentrate or whether he is ignorant of the principles involved in the arithmetic process.

SCORING

Scoring is rarely a problem with Arithmetic because of the simple pass-fail format, but one should guard against examiner bias. E. Cohen (1965) studied a sample of 13 examiners who obtained significantly different results on the WB Arithmetic subtest. Item carryover and similarities in format suggest that the phenomenum is possible on the WAIS version.

Unusual answers should be inquired into and recorded, since the method of achieving such answers can be important in assessing deviant thinking processes. An error recognized and spontaneously corrected within time limits is credited. On items where speed of performance is a factor, items #11 through #14, spontaneous corrections would be credited relative to the total elapsed time. For example, subjects frequently respond to item #14 with "48," failing to correct for the half day. If they recognize this error and spontaneously correct themselves within the 20-second time bonus interval, they would still obtain a score of 2. If the correction comes after 20 seconds but within 2 minutes, the score will be 1.

If for clinical reasons testing is continued beyond the four consecutive failures limit, successes beyond this point can be treated in the interpretation of results, but not in the computation of the raw scores.

ITEM PLACEMENT

When average raw scores on Arithmetic are compared by age level, there is a range of successes, with the high point at middle age and some decay at the older age level (Table 5–1). The adolescents (age 16 to 17) reveal an average raw score of 10. This increases to 11 for the central age ranges but

Table 5–1

ITEM PLACEMENT OF AVERAGE SCORES FOR FOUR AGE LEVELS

Age 16–17	(average raw score 10)	success through item #10
Age 25–34	(average raw score 11)	success through item #11
Age 45–54	(average raw score 11)	success through item #11
Age 65–69	(average raw score 9)	success through item #9

A raw score of 14 can be obtained without time bonuses.

Source: D. Wechsler, *Manual, Wechsler Adult Intelligence Scale* (New York: Psychological Corporation, 1955), p. 101–108.

declines to an average raw score of 9 for the older subjects (65 to 69). While time bonuses are available on this subtest, none is necessary to obtain an average score. Typically, an average score involves mastery of simple, generally one-step problems involving elementary multiplication, division, and subtraction. The total range of successes is from 100 percent passing of the initial items to 20 percent passing of the most difficult item by the standardization sample (Wechsler, 1958), indicating a limited range of items.

SIGNIFICANT DIFFERENCES BETWEEN ARITHMETIC AND OTHER SUBTESTS

In their analysis of variations between Arithmetic and the other WAIS subtests necessary to reach significance, Newland and Smith (1967) report differences of three to four scale score points necessary at the 0.05, and three to six points at the 0.01 level. Lesser differences were required for most of the verbal subtests, while Comprehension and several of the performance subtests did not reach significance until a four- to six-point difference was achieved (see Table 5–2).

ITEM COMPOSITION AND DIFFICULTY

This subtest is made up of items utilizing the four basic arithmetic operations—addition, subtraction, multiplication, and division, singly and in various combinations, the latter from item #9 on.

Table 5–2
DIFFERENCES BETWEEN ARITHMETIC AND ALL OTHER SCALED SCORES NECESSARY TO SATISFY THE 0.05 AND 0.01 CONFIDENCE LEVELS

	Confidence	*Subtests*									
CA	*level*	*I*	*C*	*S*	*D*	*V*	*DS*	*PC*	*BD*	*PA*	*OA*
18–19	0.05	3	4	3	4	3	3	4	4	4	4
	0.01	4	5	5	6	4	4	5	5	6	6
25–34	0.05	3	4	3	4	3	a	3	4	4	4
	0.01	4	5	5	5	4		5	5	6	6
45–54	0.05	3	4	4	4	3	a	3	3	4	4
	0.01	4	5	5	6	4		5	5	5	5

[a]DS omitted.
Source: From T. E. Newland and P. A. Smith, Statistically significant differences between subtest scaled scores on the WISC and the WAIS, *Journal of School Psychology*, 1967, 5, 126.

The placement of items has been analyzed by Payne and Lehmann (1966) for a large college sample. Only minor differences in rank were obtained. However, difficulty increased markedly between items #10 and #11. Although Wechsler (1958) and Shaw (1965) report this subtest to be easier for men, no sex differences were determined.

RESEARCH WITH THE ARITHMETIC SUBTEST

Saunders (1960) regards the A subtest as a measure of "ideational discipline" or concentration and views a subject's performance as compensatory to primatively determined behaviors. In the Wechsler clinical analysis (Wechsler, 1955, pp 171–172) the Arithmetic subtest score deviates from 1.5 to 2.5 units below the subjects' mean subtest scores in organic brain disease and adolescent sociopaths. Scores may not deviate in schizophrenics and *S*s manifesting anxiety states; but if deviations occur, they are usually 1.5 to 2.5 units below *S*'s mean subtest scores. A deviation of 3 or more units below *S*'s mean subtest score is said to be characteristic of mental defectives.

Ladd (1964), on the other hand, found scores for his brain-damaged and neurotic patients to deviate 1.5 to 2.5 above the mean of their other subtests, differing markedly with Wechsler's results. Bloom and Goldman (1962) did not find differences on this subtest between a Connecticut and Hawaiian psychotic population.

Experimental verification regarding utility in differential diagnosis between the various patient populations is lacking. Available research studies are limited to the relationship between anxiety and obtained test scores.

Apparently a subject's performance on this test is affected if the situation is manipulated to produce anxiety. Davis (1969) and Davis, Peacock, Fitzpatrick, and Mulhern (1969) report that prior failure experience is associated with lowered performance. Davis reasoned that Arithmetic is vulnerable to "transient emotional states." Knox and Grippaldi (1970) offer corroborative evidence. High anxiety groups showed a pattern of lower A and DS scores relative to S scores.

Not clear, however, is the relationship to an anxiety trait condition as defined by high scores on such measures as the Taylor Manifest Anxiety Scale and the Welch Anxiety Scale. In the Knox and Grippaldi study lowered scores were noted in both high anxious-anxiety state *S*s and anxiety trait *S*s. Jurjevich (1963) found no relationship between anxiety as measured by the Taylor scale and low A scores. But Siegman (1956) had reported earlier that, when combined with the D, DS, BD, and OA subtests, the resulting score enabled one to distinguish between high and low scorers on the Taylor Scale.

Callens and Meltzer (1969) provide some constructive criticism regarding the discrepant results. They argue that (1) for neurotics and schizophrenic patients, intelligence, hitherto uncontrolled, might be a complicating factor and (2) the relationship between A and D scores might be of paramount importance. D greater than A was noted for dull or nonanxious normals and dull schizophrenics. Grossman (1969) continues in a similar vein. He notes that the age variable should be considered and further points out that cautiousness, a characteristic of older subjects, lowers the Arithmetic score.

ADVANTAGES OF THE SUBTEST

The Arithmetic subtest allows a rapid estimate of number skills couched in word problems. The level of calculations is well below the educational attainment available to an individual of 16 or older. Particularly at the lower levels, this subtest measures social competency, in the sense that it is represented by ability to do at least "candy-store" arithmetic. This subtest may elicit a subject's concern about learning and education. Since attention and concentration are involved in success, the way in which a subject applies himself to a challenging task can be observed.

In addition to these contributions, Arithmetic is also a fair measure of general intelligence and can be considered fairly reliable.

Limitations of the Subtest

Men find Arithmetic somewhat easier than women, which might be a point to consider if a brief test were to be selected. Although the test is easily administered, numerous subjects find the assessment of arithmetical skills a rather threatening situation. This fact is recognized by Wechsler in his administration instructions. Further, in contrast to Information, where the subtest is considered emotionally nonthreatening, and may therefore mitigate existing anxiety, the Arithmetic subtest increases tension. In the authors' experience subjects sometimes ask to be excused on this subtest because of the severity of apprehension and anxiety it produces. Whether or not examiners tend to be overly sympathetic to the subject's plight in such situations is unknown. However, examiner variables do influence obtained scores on a test recognized as objectively easy to administer and score.

CONCLUSIONS

Arithmetic provides clues to memory and concentration, particularly when paired with Digit Span. Success on this subtest indicates meticulous attention to a task; hence some obsessives do well when they can combine speed with meticulousness. A favorable orientation toward school tasks (particularly to mathematics) is helpful in obtaining a high score, since many subjects express discomfort in mentally solving arithmetic problems.

Failures may suggest any number of problems, ranging from simple computational errors made by the overanxious and apprehensive subject, carelessness by the failure-oriented, to a loss of reality in bizarre solutions. In case of suspected mental deficiency and illiteracy, clinicians may seek clarification whether failure occurs because of inadequate conceptualization of the problem or insufficient arithmetic training, or both.

REFERENCES

Berger, L., Bernstein, A., Klein, E., Cohen, J., & Lucas, G. Effect of aging and pathology on the factorial structure of intelligence. *Journal of Consulting Psychology*, 1964, **28**, 199–207.

Bloom, B. L., & Goldman, R. K. Sensitivity of the WAIS to language handicap in a psychotic population. *Journal of Clinical Psychology*, 1962, **18**, 161–162.

Callens, C. J., & Meltzer, M. L. Effect of anxiety and diagnosis on Arithmetic and Digit Span performance on the WAIS. *Journal of Consulting and Clinical Psychology*, 1969, **33**, 630.

Cohen, E. Examiner differences with individual intelligence tests. *Perceptual and Motor Skills*, 1965, **20**, 1324.

Cohen, J. The factorial structure of the WAIS between early adulthood and old age. *Journal of Consulting Psychology*, 1957, **21**, 283–290.

Davis, W. E. Effect of prior failure on subjects' WAIS Arithmetic subtest scores. *Journal of Clinical Psychology*, 1969, **25**, 72–73.

Davis, W. E., Peacock, W., Fitzpatrick, P., & Mulhern, M. Examiner differences, prior failure, and subjects' WAIS Arithmetic scores. *Journal of Clinical Psychology*, 1969, **25**, 178–180.

Dennerll, R., Den Broeder, J., & Sokolov, S. WISC and WAIS factors in children and adults with epilepsy. *Journal of Clinical Psychology*, 1964, **20**, 236–240.

Gesell, A. *The first five years of life.* New York: Harper & Row, 1940.

Grossman, J. L. A comparison of cautious behavior of elderly and young persons on WAIS subtest performance. *Dissertation Abstracts*, 1969, **30**, 2908–2909.

Jurjevich, R. M. Interrelationships of anxiety indicies of Wechsler Intelligence Scales and MMPI scales. *Journal of General Psychology*, 1963, **69**, 135–142.

Knox, W. J., & Grippaldi, R. High levels of state or trait anxiety and performance on selected verbal WAIS subtests. *Psychological Reports*, 1970, **27**, 375–379.

Ladd, C. E. WAIS performances of brain-damaged and neurotic patients. *Journal of Clinical Psychology*, 1964, **20**, 115–117.

Newland, T. E., or Smith, P. A. Statistically significant differences between subtest scaled scores on the WISC and the WAIS. *Journal of School Psychology*, 1967, **5**, 122–127.

Payne, D. A., & Lehmann, I. J. A brief WAIS item analysis. *Journal of Clinical Psychology*; 1966, **22**, 296–297.

Rappaport, D., Gill, M. M., & Schafer, R. *Diagnostic psychological testing.* Chicago: Year Book Publishers, 1945

Riegel, K. F., & Riegel, R. M. A comparison and reinterpretation of factor structure of the W-B, the WAIS, and the HAWIE on aged persons. *Journal of Consulting Psychology*, 1962, **26**, 31–37.

Russell, E. W. A WAIS factor analysis with brain-damaged subjects using criterion measures. *Journal of Consulting and Clinical Psychology*, 1972, **39**, 133–139.

Saunder, D. R. A factor analysis of the Information and Arithmetic subtest items of the WAIS. *Psychological Reports*, 1960, **6**, 367–383.

Shaw, D. J. Sexual bias in the WAIS. *Journal of Consulting Psychology*, 1965, **29**, 590–591.

Shaw, D. J. Factor analysis of the collegiate WAIS. *Journal of Consulting Psychology*, 1967, **31**, 217.

Siegman, A. W. Cognitive, affective, and psychopathological correlates of the Taylor Manifest Anxiety Scale. *Journal of Consulting Psychology*, 1956, **20**, 137–141.

Taylor, J. B. The structure of ability in the lower intellectual range. *American Journal of Mental Deficiency*, 1964, **68**, 766–774.

Wechsler, D. *Manual, Wechsler Adult Intelligence Scale.* New York: Psychological Corporation, 1955.

Wechsler, D. *The measurement and appraisal of adult intelligence.* Baltimore: Williams & Wilkins, 1958.

Zimmerman, S. F., Whitmyre, J. W., & Fields, F. R. J. Factor analytic structure of the WAIS in patients with diffuse and lateralized cerebral dysfunction. *Journal of Clinical Psychology*, 1970, **26**, 462–465.

CHAPTER 6

SIMILARITIES

Puzzles, riddles, conundrums, and oracles are universally recognized challenges to human wit and ingenuity. These tasks appear to represent a specific application of man's ability to generalize, abstract, and find relationships that are not obvious at first. Yet, despite the recognition that a test of verbal ingenuity was highly correlated with general intelligence, items requiring that the subject make generalizations and draw abstractions were not popular in psychological tests. Wechsler (1944) himself almost omitted such items in his original scale. The fact that items used in the original Binet scales demanded considerable proficiency in language and word knowledge contributed to his reluctance. However, by careful item selection, breadth of vocabulary was relegated to a minor factor in the Wechsler Bellevue Similarities (S) subtest, and the test has been used in all subsequent Wechsler scales. In the WAIS difficulty is increased by emphasizing concept formation rather than word difficulty.

No individual can adjust to the demands of society without making implicit or explicit use of classificatory relationships. These develop through exposure to materials and information and pass through stages from the childlike recognition of differences through the conceptualization of differential degrees of abstraction, such as the concrete, the functional, and the conceptual. In the WAIS format emphasis is placed upon auditory perception and verbal expression of classificatory relationships.

WHAT THE TEST MEASURES

The degree to which the subject has assimilated similarities and differences in the objects, facts, and ideas surrounding him and his ability to order the likenesses into classes are at issue in the Similarities subtest. Memory, comprehension, and capacity for associative thinking are called into play. The early items are potentially overlearned and evoke, almost mechanically, previously learned associations. As the pairs presented grow more difficult, conceptual judgments are involved. Separation of essential from nonessential features enables qualities or levels of intellectual functioning to be distinguished. In this respect, consistency of responses at the one-point level probably reflects a person from whom less may be expected in terms of superior output. Such a result is not too likely to be due to maladjustment. Conversely, an erratic performance on the S, or on any of the subtests, is at least suggestive of a higher potential. As the items progress in difficulty, a shift in the subject's orientation from the conceptual to the concrete or functional levels can be expected.

DESCRIPTION

Similarities consists of 13 paired items, ten (77 percent) of which are retained from the Wechsler Bellevue. The added items are at the below average level, easing the difficulty of this measure slightly for average or below average patients. Also, the test is slightly extended (one weighted score point) at its top.

FACTOR ANALYSIS

In the Cohen (1957) analysis Similarities ranks as a good measure of G, 0.77 for the younger ages dropped to 0.65 for the over 60 age group. The correlation with verbal comprehension is quite low, less than 10 percent of the variance for the younger, but higher (about 20 percent of the variance) for the older age groups. Berger, Bernstein, Klein, Cohen, and Lucas (1964) in their reanalysis found that Similarities is moderately associated only with verbal comprehension throughout the age range. However, in the Birren analysis (quoted in Riegel & Riegel, 1962) Similarities reflects verbal comprehension and, to a minor extent, freedom from distractions.

For four specific groups, Similarities measures principally verbal comprehension—chronic schizophrenics (Berger et al., 1964), chronic brain-damaged (Russell, 1972), the dull and mentally retarded (Sprague and Quay, 1966; Taylor, 1964), and epileptics (Dennerll, Den Broeder, & Sokolov, 1964). For the left, right, and diffusely involved organic, the highest loading again occurred on verbal comprehension for the RI and DI groups, with lower but still significant loading for LI. However, there is still a significant loading for DI on the specific fourth factor (Zimmerman, Whitmyre, & Fields, 1970).

The Similarities subtest reflects those aspects of general intelligence that require the subject to display a capacity for verbal concept association. The factor structure remains generally stable across different age groups and different diagnostic categories, although freedom from distraction and perceptual organization at times are evident. That such is the case should not be too surprising in view of the fact that, in the process of generalizing, visual imagery and detailed examination of such are essential components, especially when concept formation must be derived from previously unconnected objects or ideas rather than learned associations. Compared to the Comprehension subtest in which emphasis is placed on social variables, this subtest requires the subject to find solutions with no immediate, everyday application. Proficiency in this task, naturally, is affected by any process that impairs thinking. However, the concepts used in the WAIS are not esoteric, and the easier ones are overlearned.

ADMINISTRATION

Many subjects find the Similarities subtest an interesting type of test. Unlike the earlier verbal subtests, the Similarities subtest begins with item #1. The examiner is allowed to explain and give a rather detailed example of the type of creditable responses only if the subject completely fails the first item. If the subject obtains a 1-point rather than a 2-point credit, no explanations are given. No further help, other than the need for clarification, is given for the remaining items. The subtest is discontinued after four consecutive zero responses.

When the WAIS is used in a test battery, scores on this subtest are lowered if administration follows that of the Rorschach (Grisso & Meadow, 1967). Therefore, clinicians will have to weigh factors carefully in sequencing the administration of the WAIS.

TESTING THE LIMITS

Because of its relationship to mental age, Similarities can prove to be too difficult for certain patients. On the Binet, Similarities are first introduced at age 7, with items of difference placed at age 6. The type of response can give gross indications of the level of abstract thinking or of the level of regression suffered. To test this further, the subject can be encouraged to give a similarity or can be led to this stage through administration of Binet, WIPPSI, or WISC items. Also, the subject might be urged on by recalling his previous successes–for example, "You said an orange and a banana are to eat. . . . Now how are a — ." The degree of prompting necessary to elicit a response should be noted. No scores can be credited as successes in testing the limits.

SCORING

Unlike Comprehension and Vocabulary, Similarities scoring did not prove to be susceptible to the halo effect (Sattler, Hillix, & Neher 1970).

A problem with scoring is that of determining the degree of abstraction achieved. However, the scoring guide is reasonably complete–the main point is that the more abstract comparisons receive a 2-point score (i.e., "A coat and a dress are clothing"), while a more functional concrete answer ("You wear 'em") receives a score of 1. Several 1-point answers on one item do not add up to a 2-point score.

If several responses are given, the credits are dependent upon the subject emphasis. Scores can be increased as for example in #2: "Same way like a fruit" is scored zero, but if the subject continues, " . . . both of them clothing," the score is then 2. On the other hand, a creditable answer can be degraded by bizarre thinking or illogical conclusions. Examples: #6: "They are senses, also nonsense, ha ha"; #11: "Both burn, being man-made." If the subject cannot clarify any further, these responses would be scored zero.

ITEM PLACEMENT

Age patterns are discernable when Similarities scores are examined (Table 6–1), with a decline observable as early as the 45- to 54-year age level. The average raw score at age 16 to 17 is 13. This pattern typically reflects success at least up to item #7 or beyond, usually with 2-point responses for the first five or six items and 1-point responses from then on. There is a 1- to 2-point increase at the young adult level (25 to 34), in contrast to the decline

Table 6–1
ITEM PLACEMENT OF AVERAGE SCORES FOR FOUR AGE LEVELS

Age 16–17	(average raw score 13)	success through item #7
Age 25–34	(average raw score 14–15)	success through item #7
Age 45–54	(average raw score 11–13)	success through item #6
Age 65–69	(average raw score 10–11)	success through item #5

Source: D. Wechsler, *Manual, Wechsler Adult Intelligence Scale* (New York: Psychological Corporation, 1955), p. 101–108.

by middle age when an average raw score of 11 to 13 is expected. A further loss for the older age level (65 to 69) results in an average raw score of 10 to 11.

The range of items is somewhat limited. Wechsler (1958) notes that 18 percent of the standardization sample could pass the most difficult items, while 7 percent received no score on the easiest item.

SIGNIFICANT DIFFERENCES BETWEEN SIMILARITIES AND OTHER SUBTESTS

According to the Newland and Smith analysis (1967), the Similarities subtest must differ three to four points from the other subtests for the difference to be significant at the 0.05 level and three to five points to be significant at the 0.01 level. Least differences were required for Information and Vocabulary, while other differences were much the same for verbal and performance subtests. (See Table 6–2.)

Table 6–2
DIFFERENCES BETWEEN SIMILARITIES AND ALL OTHER SCALED SCORES NECESSARY TO SATISFY THE 0.05 AND 0.01 CONFIDENCE LEVELS

		Subtests									
CA		*I*	*C*	*A*	*D*	*V*	*DS*	*PC*	*BD*	*PA*	*OA*
18–19	0.05	3	4	3	4	3	3	4	3	3	4
	0.01	4	5	5	5	3	4	5	4	5	5
25–34	0.05	3	4	3	4	3	a	3	3	4	4
	0.01	4	5	5	5	3		4	4	5	5
45–54	0.05	3	4	4	4	3	a	3	3	4	4
	0.01	4	5	5	5	4		5	5	5	5

[a]DS omitted

Source: From T. E. Newland and P. A. Smith, Statistically significant differences between subtest scaled scores on the WISC and the WAIS, *Journal of School Psychology*, 1967, 5, 126.

ITEM COMPOSITION AND DIFFICULTY

Items in this subtest are not esoteric, and with few exceptions they are within the experience of the average person. Payne and Lehmann (1966) in their analysis of a large college sample note a number of reversals of item placement. For example #7 and #11 appeared more difficult, while #9 appeared easier than had been expected. There was a marked dropoff of success at #11. In regard to sex differences, Wechsler (1958) observed that this subtest significantly favored men and Payne and Lehmann (1966) noted two items showing significant differences in the expected direction—#7 and #11.

RESEARCH FINDINGS WITH THE SIMILARITIES SUBTEST

Factor analytic studies have generally indicated that the subtest measures the verbal comprehension factor, although in the case of Shaw's college students (1967) the highest loading is on Perceptual Organization. Saunders (undated) notes three aspects of this subtest: (1) precision of judgment, (2) emotional control, and (3) psychological mindedness. In Wechsler's (1958 pp. 171–172) analysis of clinical groups organic brain disease is differentiated by scores 1.5 to 2.5 units below the mean subtest score. Depending on the type of schizophrenia, scores can vary from 1.5 to 2.5 units above to over 2 or more units below the subject's subtest score. For those with anxiety states, it is generally 1.5 to 2.5 units above the mean subtest score. In adolescent sociopaths it varies from 1.5 to 2.5 units below to within ± 1.5 units of the mean subtest score. For mental defectives, it varies from within ± 1.5 units to 1.5 to 2.5 units above the mean subtest score. Ladd (1964), in contrast, found his brain-damaged and neurotic patients did not vary from the mean of their other subtests on Similarities.

Renner (1969) speculated that subjects who scored high on Similarities would draw more "generalized" than stereotyped persons on the Draw a Person test. Her hypothesis was confirmed on a matched sample of 70 male high school students.

Spence (1963) studied the pattern of Similarities responses by schizophrenic and brain-damaged. Brain-damaged patients gave fewer conceptual responses, while schizophrenics, rather than admit that they did not know the answers, tended to deny similarities between concepts. However, Watson (1965) reported some contradictory findings. In his schizophrenic group there was a greater tendency, compared to organics, not to respond when uncertain. It is likely that the types of schizophrenia were not comparable.

Admission and discharge patterns of psychiatric patients were studied by McKeever, May, and Tuma (1965). For first admission patients, higher scores on Similarities were positively and significantly correlated with early release from the hospital. Price and Gentry (1968) found schizophrenics in remission less impaired in ability to abstract symbolic relations than acute schizophrenics.

In Wiener's (1957) study chronically highly distrustful subjects obtained lower scores on this subtest than did subjects not highly distrustful. Obtained scores were not affected by deliberate attempts to induce "situational" distrust. The logical application of this approach to differentiate paranoid schizophrenics or paranoid conditions have not yet been studied.

Jortner (1970) noted the presence of "overinclusive" responses (i.e., an attribute shared by so many objects that the concept is no longer delimiting, such as "both contain atoms") in 14 percent of a sample of schizophrenics and in none of the other psychiatric cases in his research.

Bloom and Goldman (1962) reported a significant difference favoring Connecticut over Hawaiian psychotic patients on this subtest.

ADVANTAGES OF THE SUBTEST

The Similarities subtest allows a survey of the ability to abstract verbally and is perhaps the one main test in the series that permits a glimpse into the subject's creative strivings. Administration time is brief, and scoring is not too difficut. Personal preoccupations are rarely expressed and, therefore, are diagnostically meaningful when they invade this subtest. Also of diagnostic value are the differential effects of schizophrenia and brain damage in lowering scores.

LIMITATIONS OF THE SUBTEST

The problem with Similarities as a subtest is that there is no chance to establish a "bottom" score for those who are unable to detect similarities.

Although it is considered a test of the ability to abstract and generalize, its easier items are often nondiscriminating since they are generally overlearned. In such cases it seems reasonable to suggest that associative memory rather than concept association is the primary factor involved.

Cultural biases are still present, despite Wechsler's efforts to eliminate them, and women tend to do better on the S test than men.

CONCLUSIONS

This subtest can relate to academic success. It may reveal character trends: meticulousness, ostentation, sophistication. There is a relationship to both creativity and visual imagery.

Good performances on the subtest have been correlated with early release from a mental hospital. High scores are also obtained by obsessives who give multiple answers, thereby increasing their chances of producing a high level response.

A Similarities score much higher than Comprehension is sometimes indicative of the dreamer whose endless abstractions preclude pragmatic fulfillment. Nevertheless, good abstraction and conceptualizing ability revealed on the test are considered the hall marks of the intelligent person.

This subtest is particularly vulnerable to disturbance and aging. For example, scores tend to be lower for active schizophrenics than for those in remission. Brain-damaged individuals who focus on the concrete are unable to cope with the test. Negative and distrustful individuals may have difficulty if they refuse to use their imaginations to search for similarities. On the other hand, overinclusive thinking, seen in some psychotics, lowers scores. A focus on differences rather than similarities may indicate mental deficiency.

REFERENCES

Berger, L. Bernstein, A., Klein, E., Cohen, J., & Lucas, G. Effect of aging and pathology on the factorial structure of intelligence. *Journal of Consulting Psychology*, 1964, **28**, 199–207.

Bloom, B. L., & Goldman, R. K. Sensitivity of the WAIS to language handicap in a psychotic population. *Journal of Clinical Psychology*, 1962, **18**, 161–162.

Cohen, J. The factorial structure of the WAIS between early adulthood and old age. *Journal of Consulting Psychology,* 1957, **21**, 283–290.

Dennerll, R. D., Den Broeder, J., & Sokolov, S. L. WISC and WAIS factors in children and adults with epilepsy. *Journal of Clinical Psychology*, 1964, **20**, 236–240.

Grisso, J. T., & Meadow, A. Test interference in a Rorschach-WAIS administration technique. *Journal of Consulting Psychology*, 1967, **31**, 382–386.

Jortner, S. Overinclusion responses to WAIS Similarities. *Journal of Clinical Psychology*, 1970, **26**, 346–348.

Ladd, C. E. WAIS performances of brain-damaged and neurotic patients. *Journal of Clinical Psychology*, 1964, **20**, 115–117.

McKeever, W. F., May, R. A., & Tuma, A. H. Prognosis in schizophrenia: prediction of length of hospitalization from psychological test variables. *Journal of Clinical Psychology*, 1965, **21**, 214–221.

Newland, T. E., & Smith, P. A. Statistically significant differences between subtest scaled scores on the WISC and the WAIS. *Journal of School Psychology*, 1967, **5**, 122–127.

Payne, D. A., & Lehmann, I. J. A brief WAIS item analysis. *Journal of Clinical Psychology*, 1966, **22**, 296–297.

Price, A. C., & Gentry, W. D. Schizophrenic thought processes: analysis of the WAIS. *Psychological Reports*, 1968, **22**, 1099–1100.

Renner, V. Abstraction ability and stereotypy of drawings. *Perceptual and Motor Skills*, 1969, **29**, 240–242.

Riegel, R. M., & Riegel, K. F. A comparison and reinterpretation of factor structure of the W-B, the WAIS, and the HAWIE on aged persons. *Journal of Consulting Psychology*, 1962, **26**, 31–37.

Russell, E. W. A WAIS factor analysis with brain damaged subjects using criterion measures. *Journal of Consulting and Clinical Psychology*, 1972, **39**, 133–139.

Sattler, J. M., Hillix, W. A., & Neher, L. A. Halo effect in examiner scoring of intelligence test responses. *Journal of Consulting and Clinical Psychology*, 1970, **34**, 172–176.

Saunders, D. R. Factor analysis of Comprehension and Similarities items from the WAIS. Unpublished paper quoted in: Saunders, D. R. & Gittinger, W. Patterns of intellectual functioning and their implications for the dynamics of behavior. Reprinted from *The role and methodology of classification and psychopathology*. Washington, D. C.: US Department of Health, Education, and Welfare, Public Health Service, undated

Shaw, D. J. Factor analysis of the collegiate WAIS. *Journal of Consulting Psychology*, 1967, **31**, 217.

Spence, J. T. Patterns of performances on WAIS Similarities in schizophrenic, brain-damaged, and normal subjects. *Psychological Reports*, 1963, **13**, 413–417.

Sprague, R. L., & Quay, H. C. A factor analytic study of the responses of mental retardates on the WAIS. *American Journal of Mental Deficiency*, 1966, **70**, 595–600.

Taylor, J. B. The structure of ability in the lower intellectual range. *American Journal of Mental Deficiency*, 1964, **68**, 766–774.

Watson, C. G. WAIS error types in schizophrenics and organics. *Psychological Reports*, 1965, **16**, 527–530.

Wechsler, D. *The measurement of adult intelligence*. Baltimore: Williams & Wilkins, 1944.

Wechsler, D. *The measurement and appraisal of adult intelligence*. Baltimore: Williams & Wilkins, 1958.

Wiener, G. The effect of distrust on some aspects of intelligence test behavior. *Journal of Consulting Psychology*, 1957, **21**, 127–130.

Zimmerman, S. F., Whitmyre, J. W., & Fields, F. R. J. Factor analytic structure of the WAIS in patients with diffuse and lateralized cerebral dysfunction. *Journal of Clinical Psychology*, 1970, **26**, 462–465.

CHAPTER 7

DIGIT SPAN

Formal assessment of immediate recall probably dates to the pioneering efforts in 1865 of Ebbinghaus (1913), who studied the acquisition process involved in the learning of nonsense syllables. The Memory for Designs test of Graham and Kendall (1960), the memory for sentences and for story content, and the memory span for digits (items originally incorporated in the Binet scales), are but variations on a theme. The memory span for digits appears to be the most popular version and in this form has been used not only as a measure of intelligence, but also as diagnostic of anxiety, organicity, negativism, and other problems, as the section on research later in the chapter will substantiate. The Wechsler variation is essentially similar to the form used in the Binet scales with two exceptions—(1) runs are grouped together and administered consecutively to failure point and (2) the subject is failed after two instead of three misses on any run.

The utility of the Digit Span (D) subtest in the battery stems from two assumptions. First, a simple memory task can be helpful in assessing those of low intelligence, and, second, Digit Span is a rapid measure of the nonintellective factor known as attention, concentration, or freedom from distractability.

Beyond minimal levels there is little correlation between digit memory and intelligence. As a matter of fact, bright people may find the task dull and uninteresting, or of minimal importance, and do relatively poorly as a result.

There are two caveats involved in the use of digit recall as an indication of memory. First, the recall involves almost no information which a subject would ordinarily use in everyday life and would hence consider important. Second, the focus is on immediate rather than delayed memory and evidence suggests the two need not be similar. Rappaport (1945) suggested that memory impairment can be found in subjects with a high Digits score. Conversely, normal or neurotics may have impaired Digit Span but excellent memory.

WHAT THE TEST MEASURES

The test measures immediate auditory recall. Even more basically, it measures attention and freedom from distractability, particularly from bizarre affects or confused thought processes. A high score based on grouping the numbers suggests a quick adaptation to the demands of the stimulus from which might be inferred a flexibility in adaptation.

A discrepancy between forward and backward digits in favor of forward can be due to poor auditory memory, anxiety, simple inattention, or low mental capacity. A higher score for reversed digits, on the other hand, can indicate a stress-resistant ability to manipulate auditory signals under difficult circumstances, or it could indicate oppositional tendencies. How much this task is intellective and how much nonintellective is an open question. Shakow thinks that digits backward are more a test of immediate learning than attention (quoted in Rappaport, Gill, & Schafer, 1945).

DESCRIPTION

The D subtest involves a simple task, repeating orally two series of numbers or digits, one forward and one backward. It is the only WAIS subtest identical to the Wechsler Bellevue in form, although a two-digit reversed is added. The two series consist of a maximum of nine digits forward and eight backward.

FACTOR ANALYSIS

In Cohen's analysis (1957) the Digit Span subtest was found to be the poorest measure of G (0.62) for the younger age group, and it was still lower

(0.48) for the 60 and over age group. It was reported, however, to be a relatively good measure of freedom from distractability (memory), which accounted for about 20 percent of its variance in the younger age group and only slightly less for the older age levels. When Berger, Bernstein, Klein, Cohen, and Lucas (1964) reanalyzed the test, Digit Span followed the same pattern as the Arithmetic subtest, in that for the 18 to 19 and over-60 age groups the primary loading is for the verbal comprehension factor, while for the 25 to 34 and 45 to 54 age groups freedom from distraction is the major factor evaluated. In the Birren sample (quoted in Riegel & Riegel, 1962) the major loading was again on verbal comprehension.

For college students, Digit Span primarily measures freedom from distraction (Shaw, 1967). Results vary with the dull and retarded; in the Sprague and Quay (1966) study the principle factor measured was freedom from distraction (loading 0.60), but in the Taylor (1964) evaluation it was verbal comprehension (loading 0.73). For epileptics (Dennerll, Den Broeder, & Sokolov, 1964), chronic organics (Russell, 1972), and schizophrenics (Berger et al., 1964), Digit Span measures freedom from distraction. On the other hand, for differentiated organics, significant and rather high loadings occur on freedom from distractibility for the RI and DI groups and on the specific fourth factor for the LI group (Zimmerman, Whitmyre, & Fields, 1970).

On the basis of the research done on the D test, one must conclude that poor reliability and comparatively low correlation with G make this subtest one of the least discriminating of the WAIS measures. Factor specificity is affected by age and sample used, although for the diagnostic categories freedom from distractability appears to be the major factor measured.

ADMINISTRATION

Most subjects recognize Digit Span as a simple memory task providing some relaxation from the thoughtful deliberations of the preceeding Similarities subtest. However, since repetition of digits is commonly a part of the routine psychiatric examination, the D may arouse a negativistic attitude. Too, some subjects occasionally criticize the task as being meaningless.

This test comprises two sections. In the first part a subject repeats a series of digits enunciated by the examiner. In the second section the subject repeats the digits in reverse order. The test begins with the subject being asked to repeat three digits. In subsequent presentations the number of digits is increased, reaching a maximum of nine. The first section is discontinued when the subject fails both trials of any given series.

In the second section the subject also starts with a series of three digits that he is to repeat in reverse order. However, if he fails both trials of the three digit series, he is given a two-digit series and the test is discontinued at this point. If he passes a three-digit series, the test is continued with the number of digits increasing for each consecutive series to a total number of eight. As previously noted for digits forward, failure on both trials of any given series terminates testing.

Examiners may use a stopwatch to assure presentation of one digit per second.

An occasional overanxious and apprehensive subject may begin to repeat the digits before the examiner has completed the series. A useful strategy is for the examiner to lower his uplifted hand upon completion as a signal for the subject to start.

Note should be made of the method a subject uses in performing the task. He can be reminded, if necessary, that it is not necessary to convert separate digits into units (582 into "five hundred eighty-two").

Responses should be recorded and compared to stimulus item. For instance, does the subject give simple runs (4–5–6–7) instead of the presented numbers? Such a response suggests emotional disturbance or retardation. A much lower score on backward than forward digits suggests seriously impaired attention.

The types of excuses that the subject puts forth can be interesting: "I lost it" suggests temporary inefficiency but some effort. "Nope, beyond me" suggests lack of effort, either in the sense of avoidance or in the recognition of one's limitations (at the upper level).

Reversal of digits forward is worth study: inefficiency or negativism might be indicated.

The D is one of the less reliable subtests. Attempts to achieve greater reliability have not been too successful. Blackburn and Benton (1957) reverted to the Binet Digit Memory format by adding a third item to each series. They suggested termination after three consecutive failures. Reliability of the digits forward was increased under this condition, but digits backward was not made any more reliable.

Further evidence of unreliability is suggested by Grisso and Meadows (1967). They noted that if the WAIS follows the Rorschach in a test battery, the score on the D subtest is likely to deteriorate.

TESTING THE LIMITS

Testing the limits on Digit Span is accomplished by giving additional series after the failure limit has been reached in order to determine whether a simple lack of attention existed or other factors were responsible. A single run series (3–4–5) can be added. Failure here suggests severe disorganization.

SCORING

No problem in scoring is encountered with the D. The most common problem is noise or interruption, which can spoil the presentation of an item. The beginning examiner should be reminded that the score consists of the number of digits in the highest series performed correctly.

DIGIT SPAN ITEM PLACEMENT

The range of average scores is only from 9 to 11, based on the combined scores of digits forward and backward (see Table 7–1).

At age 16 a raw score of 10 to 11 is average, typically obtained by passing six digits forward and five backward. By age 25 to 34 the average raw score is 11. This drops slightly, to 10, for the middle-age sample (45 to 54). For the older age level, the average raw score reduces slightly to 9 to 10, typically five digits forward and four backward. The relatively few items on this subtest make the age changes more meaningful than might be expected with a longer measure.

SIGNIFICANT DIFFERENCES BETWEEN DIGIT SPAN AND OTHER SUBTESTS

In the Newland and Smith analysis (1967) the differences required between Digit Span and all other subtests to reach the 0.05 confidence level was most frequently four scale score points, rising to five or six points when

Table 7–1
ITEM PLACEMENT OF AVERAGE SCORES FOR FOUR AGE LEVELS

Age 16–17	(average raw score 10–11)	success on 5 or 6 digits forward, 4 or 5 digits backward
Age 25–34	(average raw score 11)	success on 6 digits forward, 5 digits backward
Age 45–54	(average raw score 10)	success on 5 or 6 digits forward, 4 or 5 digits backward
Age 65–69	(average raw score 9–10)	success on 5 or 6 digits forward, 4 or 5 digits backward

Source: D. Wechsler, *Manual, Wechsler Adult Intelligence Scale* (New York: Psychological Corporation, 1955), p. 101–108.

Table 7–2
DIFFERENCES BETWEEN DIGIT SPAN AND ALL OTHER SCALED SCORES NECESSARY TO SATISFY THE 0.05 AND 0.01 CONFIDENCE LEVELS

CA	*Confidence level*	*Subtests* *I*	*C*	*A*	*S*	*V*	*DS*	*PC*	*BD*	*PA*	*OA*
18–19	0.05	4	4	4	4	3	4	4	4	4	4
	0.01	5	5	6	5	5	5	5	5	6	6
25–34	0.05	4	4	4	4	4	a	4	4	5	5
	0.01	5	6	5	5	5		5	6	6	6
45–54	0.05	4	4	4	4	4	a	4	4	4	4
	0.01	5	6	6	5	5		5	5	6	6

[a] DS omitted

Source: From T. E. Newland and P. A. Smith, Statistically significant differences between subtest scaled scores on the WISC and the WAIS, *Journal of School Psychology,* 1967, 5, 126.

the 0.01 level was required. Significant differences between Digit Span and the other subtests were uniformly larger than those required for any other verbal subtest (Table 7–2).

ITEM COMPOSITION AND DIFFICULTY

Item placement, composition, and difficulty are not a problem on Digit Span.

RESEARCH WITH THE DIGIT SPAN SUBTEST

Factorially complex and unstable, the least reliable of all the WAIS subtests, Digit Span, nevertheless, has been subjected to more studies than any other of the WAIS tests. Saunders (1960) describes it as a measure of "the strength of the primitive tendency toward 'internalization.' " In Wechsler's (1958) analysis of clinical groups a deviation in excess of 3 units below *S*'s mean subtest score can be expected in organic brain disease. A deviation of 1.5 to 2.5 units below *S*'s mean subtest score can be expected in anxiety states, while scores appear relatively unaffected in schizophrenia. Adolescent sociopaths also do not show much deviation, or, if they do, it tends to be 1.5 to 2.5 units below the mean. Mental defectives demonstrate a pattern of 1.5 to 2.5 units below their mean subtest score, but scores could also remain ± 1.5 units within the mean.

Ladd (1964) found that his neurotic patients scored similarly to Wechsler's, but, in contrast, his brain-damaged sample showed no deviation from the mean of their other subtests on Digit Span, while Wechsler reported a marked drop. Bloom and Goldman (1962) did not find a significant difference between Connecticut and Hawaiian psychotic patients on this subtest, although the former did do slightly better.

In general, the bulk of the research has been based on the assumption that Digit Span as a measure of attention can be disrupted by anxiety. A study by Maupin and Hunter (1966) attempted to validate the assumption that Digit Span does measure attention. They correlated the Digit Span performance with receptivity to subliminal visual stimulation via a tachistoscope using 120 college students. The correlation was insignificant.

But if attention is not measured, there are studies that indicate that performance on the subtest does deteriorate under frustrating conditions. In the Maupin and Hunter study, for example, a simple clerical test and a flickering light presented at the same time the D test was being administered disrupted performance.

The degree of frustration necessary for the production of deterioration appears greater than previously assumed. Guertin (1959).reported that the presence of noise versus relative silence did not appreciably affect performance. Using visual distraction, Craddick and Grossman (1962) reached similar conclusions.

Studies in which deterioration of performance are noticeable are typically those where the experimenter deliberately set about to create a stressful situation by degrading *S*'s ability prior to testing (Pyle & Agnew 1963; Walker & Spence, 1964). Results are still inconclusive regarding the relationship between anxiety trait (proneness to anxiety as measured by various anxiety scales—for example, the Taylor Manifest Anxiety Scale) and D performance. While Jackson and Bloomberg (1958) and Walker and Spence (1964) report no relationship, Jurjevich (1963) states that anxiety prone *S*s do poorly on this subtest. Boor and Schill (1968) and Edwards (1966) corroborate. Hodges and Spielberger (1969) feel that decriment in D performance is characteristic of an anxiety state (subjective feelings of apprehension and concern presumably situationally based) but that performance is unaffected by the subject's proneness to anxiety (anxiety trait).

Two other lines of research have been pursued: (1) that D performance is affected by organicity and (2) that digits reversed greater than digits forward is indicative of negativism. Support for low scores in organic conditions come from Tolor (1958), Evans and Marmorston (1964), and Templer (1967). A contrary finding is offered by Sterne (1969), who found no differences between normal, nonclassified, and organic groups on total digits and number of digits forward or backward. Similarly, Ladd (1964) found no difference between neurotic and brain-damaged *S*s in terms of their D performance. It is possible that organics are too loosely defined and that this in part may be a confounding factor. Russell (1972), for example, noted that D is significantly more impaired by left-hemisphere damage.

The role of the digit performance in negativism stems from the suggestion of Rappaport et al. (1945, p. 180). Fox and Blatt (1969) report that a group of 14 Ss with a profile of digits backward greater than digits forward obtained significantly greater white space (S) Rorschach scores, long considered a measure of negativism, than did two control groups. Replication and correlation studies are needed.

ADVANTAGES OF THE SUBTEST

Digit Span allows a rapid check on verbal memory and attention, particularly at the lower levels. The task is neutral in that it does not involve emotionally loaded material. There is minimal cultural loading. Digit Span is rapidly administered, and individuals are not usually aware of or concerned about their errors. Frustration tolerance, especially for longer sequences or reversed sequences, can be studied. Inability to rally to such a simple task will indicate the degree of invasion of thinking disorders or limitations. Even a 3-year-old child is able to recall a three-digit sequence.

LIMITATIONS OF THE SUBTEST

The range of scores is limited. The reliability of the subtest is low, and Digit Span is the poorest measure of general intelligence in the WAIS. Temporary disturbance can affect scores. Score dispersion at the uppermost range is spotty. A raw score of 16 results in a corresponding weighted score of 16 in the table of scale score equivalents. A raw score of 17, however, gives a weighted score equivalent of 19.

CONCLUSIONS

The areas of attention and concentration are apparently being measured in Digits, but the stability of the measurement is questionable. Of all the verbal subtests, Digit Span is particularly sensitive to a less than ideal testing environment. The hard-of-hearing person who otherwise performs well may do poorly. Spoken sentences expressing ideas can be deciphered in terms of the sense they make, even if a word is missed. The individual missing one number in a random sequence automatically fails the item.

High scores can indicate ability to rally to a simple task. Classic is the success in an otherwise hysterical setting, the "belle indifference" that allows a "disturbed" individual to temporarily put aside concerns to attend to a simple and easily mastered task. In schizoid cases Digit Span may surpass Arithmetic.

Low scores can indicate the vulnerability of attention. Situational transient anxiety tends to lower scores in normal subjects.

Differential success can be diagnostic. Digits backward better than forward may result when a subject suddenly conceives of the subtest as a challenge rather than mere repetition of inconsequential numbers. Oppositional tendencies are also suggested, as are independence of thought and lack of rigidity. Digits forward two or more numbers better than backward may indicate the avoidance of effortful striving, and concrete thinking, in the sense that the concept of reversal is not understood.

REFERENCES

Berger, L., Bernstein, A., Klein, E., Cohen, J., & Lucas, G. Effect of aging and pathology on the factorial structure of intelligence. *Journal of Consulting Psychology*, 1964, **28**, 199–207.

Blackburn, H. L., & Benton, A. L. Revised administration and scoring of the Digit Span test. *Journal of Consulting Psychology*, 1957, **21**, 139–143.

Bloom, B. L., & Goldman, R. K. Sensitivity of the WAIS to language handicap in a psychotic population. *Journal of Clinical Psychology*, 1962, **18**, 161–162.

Boor, M., & Schill, T. Subtest performance on the WAIS as a function of anxiety and defensiveness. *Perceptual and Motor Skills*, 1968, **27**, 33–34.

Cohen, J. The factorial structure of the WAIS between early adulthood and old age. *Journal of Consulting Psychology*, 1957, **21**, 283–290.

Craddick, R. A., & Grossman, K. Effects of visual distraction upon performance on the WAIS digit Span. *Psychological Reports*, 1962, **10**, 642.

Dennerll, R. D., Den Broeder, J., & Sokolov, S. L. WISC and WAIS factors in children and adults with epilepsy. *Journal of Clinical Psychology*, 1964, **20**, 236–240.

Ebbinghaus, H. Memory, a contribution to experimental psychology. In *Auditory memory span*. Translated by H. A. Ruger and Clare F. Bussinius. New York: Columbia University Press, 1913.

Edwards, G. A. Anxiety correlates of the WAIS. *California Journal of Educational Research*, 1966, **17**, 144–147.

Evans, R. B., & Marmorston, J. Perceptual test signs of brain damage in cerebral thrombosis. *Perceptual and Motor Skills*, 1964, **18**, 977–988.

Fox, E., & Blatt, S. J. An attempt to test assumptions about some indications of negativism on psychological tests. *Journal of Consulting and Clinical Psychology*, 1969, **33**, 365–366.

Graham, F. K., & Kendall, B. S. Memory for Designs Test, Revised General Manual. *Perceptual and Motor Skills*, 1960, **11**, 147–188.

Grisso, J. T., & Meadow, A. Test interference in a Rorschach-WAIS administration technique. *Journal of Consulting Psychology*, 1967, **31**, 382–386.

Guertin, W. H. Auditory interference with Digit Span performance. *Journal of Clinical Psychology*, 1959, **15**, 349.

Hodges, W., & Spielberger, C. Digit Span: an indication of trait or state anxiety? *Journal of Consulting and Clinical Psychology*, 1969, **33**, 430–434.

Jackson, D. N., & Bloomberg, R. Anxiety: unitas or multiplex. *Journal of Consulting Psychology*, 1958. **22**, 220–223.

Jurjevich, R. M. Interrelationships of anxiety indices of Wechsler Intelligence Scales and MMPI scales. *Journal of General Psychology*, 1963, **69**, 135–142.

Ladd, C. E. WAIS performance of brain-damaged and neurotic patients. *Journal of Clinical Psychology*, 1964, **20**, 114–117.

Maupin, E., & Hunter, D. Digit Span as a measure of attention: attempted validation studies. *Psychological Reports*, 1966, **18**, 451–458.

Newland, T. E., & Smith, P. A. Statistically significant differences between subtest scaled scores on the WISC and the WAIS. *Journal of School Psychology*, 1967, **5**, 122–127.

Pyle, S., & Agnew, N. M. Digit Span performance as a function of noxious stimulation. *Journal of Consulting Psychology*, 1963, **27**, 281.

Rappaport, D., Gill, M. M., & Schafer, R. *Diagnostic psychological testing*. Chicago: Year Book Publishers, 1945.

Riegel, R. M., & Riegel, K. F. A comparison and reinterpretation of factor structures of the W-B, the WAIS, and the HAWIE on aged persons. *Journal of Consulting Psychology*, 1962, **26**, 31–37.

Russell, E. W. A WAIS factor analysis with brain damaged subjects using criterion measures. *Journal of Consulting and Clinical Psychology*, 1972, **39**, 133–139.

Saunders, D. E. Further implications of Mundy-Castle's correlations between EEG and Wechsler Bellevue variables. *Journal, National Institute of Personality Research*, 1960, **8**, 91–101.

Shaw, D. J. Factor analysis of the collegiate WAIS. *Journal of Consulting Psychology*, 1967, **31**, 217.

Sprague, R. L., & Quay, H. C. A factor analytic study of the responses of mental retardates on the WAIS. *American Journal of Mental Deficiency*, 1966, **70**, 595–600.

Sterne, D. M. The Benton, Porteus, and WAIS Digit Span tests with normal and brain-injured subjects. *Journal of Clinical Psychology*, 1969, **25**, 173–175.

Taylor, J. B. The structure of ability in the lower intellectual range. *American Journal of Mental Deficiency*, 1964, **68**, 766–774.

Templer, D. I. Relation between immediate and short-term memory and clinical implications. *Perceptual and Motor Skills*, 1967, **24**, 1011–1012.

Tolor, A. Further studies on the Bender Gestalt test and the Digit Span test as measures of recall. *Journal of Clinical Psychology*, 1958, **14**, 14–18.

Walker, R. E., & Spence, J. Relationship between Digit Span and anxiety. *Journal of Consulting Psychology*, 1964, **28**, 220–223.

Wechsler, D. *The measurement and appraisal of adult intelligence*. Baltimore: Williams & Wilkins, 1958.

Zimmerman, S. F., Whitmyre, J. W., & Fields, F. R. J. Factor analytic structure of the WAIS in patients with diffuse and lateralized cerebral dysfunction. *Journal of Clinical Psychology*, 1970, **26**, 462–465.

CHAPTER 8

VOCABULARY

Vocabulary is generally considered the best single measure of general intelligence. Some assessment of word knowledge is included in most individual and group scales. In tests such as the Peabody Picture Vocabulary and Ammons Picture Vocabulary it is used as the only criterion of intellectual functioning. Despite the common acceptance of vocabulary as an indicator of intelligence, the Vocabulary subtest (V) was used only as an alternate test in the Wechsler Bellevue I because of the then current feeling that it might be unfair to illiterates and the foreign-born. By 1941, however, Wechsler was recommending that Vocabulary be incorporated into the scale as a regular test. In the WAIS it is an integral part of the scale.

Vocabulary reflects an individual's familiarity with words as well as his ability to express himself through word usage. This kind of information seems clearly an important element of intelligence. The assumption can even be made that in any society, literate or nonliterate, the persons with the greatest verbal fluency are likely to be considered the most intelligent members of that society.

Ideas, associations, even feelings are verbalized better by some than by others. This ability to make meaningful his ideas and to conceptualize experiences in terms of word definitions is one indication of the individual's approach to his environment, which is strongly suggestive of his level of intelligence.

WHAT THE TEST MEASURES

In using vocabulary as a measure of intelligence it is assumed that all subjects experience a reasonably uniform background of education and culture. The Vocabulary subtest is indicative of early education and environment as well as later schooling and life experience. Vocabulary indicates sensitivity to new information and ideas and the ability to store and associatively regroup these as the occasion demands. By inference, it reveals classificatory and conceptualizing skills.

The same qualitative aspects that were seen in the Information, Comprehension, and Similarities subtests appear in Vocabulary, serving to indicate the relative degree of poverty or richness of the subject's thought processes and his environment. Also, as in the other subtests, word definition is sometimes sensitive to feelings, particularly fears or preoccupations, to irrelevancy of thought, and to bizarre associations.

It is necessary to be alert to the distinction between old, overlearned, rote responses and the vigorous striving of an individual attempting to restructure current experiences. A much different performance can be expected from persons who are stagnant mentally than from those in the second, striving group.

Vocabulary deteriorates least of all subtests with age. It does deteriorate, however, in the sense that the level of definition drops. Feifel (1949) distinguishes four types of definition that are separable from one another:

1. Synonyms
2. Use of description
3. Explanation
4. Inferior explanation, illustration, demonstration

DESCRIPTION

The V subtest is composed of 40 words (versus 42 on the Wechsler Bellevue I) to be defined. They are listed in estimated order of difficulty. Unlike any of the other WAIS subtests, there is no overlap of items from the Wechsler Bellevue, and all the words are new. Also, the emphasis upon the four parts of speech is better balanced: equal numbers of nouns and verbs, with half as many adjectives, and one lone adverb, versus an almost exclusive reliance on nouns in the Wechsler Bellevue. This results in greater stress on process, action, and change and taps personal feelings as well as ways of dealing with control, guilt, depression, frustration, and competitiveness, all aspects of social living (Barnes, 1969).

Vocabulary is the only subtest in the verbal section in which the subject does not have to depend on the examiner's diction. A word list given to the subject allows him to read as well as hear each word.

FACTOR ANALYSIS

The Vocabulary subtest is unexcelled as a measure of G up through middle age. Cohen (1957) reports a correlation of 0.83 for the standardization group. However, for the aged, the correlation drops to 0.66. In terms of percentages, this represents a shift from 69 percent to 43 percent.

Vocabulary is also a good measure of verbal comprehension, although in Cohen's analysis, memory becomes the more important factor for the aged. In the Berger, Bernstein, Klein, Cohen, and Lucas reanalysis (1964) it remains a pure measure of verbal comprehension at all age levels. (Birren, as quoted in Riegel and Riegel, 1962, does not report on subtest specificity for this subtest.)

Vocabulary continues as a pure measure of verbal comprehension for college students (Shaw, 1967), chronic schizophrenics (Berger et al., 1964), chronic brain-damaged patients (Russell, 1972), epileptics (Dennerll, Den Broeder, & Sokolov, 1964), and the dull and mentally retarded (Taylor, 1964; Sprague & Quay, 1966). However, in the Sprague and Quay sample, curiously, the correlation with general intelligence is quite low (0.07). This finding cannot be explained at the present. Factorial purity is also reported on the differentiated groups of organics studied by Zimmerman, Whitmyre, and Fields (1970), and here, factorial loadings appear similar to those found with the Comprehension subtest.

The Vocabulary subtest measures those aspects of general intelligence that show the comprehension of words and meanings as a basic requirement for everyday functioning. Language development, which is a key factor in the assessment of the developing infant, assumes a position of preeminence by late childhood. It is difficult to conceive of man being able to survive in present-day society without the ability to understand the spoken or written word and to communicate his thoughts and ideas through language.

The capacity to learn new words and their meanings appear to be a continuing life process. Age appears to affect the speed and ease of the learning process. Generally, the younger child is much more adept at this acquisition than the older person, as any student of foreign language skills will wearily attest. Rate of accumulation can also be affected by one's attitude and sociocultural opportunities.

ADMINISTRATION

The last of the verbal subtests, Vocabulary is readily accepted by most subjects as a reasonable task. The examiner should be sure to pronounce all words correctly and use the word list provided for the subject.

Vocabulary has a format reminiscent of Information, with an easy run of items at the beginning. The first three words serve as buffers, being credited automatically unless the subject falters on the usual beginning item #4. Zero scores on any of items #4 to #8 necessitate administration of the earlier items. Testing continues until five consecutive failures (zero scores) have been amassed.

A problem in administering this subtest to bright subjects can be a too casual definition of early, easy words (breakfast—"a meal") to meet the 2-point criterion. Constant attention and proper questioning (to explain further) are required.

Hesitation or uncertainty suggests need for encouragement and further inquiry. Such action by the subject might indicate fear of failure or, on the other hand, mask bizarre associations. The value of an individually administered examination lies in the opportunity to explore what is in the mind of the subject rather than settle for a pass-fail approach.

Difficulty of the WAIS Vocabulary items can change with current fads. "Tranquil," for instance, has become a household word since the test was introduced. On the other hand, the WAIS Vocabulary has a tremendous loading of French cognates (DeMilan, 1965), approximating 62 percent, so that item difficulty is changed for many foreign-born subjects. Questioning as to language background is helpful in such cases.

With subjects revealing limited verbal skills, the examiner often encounters such comments as "I know what it means, but can't say it". Suggesting that the subject might express what he feels, or use the word in a sentence, can often overcome this problem. The examiner should also encourage the subject to continue or elaborate on his definitions in those cases where it is difficult to determine whether the subject does or does not know the meaning.

This is one subtest that can be reduced in length without too much loss in reliability. Brown (1968) indicates that the Jastak Short Form (Jastak &

Jastak, 1964) of this subtest correlates 0.94 for males and 0.99 for females with the full Vocabulary score. However, Burton (1968) suggests that the obtained score may be too low (by one point).

TESTING THE LIMITS

A slight variation in testing procedures allows for some hints as to reading skills. Using the vocabulary list given him, the subject is asked to read the word aloud before giving the definition. Mispronunciation can then be separated from inability to recognize a particular word. Note should be made if a person unable to recognize a word in printed form can, nevertheless, give an acceptable definition once he hears it pronounced by the examiner. Difficulty here can be checked with the Jastak Wide Range Achievement Test reading section (Jastak, Bijou, & Jastak, 1965).

Easier words from the WISC or Binet can be introduced. Subjects who seem at a loss in verbalizing might be given the Peabody Picture Vocabulary Test (Dunn, 1959) to see if there is a marked difference between expressive and receptive vocabulary.

Because of the heavy loading of French cognates, as mentioned, it may be useful to go beyond the five-failure level in order to test the limits. Foreign-born subjects may show greater success with such an approach. Testing the limits can also include using the word in a sentence in order to ascertain whether the subject knows more than would appear from the standardized administration.

SCORING

The three-level scoring (2, 1, 0) makes scoring the Vocabulary subtest more difficult than a simple plus-minus differentiation would be and adds to the total test time considerably. Jastak and Jastak (1964) tackle these problems directly, first by detailing the criteria for scoring and, second, by producing their own short form. In a general approach, they suggest that the 2-point response would be sufficiently abstract as well as accurate. In contrast, the 1-point responses are those that are descriptive, concrete, functional, or vague. A suggestive clue is that responses beginning with "something" are often scored 1 point (breakfast—"something you eat").

The general rules for multiple responses vary a bit from those mentioned in Comprehension scoring. If a second, better response follows the initial one, the better response is scored. Choice need not be indicated. However, a 1-point response followed by an elaboration which is confused or mistaken loses all credit. In other words, giving several different definitions of varying levels of accuracy need not involve the judgment factor and, therefore, does not "spoil" the item as does a confused elaboration of the original definition.

Following are the criteria used by Jastak and Jastak (1964) in scoring Vocabulary items:

Score 2 points for:

1. Adequate synonym with or without category differentiation except when specified. (For example: Slice = cut or thin cut[1])
2. Proper classification with or without further subdivision. (For example: slice = a piece or thin piece[1])
3. Relevant part of speech, i.e., noun defined in terms of a noun, verb in terms of a verb, adjective in terms of an adjective. (For example: fabric = a material; ponder = to think; tangible = touchable.) If the same item is used as a noun or a verb, either response is acceptable. (For example: slice = a piece or to cut)

Score 1 point for:

1. Inferior synonym or inexact classification. (For example: fabric = piece of clothing)
2. Description in terms of use and function. (For example: fabric = something you wear)
3. Enumeration of parts, composition, and other characteristics. (For example: breakfast = ham and eggs)
4. Substitution of one part of speech for another in the definition. (For example: commence = a beginning)
5. Illustrative phrase or sentence in which the stimulus word may or may not be repeated but is clearly qualified by associative concepts showing a reasonable understanding of the word. (For example: slice = to slice an apple)[2]

Scoring problems are even more complex than defining adequate responses. Sattler, Hillix, and Neher (1970) note that ambiguous Vocabulary responses were susceptible to a halo effect when the examiner was convinced that the subject was bright or dull. As noted earlier, initial, easier words may be defined too casually to meet the Wechsler scoring criteria. Others are surprisingly hard to define or to classify; Jastak and Jastak (1964) specifically mention "fabric," "slice," and "sentence". Other words seem to elicit 1-point responses, like "enormous," where "big" rather than "very big" is common. Ironically, at difficult levels the probability of a 2-point answer can increase significantly (Fink & Shontz, 1958). Difficult or abstract words are often known well or not at all. Certain words appear to have an age loading. "Edifice," for example, was much easier for older subjects seen by Looft

[1] The WAIS manual requires the concept of "thin" to reach a 2-point score.

[2] J. F. Jastak and S. R. Jastak. Short forms of the WAIS & WISC Vocabulary subtests *Journal of Clinical Psychology* 1964 Monograph Supplement 18, 1–35 (pp. 6–7).

(1970). Other words are easier for men than for women, and vice versa (Jastak & Jastak, 1964; Payne & Lehmann, 1966).

All the points made here limit the interpretation of interetest scatter on this subtest.

ITEM PLACEMENT

Vocabulary has long been considered the subtest least likely to be subject to deterioration. However, an analysis of the average raw scores indicates considerable variation over the years (Table 8–1).

At age 16 to 17 the average individual achieves a raw score of 29 to 33, typically indicating successes to at least item #15 or beyond. At the young adult level (25 to 34) a considerable increase in scores occurs, with the average raw score rising to 41 to 47, typically indicating success beyond item #21. However, average scores decline in the following years: at age 45 to 54, the average raw score drops to 39 to 45, or success beyond #20, and at the older age level, 65 to 69, an average raw score of 35 to 42, or success beyond #18 is expected.

Like Information, the raw scores on Vocabulary indicate the wide range and good selection of items. The easiest items were passed by all of the standardization sample, while the most difficult items were passed by almost none (Wechsler, 1958).

SIGNIFICANT DIFFERENCES BETWEEN THE VOCABULARY AND OTHER SUBTESTS

The reliability of the Vocabulary subtest is indicated by the relatively small differences between this subtest and all others to reach the 0.05 and 0.01 level of significance. According to the Newland and Smith analysis (1967), differences between two and five subtest weighted score points would

Table 8–1
ITEM PLACEMENT OF AVERAGE SCORES FOR FOUR AGE LEVELS

Age 16–17	(average raw score 29–33)	success through item #15
Age 25–34	(average raw score 41–47)	success through item #21
Age 45–54	(average raw score 39–45)	success through item #20
Age 65–69	(average raw score 35–42)	success through item #18

Source: D. Wechsler, *Manual, Wechsler Adult Intelligence Scale* (New York: Psychological Corporation, 1955), p. 101–108.

reach the 0.05 level, and differences from three to seven points would reach the 0.01 level (Table 8–2).

ITEM COMPOSITION AND DIFFICULTY

Item placement has been studied by several authorities. Certain words tend to elicit reactions of clinical significance. For example, #13 (sentence) may spark ideas of jail in terms of personal reference; #17, (cavern) is frequently confused with or associated with tavern; #21 (terminate) often elicits "to rub out," which suggests excessive devotion to late movies on TV; #25 (matchless) may lead to a concrete "without a match" response. Personal references often enhance rather than mar definitions; for example, #27 (calamity) and #29 (tranquil) may be connected with the presenting illness of the patient.

Item placement is not seriously questioned by Payne and Lehmann (1966) in their review of a large college sample. There were only six items which changed ranks by as much as three steps; #12, #18, and #33 were easier than noted; and #22, #26, and #30 were harder than noted. Wechsler (1958) observes that Vocabulary is one of the subtests favoring women. However, Payne and Lehmann (1966) identified only #8, #16, #23, and #31 as significantly favoring women, while #39 was notably easier for men.

Jastak and Jastak (1964) repositioned items and dropped half of them to form a short version of the Vocabulary subtest. Of those items remaining, #16 and #22 were put in sequence, considerably out of line with the original

Table 8–2
DIFFERENCES BETWEEN VOCABULARY AND ALL OTHER SCALED SCORES NECESSARY TO SATISFY THE 0.05 AND 0.01 CONFIDENCE LEVELS

	Confidence	*Subtests*									
CA	*level*	*I*	*C*	*A*	*S*	*D*	*DS*	*PC*	*BD*	*PA*	*OA*
18–19	0.05	2	3	3	3	3	2	3	3	4	4
	0.01	3	4	4	3	5	3	4	3	5	5
25–34	0.05	3	3	3	3	4	a	3	3	5	4
	0.01	4	4	4	3	5		3	4	7	5
45–54	0.05	2	3	3	3	4	a	3	3	3	3
	0.01	3	4	4	4	5		3	3	4	4

[a] DS omitted.

Source: From T. E. Newland and P. A. Smith, Statistically significant differences between subtest scaled scores on the WISC and the WAIS, *Journal of School Psychology*, 1967, 5, 126.

positions. They noted two words easier for men than women—#39 and #40, the most difficult in the scale—while the following Vocabulary items were easier for women—#7, #12, #16, #27, #30, #32, and #34. Five of the seven are discriminating in the same direction for Payne and Lehmann (1966).

Another study specifically compared younger (age 19) and older (age 77) subjects on Vocabulary (Looft, 1970). The younger subjects, more homogenous but equal to the older in education, were more inclined to give 2-point answers. However, older subjects were superior on three items: #20, #30, and #36, words perhaps somewhat archaic for the young, who gave significantly more high level responses to these items: #4, #14, #18, #22, #24, #26, #28, #29, and #32. These response differences tend to confirm Feifil's (1949) observation that the kind of response, rather than word knowledge, changes with age.

Barnes (1969) notes the stress on more dynamic aspects and social-living items characteristic of the WAIS Vocabulary as compared to the Wechsler Bellevue I version.

RESEARCH FINDINGS WITH THE VOCABULARY SUBTEST

Saunders and Gittinger (undated) describe the Wechsler Vocabulary subtest as a measure of "symbolic range." Blatt and Allison (1968) refer to V as the breadth of concepts, ideas, and experience gained during one's lifetime. Conry and Plant (1965) rate the WAIS Vocabulary as the equal of any combination of WAIS subtests for ranking high school graduates. This subtest is also assumed to be stable over time and relatively insensitive to neurological deficit (Blatt & Allison, 1968; Wechsler, 1958). In his analysis of diagnostic and clinical features Wechsler (1958, pp. 171–172) suggests that the Vocabulary score deviates 3 or more points above *S*'s mean subtest scores in organic brain disease and schizophrenia, 1.5 to 2.5 points above the mean subtest score in anxiety states. Adolescent sociopaths and mental defectives are the only clinical groups with average or slightly above average scores (within ± 1.5 of mean subtest scores to ± 1.5 units above mean subtest score).

No deviation from the mean of their other subtests for brain-damaged and neurotic samples was noted by Ladd (1964), which was in contrast to the well above average scores reported by Wechsler. Ladd's findings were usually higher than Wechsler's; only on Vocabulary was the deviation in the other direction.

Bloom and Goldman (1962) found their hypothesis of a language handicap in a Hawaiian psychotic population confirmed when the group was compared to a Connecticut sample. Differences were significant at the 0.01 level.

A check of references suggests that conclusions of Blatt and Allison (1968) regarding clinical implications are based on studies using the Wechsler Bellevue I Vocabularly subtest (no overlap of items). That the two may not be comparable is suggested by Wechsler (1958, p. 84) and DeMilan (1965), who points out that words with French cognates comprise 33 percent of the Wechsler Bellevue I Vocabulary versus 62 percent for the WAIS Vocabulary. Further investigations will be necessary to substantiate assumed claims.

Stability of the WAIS in organic disease is questioned by Evans and Marmorston (1964). They compared known brain-damaged subjects suffering from cerebral thrombosis with those suffering myocardiac infraction but with no known brain damage. The Vocabulary subtest was lower for the brain-damaged group. However, they concluded that the number of patients misclassified limited the usefulness of this sign as a reliable single measure. Goren and Brown (1968) note that the vocabulary scores can fluctuate with the disease process and that stability may be evidenced only in cases with mild or moderate degree of neurological impairment. Rennick, Wilder, Sargent, and Ashley (1968) substantiate this hypothesis for cases with mild chronic cerebral dysfunction. Using a diagnostic approach, Parsons, Vega, and Burn (1969) suggested that left-hemisphere damage is associated with Block Design scores significantly higher than Vocabulary scores. The reverse was true for right-hemisphere damaged *S*s. Woo-Sam (1971) argued that such results were compromised by the use of age-corrected scale scores and suggested that the reported differences would not be evident when standard scores were used. A subsequent paper by Simpson and Vega (1971), in which standard scores are published, confirmed Woo-Sam's argument. Regardless of which hemisphere was damaged, right, left, or bilateral, the standard scaled scores for the Vocabulary subtest was always higher than that for the Block Design subtest.

Finally, Sherman and Blatt (1968) contend that scores on this subtest are not affected by situational or induced stress. Chronic anxiety, however, does lower performance (Sarason & Minard, 1962).

ADVANTAGES OF THE SUBTEST

The V subtest is generally accepted as the best single measure of intelligence. Its reliability is the highest of all the subtests. The range of items is excellent and is paralleled by the variety in content. The whole intellectual spectrum is covered. In addition, this subtest is a strong measure of verbal comprehension.

Vocabulary gives an estimate of cultural level and indicates early educational and cultural environment. The subtest is of interest in that while emotional reactions are elicited by the dynamic content of the words, failures in such cases are not automatic, as words can be adequately defined this way. Indeed, definitions need not be worded well. The only requirement is that the examiner is convinced that the subject is aware of the meaning. It is not surprising then that this subtest is one of the least vulnerable to pathology of any kind and is generally felt to provide a reliable estimate of premorbid functioning in a person suspected of suffering intellectual deterioration.

LIMITATIONS OF THE SUBTEST

Scoring tends to be subjective, lengthy, and unreliable. The subtest itself is lengthy to administer. There is a cultural loading penalizing the more action-oriented. The current word list has a loading of French cognates, which changes its composition for foreign-born subjects who speak a Latin-based language. The V subtest is easier for women than for men.

CONCLUSIONS

An examination of the kinds of word definitions given by the subject and the content involved can give clues to a subject's status and background. The range and richness of his ideas and the level of abstract thinking can be tapped.

High scores may reflect erudition, sophistication, and intellectual striving. Obsessives, paranoid subjects, anxiety and depressive patients, and certain preschizophrenics are among the pathological groups described as doing well on this subtest.

Language and thought disturbances may be reflected in low scores, as in cases where bizarre definitions, clang associations (cavern—tavern), incoherent running together of words, word salad, and perseveration of inadequate responses are observable.

REFERENCES

Ammons, R. B., & Ammons, H. S. *The Full-Range Picture Vocabulary Test.* New Orleans: Author, 1948.

Barnes, C. Trends in the adult Wechsler individual intelligence scales from the 1939 WB I to the new 1968 Spanish EIWA. Paper given at California State Psychological Association Convention, January 1969.

Berger, L., Bernstein, A., Klein, E., Cohen, J., & Lucas, G. Effect of aging and pathology on the factorial structure of intelligence. *Journal of Counsulting Psychology*, 1964, 28, 199–207.

Blatt, S. J., & Allison, S. The intelligence test in personality assessment. In A. Rabin (Ed.). *Projective techniques in personality assessment.* New York: Springer, 1968. Pp. 421–460.

Bloom, B. L., & Goldman, R. K. Sensitivity of the WAIS to language handicap in a psychotic population. *Journal of Clinical Psychology*, 1962, 18, 161–163.

Brown, F. Applicability of the Jastak short-form revision of the WAIS Vocabulary subtest to psychiatric patients. *Journal of Clinical Psychology*, 1968, 24, 454–455.

Burton, D. A. The Jastak short form WAIS Vocabulary applied to a British psychiatric population. *Journal of Clinical Psychology*, 1968, 24, 345–347.

Cohen, J. The factorial structure of the WAIS between early adulthood and old age *Journal of Consulting Psychology*, 1957, 21, 283–290.

Conry, R., & Plant, W. T. WAIS and group test predictions of an academic services criterion: high school and college. *Educational and Psychological Measurement*, 1965, 25, 493–500.

DeMilan, J. Bilingualism and the Wechsler Vocabulary scales. *Journal of Clinical Psychology*, 1965, 21, 298.

Dennerll, R. D., Den Broeder, J., & Sokolov, S. WISC and WAIS factors in children and adults with epilepsy. *Journal of Clinical Psychology*, 1964, 20, 236–240.

Dunn, L. M. *Manual, Peabody Picture Vocabulary Test.* Minneapolis: American Guidance Service, 1959.

Evans, R. B., & Marmorston, J. Psychological test signs of brain damage in cerebral thrombosis. *Psychological Reports*, 1963, 12, 915–930.

Feifel, H. Qualitative differences in the vocabulary responses of normals and abnormals. *Genetic Psychology Monograph*, 1949, 39, 151–204.

Fink, S. L., & Shontz, F. C. Inference of intellectual efficiency from the WAIS Vocabulary subtest. *Journal of Clinical Psychology*, 1958, 14, 409–412.

Gonen, J. G., & Brown, L. Role of vocabulary in deterioration and restitution of mental functioning. *Proceedings*, American Psychological Association, 1968, 3, 464–470.

Jastak, J. F., Bijou, S. W., & Jastak, S. R. *Wide Range Achievement Test.* Wilmington, Delaware, Guidance Associates, 1965.

Jastak, J. F., & Jastak, S. R. Short forms of the WAIS and WISC Vocabulary subtests. *Journal of Clinical Psychology*, 1964, Monograph Supplement 18, 1–35.

Ladd, C. E. WAIS performances of brain-damaged and neurotic patients. *Journal of Clinical Psychology*, 1964, 20, 115–117.

Looft, W. R. Note on WAIS Vocabulary performance by young and old adults. *Psychological Reports*, 1970, 26, 943–946.

Newland, T. E., & Smith, P. A. Statistically significant differences between subtest scaled scores on the WISC and the WAIS. *Journal of School Psychology*, 1967, 5, 122–127.

Parsons, O., Vegas, A. J., & Burn, J. Different psychological effects of lateralized brain damage. *Journal of Consulting and Clinical Psychology*, 1969, 33, 551–557.

Payne, D. A., & Lehmann, I. J. A brief WAIS item analysis. *Journal of Clinical Psychology*, 1966, 22, 296–297.

Rennick, P. M., Wilder, R. M., Sargent, J., & Ashley, B. J. Retinopathy as an indicator of cognitive-perceptual-motor impairment in diabetic adults. *Proceedings*, American Psychological Association, 1968, 3, 473–474.

Riegel, R. F., & Riegel, R. M. A comparison and reinterpretation of factor structures of the W-B, the WAIS, and the HAWIE on aged persons. *Journal of Consulting Psychology*, 1962, **26**, 31–37.

Russell, E. W. A WAIS factor analysis with brain-damaged subjects using criterion measures. *Journal of Consulting and Clinical Psychology*, 1972, **39**, 133–139.

Sarason, I. G., & Minard, J. Test anxiety, experimental instructions, and the WAIS. *Journal of Educational Psychology*, 1962, **58**, 299–302.

Saunders, D. R. & Gittinger, W. Patterns of intellectual functioning and their implications for the dynamics of behavior. Reprinted from *The role and methodology of classification and psychopathology.* Washington, D. C.: US Department of Health, Education, and Welfare, Public Health Service, undated.

Shaw, D. J. Factor analysis of the collegiate WAIS. *Journal of Consulting Psychology*, 1967, **31**, 217.

Sherman, A. R., & Blatt, S. J. WAIS Digit Span, Digit Symbol, and Vocabulary performance. *Journal of Consulting and Clinical Psychology*, 1968, **32**, 407–412.

Simpson, C. D., & Vega, A. Unilateral brain damage and patterns of age-corrected WAIS subtest scores. *Journal of Clinical Psychology*, 1971, **27**, 204–208.

Sprague, R. L., & Quay, H. C. A factor analytic study of the responses of mental retardates on the WAIS. *American Journal of Mental Deficiency*, 1966, **70**, 595–600.

Taylor, J. B. The structure of ability in the lower intellectual range. *American Journal of Mental Deficiency*, 1964, **68**, 766–774.

Wechsler, D. *The measurement and appraisal of adult intelligence.* Baltimore: Williams & Wilkins, 1958.

Woo-Sam, J. Lateralized brain damage and differential psychological effects: Parsons et al. re-examined. *Perceptual and Motor Skills*, 1971, **33**, 259–262.

Zimmerman, S. F., Whitmyre, J. W., & Fields, F. R. J. Factor analytic structure of the WAIS in patients with diffuse and lateralized cerebral dysfunction. *Journal of Clinical Psychology*, 1970, **26**, 462–465.

CHAPTER 9

DIGIT SYMBOL

Wechsler (1958) notes that "the digit symbol or substitution test is one of the oldest and best established of all psychological tests" (p. 81). Items of this nature were incorporated in the original Army Performance Tests and were included in the Cornell-Coxe Performance Scale and the Chicago Non-Verbal Scale. The test is easily modified to suit a variety of situations. For example, in the Army Beta it can be given through pantomime instructions, and, as used in the Leiter, pencil skills are not required. The form used by Wechsler is adapted from the Army Beta of World War I vintage.

In security work coding and "intelligence" are synonomous. This subtest does not, of course, tap the high level of specialized coding skills used in such an act. However, it does involve the ability to master a new and essentially alien task within a brief time span. The Digit Symbol (DS) subtest is predicated upon the assumption that the ability to learn relationships between specific symbols and numbers and to reproduce them rapidly in a paper-and-pencil task is one measure of intelligence. Rappaport, Gill, & Schafer (1945) specifically mentioned three kinds of learning involved: (1)

what symbol goes with what digit, (2) where it is placed, (3) how efficiently it is written. Difficulty at any stage will seriously impair success.

WHAT THE TEST MEASURES

Digit Symbol presumably calls for ability to learn an unfamiliar task. Other considerations are visual-motor dexterity, degree of persistence in sticking to an unattractive task, and speed of performance. Alert, creative individuals actually may fare worse on this test than those who are motivated by the compulsive need to conform.

Deficiencies in visual acuity and visual motor coordination affect performance markedly. Motor behavior is more important than in any other subtest. It is of interest to observe to what degree the symbols are memorized, for this may play an exceedingly important role in determining the score. Efficient memorization under pressure can be considered one measure of intelligence.

DESCRIPTION

The test requires the subject to fill in empty spaces with symbols associated with the numerals 1 through 9. The symbols to be substituted are always visible in a key printed above the blank.

Twenty-three additional items have been added to the Wechsler Bellevue I version. In addition to lengthening the test, there is one minor change from the WB. The symbol associated with the number 2, a И, has been replaced by the symbol ⊥. Experience with the earlier version led to the observation that subjects frequently wrote this symbol as an N. No diagnostic value had been attached to this common error.

FACTOR ANALYSIS

Through middle age, the DS subtest is one of the poorest measures of G. However, in the Cohen (1957b) analysis the correlation reaches a respectable 0.71 for the aged. What Digit Symbol measures beyond this could not be interpreted, although for the aged there were weak loadings on perceptual organization (0.26) and freedom from distraction (0.21). In the Berger, Bernstein, Klein, Cohen, and Lucas (1964) reanalysis of the standardization data, age differentials were quite important. For the 18 to 19 age group, the primary specific factor measured was verbal comprehension, with a weak although still significant loading on freedom from distractability and on an unspecified fourth factor. For the 25 to 34 age group, Digit Symbol correlated weakly with both verbal comprehension and perceptual organization; for the 45 to 54 age group, the only significant correlation was with the unspecified factor four. For the aged, the primary aspect measured was perceptual organization. In contrast, the Birren composite group (quoted in Riegel & Riegel, 1962) had good loading on verbal comprehension but a substantial negative loading on perceptual organization.

In Shaw's (1967) study of college students Digit Symbol appears to reflect "perceptual speed," while chronic schizophrenics showed substantive correlations on both perceptual organization and the unspecified fourth factor (Berger et al., 1964). For chronic brain-damaged patients, this subtest is highly correlated with perceptual organization (Russell, 1972); for the mentally retarded, it measures freedom from distraction (Sprague & Quay, 1966). On the other hand, for the borderline and dull normal, Digit Symbol is considered to measure primarily a verbal-numerical-educational factor (Taylor, 1964). Low positive loadings are reported for epileptics on perceptual organization and freedom from distractability, low negative loadings on an unspecified four factor (Dennerll, Den Broeder, & Sokolov, 1964). Differentiated organics of the RI group have a significant and high loading on perceptual organization; the DI group, a lower but still significant loading on this factor; and the LI group, a significantly high loading on freedom from distractability (Zimmerman, Whitmyre, & Fields, 1970).

In summary, the Digit Symbol subtest appears to be a mediocre measure of general intelligence. The particular aspects of intelligence evaluated seems to vary across age groups and diagnostic categories. The variation across diagnostic categories is a potentially favorable characteristic, if it can be shown to be static within diagnostic categories or subcategories. Given these circumstances, differential diagnosis is strengthened. If the findings with the dull and mentally retarded are indicative of instability within other diagnostic groups, this particular use is limited. Further studies should explore the possibility. The Zimmerman et al. study (1970) seems promising.

ADMINISTRATION

As the only paper-and-pencil task in the WAIS, the DS can be a problem for those not accustomed to writing, those with a learning disorder in which motor faculties are particularly affected, those with failing vision, and those with low motivation.

Total time for the subtest is 90 seconds plus the brief period allowed for sample items, making it potentially the most rapidly administered of all the

WAIS tasks. To begin, the examiner fills in the first three symbols of the sample to illustrate the proper procedure. The subject is asked to fill in the next seven. This procedure insures adequate rehearsal and understanding before the subject begins the task, unlike the earlier Wechsler Bellevue I where practice was limited to three symbols. There is also opportunity to familiarize oneself with six of the nine symbols used. Help may be given throughout the sample items.

Only three items (#2, #3, and #7, reversed or inverted letters) are outside general writing experience. Four of the symbols are letters (L, U, O, and X), and two others are common notations (a dash and an equals symbol). Easily verbalized symbols are readily memorized. Obviously, the literate and those accustomed to writing have an advantage here.

The most common errors tend to be perseverative runs in the first line, the only place where sequences of any kind occur. Writing the symbols for 2 and 3 may stimulate entering the one for 4 instead of the one for 5 as required.

A particular problem in administration of the Digit Symbol subtest to left-handed subjects is to ascertain that the key is observable. While most left-handed subjects have no difficulty with this, those who write in the "crooked" position tend to cover up the symbols as they work and are thus penalized unless another copy with a visible key is available.

The subject is told to fill in the symbols in order, not to erase, and not to skip any. For some subjects it may be necessary to stress that perfect symbol reproduction is not essential. These instructions can be given during the sample period without affecting the administration.

The examiner should be alert to a very common occurrence on this subtest, the subjec's failure to continue beyond the first line. When this happens, manual directions must be ammended and the subject urged to continue until his time is up.

Changes in speed of performance are worth noting. Fatigue and attention factors may be involved. Sudden improvement can occur when the subject has memorized some or all of the symbols. When variability is marked, it can be useful to ask the subject how he proceeded—that is, once the subtest is completed. Peculiar symbols should be questioned; they may possess idiosyncratic meaning for the subject.

Inability to follow the nonsequential ordering of the numbers can provide useful information regarding motor planning, concentration, and flexibility in adapting to stimulus changes.

TESTING THE LIMITS

When either motor skills or literacy are in question, the subject might be asked to write his own name, letters, or numbers. Jastak, Bijou, and Jastak

(1964) give grade level equivalents for such tasks. Another area to be explored is that of visual disturbance. Having the subject write each symbol in turn may clarify his ability to distinguish such details.

SCORING

One half credit is given for reversed items; otherwise scoring is fairly straightforward. It should be remembered that the sample items are not credited. There is no mention of early termination, presumably because of the brief time period, which runs out before those having difficulty can suffer too much trouble from failure. It is extremely rare for anyone to complete the entire series.

ITEM PLACEMENT

No other subtest is so critically influenced by time limits as is Digit Symbol. The average raw scores decline markedly with advancing age (Table 9–1). At age 16 to 17 the average score is 51 to 54, or completion of items to the middle of the third line. This average score changes very little for the next age level, CA 25 to 34 (51 to 56). By the middle-age level, 45 to 54, an average score drops to 38 to 42, or the end of the second line. The decline is particularly marked by age 65 to 69, where a score of 26 to 28 is average (middle of the second line).

SIGNIFICANT DIFFERENCES BETWEEN THE DIGIT SYMBOL AND OTHER SUBTESTS

Since the Digit Symbol could not be utilized in a split half approach to reliability data, Wechsler (1955) limited his study to a separate sample of

Table 9–1
ITEM PLACEMENT OF AVERAGE SCORES FOR FOUR AGE LEVELS

Age 16–17	(average raw score 51–54)	success through items 51–54, or beyond the middle of the third row
Age 25–34	(average raw score 51–56)	success through items 51–56, or beyond the middle of the third row
Age 45–54	(average raw score 38–42)	success through items 38–42, or end of the second row
Age 65–69	(average raw score 26–28)	success through items 26–28, or before the middle of the second row

Source: D. Wechsler, *Manual, Wechsler Adult Intelligence Scale* (New York: Psychological Corporation, 1955), p. 101–108.

Table 9–2
DIFFERENCES BETWEEN DIGIT SYMBOL AND ALL OTHER SCALED SCORES NECESSARY TO SATISFY THE 0.05 AND 0.01 CONFIDENCE LEVELS

CA	Confidence level	*I*	*C*	*A*	*S*	*D*	*V*	*PC*	*BD*	*PA*	*OA*
		Subtests									
18–19	0.05	2	3	3	3	4	2	3	3	4	4
	0.01	3	4	4	4	5	3	4	4	5	5
25–34	a										
45–54	a										

[a] DS analysis omitted for these age levels.
Source: From T. E. Newland and P. A. Smith, Statistically significant differences between subtest scaled scores on the WISC and the WAIS, *Journal of School Psychology*, 1967, 5, 126.

subjects age 18 to 19 who were tested twice to calculate a test-retest reliability coefficient. For this younger group, differences between Digit Symbol and the other subtests needed to be between two and four points to reach the 0.05 level and between three and five points to reach the 0.01 level. The least differences were required for Information and Vocabulary, while the largest differences were needed for Digit Span, Picture Arrangement, and Object Assembly (Table 9–2).

ITEM COMPOSITION AND DIFFICULTY

Since there is no increase in difficulty over the subtest span, item placement and difficulty are not problems on Digit Symbol. The items are simple, and, of the nine, only three (#2, #3, and #7) are not easily verbalized symbols. Thus two-thirds of the items can be relatively easy to memorize for those utilizing verbal mediation, an indication of mental ability. Wechsler (1958) and Shaw (1965) found that DS favored women.

RESEARCH WITH THE DIGIT SYMBOL SUBTEST

This subtest is factorially complex, and the hypotheses concerning it cover a wide and seemingly unrelated list of behavioral activities ranging from anxiety, promptness, and energy output to the effect of organicity, use of nonpreferred hand, and school achievement. The majority of the studies need replication.

Saunders (undated) defines DS as a measure of "psychometabolic rate" influenced by such variables as drugs, brain damage, and the psychological state. To the present authors' knowledge there have been no studies on the effect of drugs.

In the Wechsler (1958, pp. 171–172) diagnostic profiles organics are expected to do quite poorly on this subtest (more than 3 units below *S*'s mean subtest scores) while in schizophrenia and anxiety state reaction the expectation is that scores should deviate 1.5 to 2.5 units below the mean subtest scores. For both adolescent psychopathics and mental defectives, scores may remain ± 1.5 units within the mean subtest score. However, when deviations are encountered, the scores drop 1.5 to 2.5 units below that of *S*'s mean subtest score. Ladd's findings (1964) tended to confirm Wechsler's results for a neurotic sample and were identical for a brain-damaged group.

Low scores as an indicator of organic brain damage is suggested by Rennick, Wilder, Sargent, and Ashley (1968). They found that diabetic patients with perceptual-motor impairment scored lower on DS both on an absolute and relative level (compared to other performance subtests). Russell (1972) and Simpson and Vega (1971) concur that the DS test is especially affected in organicity. DeWolfe (1971) asserts that the pattern DS greater than C characterized schizophrenia, while DS lower than C predicted organicity. Bloom and Goldman (1962) found no difference between Connecticut and Hawaiian psychotic patients on Digit Symbol.

The effect of anxiety needs further clarification. For anxiety-prone subjects, there seems to be no difference in scores obtained by those who test high on this trait versus those who test low (Sarason & Minard, 1962; Wachtel & Blatt, 1965). Relative to situational anxiety, Gallagher (1964), Sherman & Blatt (1968), and Sarason & Minard (1962) report that threat of failure tends to increase DS scores. However, Moon and Lair (1970) noted a significant depression in DS scores when subjects viewed a stressful film prior to taking the test. They also observed that anxiety-prone subjects showed significantly greater improvement on a post test trial, regardless of the stress condition.

The motor aspects of the test were studied by Briggs (1960), who reported a significant drop in scores when the nonpreferred hand was used, and by Kaufman (1966), who proposed on oral version for those with writing impairment. He notes that performance falls off less rapidly with aging for the oral version as compared to the written test. Fogel and Blumlotz (1965) also report that *S*s administered a task that inhibited motor functioning prior to administration subsequently did poorer on the DS test than did the controls.

Relative to academic behavior, Wolfson and Weltman (1963) found that students who applied very late for admission to nursing school ("short-term planners") made more errors on DS than students who applied early. However, Wolfson and Lo Cascio (1961) found no support for the conclusion attributed to Wechsler that nursing school applicants in general do poorer on this subtest than do other groups. A study by Wachtel and Blatt (1965) found a positive relationship between academic performance and DS performance. Students who were in the upper third of their class but equal in overall intelligence (measured by WAIS Vocabulary and by College Board tests) produced higher scores than *S*s in the lower third of the class.

Davis, Dizzonne, and DeWolfe (1971) compared schizophrenic patients. They concluded that reactive schizophrenics scored higher than process schizophrenics on this subtest.

Lastly, Kahn and Fisher (1968) report that DS scores correlate significantly with REM sleep. A tau of 0.49, significant at the $p = 0.01$ was found for aged subjects. Apparently, DS was related to physical vigor.

ADVANTAGES OF THE SUBTEST

This subtest is one of the most rapidly administered and scored tests in the WAIS and provides a quick measure of ability to learn a simple substitution task. Evidence suggests that performance on DS can be extended to predict various aspects of learning. Generally, Digit Symbol appears to be reliable and culture-fair. Subjects unaccustomed to such a task are provided with an adequate practice period.

LIMITATIONS OF THE SUBTEST

Digit Symbol is a mediocre measure of general intelligence. It is the only subtest requiring pencil work and can be objectionable to those not used to such tasks. Also, unlike other subtests, it must be done with the dominant hand, limiting its use in certain cases of disability. Individuals not at ease in speeded tasks can be seriously penalized. Careful workers are included in this group. The implications of Digit Symbol vary with both age and diagnosis. It also appears considerably easier for women.

CONCLUSIONS

The need for rapid learning and copying new symbols makes this a quasi-clerical task that must be mastered within a very short time limit.

High scores may indicate clerical skills, or tolerance of such a task. Speed and vigor are at least temporarily necessary. Accuracy achieved without the need for checking results is required for success. The subtest measures effort in a concentrated task. A good memory and reliance on verbal mediation will aid a speedy performance. Coordination is required and freedom from distractability at certain levels.

Low scores may indicate a dominance problem. Since this task cannot be done adequately with the nondominant hand, the influence of a stroke, for example, might be assessed here. Specific visual defects can be penalizing: the type of error, the visual approach (peering, etc.) may give a clue. Failures may indicate only a slap-dash approach from an individual who is action-oriented, impulsive, or unwilling to tackle this kind of task. The perseveration of the same symbol or skipping across the page to do just one symbol can indicate rigidity such as seen in the brain-damaged. Left-handed writers may cover the sample as they write; a second blank is then required. Those overly concerned with accuracy will work too slowly to do well. Depressives may show motor retardation as part of their symptomatology. For others, doubt and hesitancy leading to constant rechecking can be penalizing. Process schizophrenics do less well than reactive schizophrenics, suggesting motor inhibition in the former. Such a rote task may not challenge the bright subject enough to elicit a high level response. Low scores have been reported for the brain-damaged, anxious, depressed, dissociated, schizophrenics, and hyperactives unable to attend adequately to the task.

REFERENCES

Berger, L., Bernstein, A., Klein, E., Cohen, J., & Lucas, G. Effects of aging and pathology on the factorial structure of intelligence. *Journal of Consulting Psychology*, 1964, **28**, 199–207.

Bloom, B. L., & Goldman, R. K. Sensitivity of the WAIS to language handicap in a psychotic population. *Journal of Clinical Psychology*, 1962, **18**, 161–163.

Briggs, P. F. The validity of WAIS performance subtest completed with one hand. *Journal of Clinical Psychology*, 1960, **16**, 318–320.

Cohen, J. A factor-analytically based rationale for the WAIS. *Journal of Consulting Psychology*, 1957, **21**, 451–457. (a)

Cohen, J. The factorial structure of the WAIS between early adulthood and old age. *Journal of Consulting Psychology*, 1957, **21**, 283–290. (b)

Davis, W. E., Dizzonne, M. F., & DeWolfe, A. S. Relationships among WAIS subtest scores, patient's premorbid history, and institutionalization. *Journal of Consulting and Clinical Psychology*, 1971, **35**, 400–403.

Dennerll, R. D., Den Broeder, J., & Sokolov, S. L. WISC and WAIS factors in children and adults with epilepsy. *Journal of Clinical Psychology*, 1964, **20**, 236–240.

DeWolfe, A. S. Differentiation of schizophrenia and brain damage with the WAIS. *Journal of Clinical Psychology*, 1971, **27**, 207–211.

Fogel, M., & Blumlotz, P. Effect of different training tasks on Digit Symbol performances. *Journal of Clinical Psychology*, 1965, **21**, 109–111.

Gallagher, P. J. Effect of increased verbal scale difficulty and failure on WAIS Digit Symbol performances. *Dissertation Abstracts*, 1964, **24**, 5544.

Jastak, J. F., Bijou, S. W., & Jastak, S. R. *Wide Range Achievement Test.* Wilmington, Del. Guidance Associates, 1965.

Kahn, E., & Fisher, C. The relationship of REM sleep to various measures in the aged. *Psychophysiology*, 1968, **5**, 228–229.

Kaufman, A. An oral Digit Symbol test. *Journal of Clinical Psychology*, 1966, **27**, 180–183.

Ladd, C. E. WAIS performance of brain-damaged and neurotic patients. *Journal of Clinical Psychology*, 1964, **20**, 114–117.

McCarthy, D. Administration of Digit Symbol and Comprehension subtests of the WAIS and WISC to left-handed subjects. *Psychological Reports*, 1961, **8**, 407–408.

Moon, W. H., & Lair, C. V. Manifest anxiety, induced anxiety, and Digit Symbol performance. *Psychological Reports*, 1970, **26**, 947–950.

Rappaport, D., Gill, M. M., & Schafer, R. *Diagnostic psychological testing*. Chicago: Year Book Publishers, 1945.

Rennick, P. M., Wilder, R. M., Sargent, J., & Ashley, B. J. Retinopathy as an indicator of cognitive-perceptual-motor impairment in diabetic adults. *Proceedings*, American Psychological Association, 1968, **3**, 473–474.

Riegel, R. M., & Riegel, K. F. A comparison and reinterpretation of factor structures of the W-B, the WAIS, and the HAWIE on aged persons. *Journal of Consulting Psychology*, 1962, **26**, 31–37.

Russell, E. W. A WAIS factor analysis with brain damaged subjects using criterion measures. *Journal of Consulting and Clinical Psychology*, 1972, **39**, 133–139.

Sarason, I. G., & Minard, J. Test anxiety, experimental instructions, and the WAIS. *Journal of Educational Psychology*, 1962, **53**, 299–302.

Saunders, D R. Patterns of intellectual functioning and their implications for the dynamics of behavior. Reprinted from *The role and methodology of classification in psychiatry and psychopathology.* Washington, D. C.: U.S. Department of Health, Education, and Welfare, Public Health Service, undated.

Shaw, D. J. Sexual bias in the WAIS. *Journal of Consulting Psychology*, 1965, **59**, 590–591.

Shaw, D. J. Factor analysis of the collegiate WAIS. *Journal of Consulting Psychology*, 1967, **31**, 217.

Sherman, A. R., & Blatt, P. J. WAIS Digit Span, Digit Symbol, and Vocabulary performance as a function of prior experiences of success and failure. *Journal of Consulting and Clinical Psychology*, 1968, **32**, 407–412.

Simpson, C. D., & Vega, A. Unilateral brain damage and patterns of age corrected WAIS subtest scores. *Journal of Clinical Psychology*, 1971, **21**, 204–208.

Sprague, R. L., & Quay, H. C. A factor analytic study of the responses of mental retardates on the WAIS. *American Journal of Mental Deficiency*, 1966, **70**, 595–600.

Taylor, J. B. The structure of ability in the lower intellectual range. *American Journal of Mental Deficiency*, 1964, **68**, 766–774.

Wachtel, P. L., & Blatt, S. J. Energy deployment and achievement. *Journal of Consulting Psychology*, 1965, **29**, 302–308.

Wechsler, D. *Manual, Wechsler Adult Intelligence Scale.* New York: Psychological Corporation 1955.

Wechsler, D. *The measurement and appraisal of adult intelligence.* Baltimore: Williams & Wilkins, 1958.

Wolfson, W., & Lo Cascio, R. Digit Symbol performance of nursing school applicants. *Journal of Clinical Psychology*, 1961, **17**, 59.

Wolfson, W., & Weltman, R. E. Visual-motor efficiency of long- and short-term planners. *Perceptual and Motor Skills*, 1963, **17** 908.

Zimmerman, S. F., Whitmyre, J. W., & Fields, F. R. J. Factor analytic structure of the WAIS in patients with diffuse and lateralized cerebral dysfunction. *Journal of Clinical Psychology*, 1970, **26**, 462–465.

CHAPTER 10

PICTURE COMPLETION

The ability to comprehend perceptually the major components of familiar objects begins at an early age, with the child's recognition of those parts of the body used in everyday activities apparently forming the basis for later discriminations. With increasing age and experience familiarity extends over a greater diversity of objects, and functions of the major components of such objects become more sharply defined. There are two general methods for evaluating the level of perceptual discrimination: (1) by asking the subject to recognize a given object from a partial sampling of major components (incomplete pictures, for example) and (2) by asking the subject to identify the major missing component in an incomplete or mutiliated object. The latter is by far the more popular approach. In one form or another, this measure has appeared in group tests, such as the Army Beta and the Pintner Non-Language Scale, or in individual tests, such as the Binet series and the Wechsler scales.

To recognize modifications in familiar surroundings, objects, or structures and as a result make corresponding adjustments is something people do routinely. A newly placed road sign along a familiar road, warns of an unexpected contingency; a missing limb in an otherwise exquisitely carved statue outrages our sense of esthetics. We quickly by-pass the unrepaired chair as we seek seating accomodations, and we stay away from walls on which the wet paint sign is posted. In folklore and mythology we are not fooled by the human form of the vampire since this form casts no shadow nor is it reflected.

Honed and refined, this perceptual skill is used with telling efficacy by the master sleuth, and, as practiced by Doyle's Sherlock Holmes, the uncanny ability to capitalize on minute and often overlooked details engenders universal admiration.

Only one facet of this skill appears reflected in the Picture Completion (PC) task of the WAIS, that of the visual identification of missing elements in sketched figures. Taste, smell, touch, and hearing, senses that play equally important roles in real life situations are not tapped in this artificial task.

WHAT THE TEST MEASURES

In order to recognize visually that some essential element is missing in an otherwise completed sketch, one must know the object or situation represented, the particular perspective presented, and the interrelationship between the various major elements that are visible. Secondarily, when this element is not readily perceived, one must be able to concentrate and resist distractions.

Since culture determines the particular artifacts present in any society, there is a built-in cultural bias in this test. Furthermore, socioeconomic variables help determine one's acquaintance with existing cultural artifacts. Unless objects and situations represented are equally familiar to subjects at all socioeconomic levels, this is also a source of bias. Wechsler recognized this problem by avoiding unfamiliar, specialized, and esoteric subject matter; however, he felt that sex differences would remain a factor. (Wechsler, 1958).

A subject's performance on the PC subtest, by inference, can offer valuable clues to the personality integration. The pointing out of tiny gaps in the lines of the sketch, the inability to identify simple objects, or the tendency to designate them in some bizzare scheme, all suggest distortion of reality. Likewise, although there are time limits, these limits have proved adequate even for dull subjects. Thus, an inability to make identification within the time limits have come to be associated with the slowness characteristic of individuals known to be brain damaged.

DESCRIPTION

One of the two picture tests in the WAIS, Picture Completion is composed of 21 pictures in each of which a significant element is omitted. Eleven items have been retained from the earlier Wechsler Bellevue, although pictures have been redrawn for clarity. New items are introduced at all intellectual levels, providing a good range.

Noteworthy is that this is the only performance test in which no visual motor manipulation, or in other words, "performance," is called for. The 20-second time limit per item is rarely a factor, and time bonuses do not play any part in success.

FACTOR ANALYSIS

The PC has the highest loading on the G factor of all the nonverbal subtests. In the Cohen (1957b) analysis of the standardization sample it correlates an average of 0.75 for the middle-aged and aged. However, just what specific aspect of G is being measured is not known. Cohen noted that Picture Completion measured at a low level an unspecified factor D for both the younger through middle-age levels and the aged, while in the Berger, Bernstein, Klein, Cohen, & Lucas (1964) reanalysis the primary loading was on perceptual organization through the middle-age level, shifting to freedom from distractability for the aged. Birren (quoted in Riegel & Riegel, 1962) found substantial loadings occurred on both verbal comprehension and freedom from distinction.

College students had a low but significant loading only on verbal comprehension (Shaw, 1967), while chronic schizophrenics loaded primarily on perceptual organization, with minor loadings on verbal comprehension (Berger et al., 1964). Chronic organics revealed a picture roughly similar to chronic schizophrenics in that the primary factor was perceptual organization; however, verbal comprehension for this group was also a substantial factor (Russell, 1972). For the dull and mentally retarded, the primary emphasis was on a factor similar to perceptual organization (Sprague & Quay, 1966; Taylor, 1964). The picture is less clear for epileptics (Dennerll, Den Broeder, & Sokolov, 1964), with low positive loadings on perceptual organization and two other nonspecific factors. Differentiated organics (Zimmerman, Whitmyre, & fields, 1970) had significant but low loadings on perceptual organization for both the LI and DI groups, on an unspecified fourth factor for the RI group, and on an unspecified fifth factor for the DI group.

From the research it can be concluded that PC has a high loading with general intelligence, measuring different aspects at different age levels and across categories and subcategories. Factorial complexity is evident in that depending upon subjects, age, and diagnostic category, Picture Completion can reflect any one of the three specific factors (verbal comprehension, perceptual organization, and freedom from distractability) and the two nonspecific factors originally described in the Cohen (1957a) analysis. However, by and large, there tends to be factor specificity across diagnostic groups, a potentially useful attribute. That such complexity exists should not be too surprising since in the act of discovering missing elements in familiar objects any number of approaches can be used. Even the manual allows for either verbalization or pointing as acceptable problem-solving approaches.

ADMINISTRATION

The simple picture task of PC is typically seen as pleasant and nonthreatening. Trying to find what is missing in a picture interests most subjects, since similar puzzles have been presented to them from childhood.

Like all performance tasks, timing is involved, but the 20-second limit is more than ample, and the test is short enough to be completed within 10 minutes. After asking what important part is missing, the examiner may help the subject by giving the correct answer for items #1 and #2, as necessary. However, a hint as to the essential aspect of a missing part can be given only once by saying "Yes, but what is the most important thing missing?" After this, no comment may be made. All items must be given; no provision is made for discontinuing after a run of failures. This point is pertinent since in the WISC version termination occurs after four successive failures. Quershi (1968) reported identical results when a six-failure cut off was substituted for administering all items.

Reaction times should be noted, particularly the extremes. Long reaction time might suggest temporary inefficiency, while overly rapid responses connote impulsivity.

Answers should be recorded exactly, and some inquiry made into peculiar responses. Guessing should be encouraged. Some subjects may hesitate for fear of making an error. Others might not be able to express themselves verbally. Still others may reveal suspicious attitudes ("There is nothing missing!"). Certain answers may indicate defective reality testing. For those subjects unable to verbalize responses, pointing may be substituted.

TESTING THE LIMITS

Testing set may be grossly evaluated by modifying instructions. The subject could be asked, for example, to list all important elements missing. Often a request to name the object itself might clarify the role of a limited environment in determining failures. WISC items can be used to extend the lower limits of the test.

SCORING

Scoring is routine, each correctly identified element credited with one point. The only problem that can occur stems from those situations when the subject is unable to verbalize his response and utilizes pointing. The examiner must be certain that the subject identifies the correct location of the missing element.

ITEM PLACEMENT

When an analysis of average raw scores for this subtest is made, at age 16 to 17, adolescents typically obtain a score of 13 (see Table 10–1). This rises to 14 at the young adult level, 25 to 34, but regresses to 11 to 12 at middle age, 45 to 54, and declines to a low of 9 at the older age level, 65 to 69. In spite of a wide spread of items, 22 percent of the standardization sample were able to pass the most difficult items (Wechsler, 1958).

SIGNIFICANT DIFFERENCES BETWEEN PICTURE COMPLETION AND OTHER SUBTESTS

Newland and Smith (1967) reported that for a significant difference to occur between Picture Completion and another subtest, a three- or four-point

Table 10–1
ITEM PLACEMENT OF AVERAGE SCORES FOR FOUR AGE LEVELS

Age 16–17	(average raw score 13)	success through item #13
Age 25–34	(average raw score 14)	success through item #14
Age 45–54	(average raw score 11–12)	success through item #11
Age 65–69	(average raw score 9)	success through item #9

Source: D. Wechsler, *Manual, Wechsler Adult Intelligence Scale* (New York: Psychological Corporation, 1955), p. 101–108.

Table 10–2
DIFFERENCES BETWEEN PICTURE COMPLETION AND ALL OTHER SCALED SCORES NECESSARY TO SATISFY THE 0.05 AND 0.01 CONFIDENCE LEVELS

CA	Confidence level	Subtests *I*	*C*	*A*	*S*	*D*	*V*	*DS*	*BD*	*PA*	*OA*
18–19	0.05	3	4	4	4	4	3	3	3	4	4
	0.01	4	5	5	5	5	4	4	4	5	5
25–34	0.05	3	4	3	3	4	3	a	3	4	4
	0.01	4	5	5	4	5	3		4	5	5
45–54	0.05	3	4	3	3	4	3	a	3	3	4
	0.01	4	5	5	5	5	3		4	4	5

[a] DS omitted.

Source: From T. E. Newland and P. A. Smith, Statistically significant differences between subtest scores on the WISC and the WAIS, *Journal of School Psychology*, 1967, 5, 126.

discrepancy must occur to reach the 0.05 level, and a three- to five-point discrepancy to reach the 0.01 level. There was relatively little difference between verbal and performance measures. (See Table 10–2).

ITEM COMPOSITION AND DIFFICULTY

The everyday objects in the PC are not likely to be failed because of their absence in the environment of the average United States citizen, although obviously several favor "north" Americans: #11 (stars), #12 (dog tracks), #13 (Florida), and #20 (snow).

Payne and Lehmann (1966) note some change in ranks for a college population: specifically, items #10 and #12 were easier, and items #13, #15, and #16 were harder than the present item placement would suggest. Agreeing with Wechsler (1958), Payne and Lehmann found five items easier for men than woman—these were #10, #11, #12, #14, and #17. At items #17 and #18 there appears to be a sudden increase in item difficulty.

Typical and pathological errors on this subtest were analyzed by Wolfson and Weltman (1960). Common errors without pathological concomitants occurred on eleven of the pictures—#3, ear; #10, socket; #11, staff, more stripes; #12, man's foot, boots, shoes; #13, states, name; #15, tail, eyes, head; #16, arm, part of chair or table; #17, pockets, ear, a clothes item; #18, hand, path, ground, grass; #19, person, saddle horn.

Pictures that elicited both normal and pathological errors made up nine of the 21 items. These were #4 wheel(s) as a "normal" error versus (titled) person, steering wheel as pathological errors; #6, person (normal) versus water in the glass (pathological); #7, part of nose (normal) versus shoulder (pathological); #8 bow, string(s) (normal) versus person, fiddler (pathological); #9, untitled person (normal) versus titled person—captain, etc. (pathological); #14, sails, deck, top of ship (normal) versus humans (pathological); #20, chimney, part of fence (normal) versus humans (pathological); and #21, ear, shoulder (normal) versus hat (pathological).

Only one item, #5, elicited only pathological errors, specifically, deck, other cards (i.e., ace).

Comparing a psychotic population with a control group, Wolfson and Weltman (1960) reported that 81 percent of the former gave pathological responses, particularly schizophrenics. On the other hand, no patients diagnosed as primary behavior disorder, organic, or alcoholic and no controls gave such a response.

RESEARCH WITH THE PICTURE COMPLETION SUBTEST

Although the PC correlates highly with general intelligence and is apparently useful in discriminating between groups, research with the test has, nevertheless, been extremely limited. Saunders (1960) reported three major factors affecting performance on PC: (1) a maintenance of contact, (2) a maintenance of perspective, and (3) the effect of uncertainty. In the Wechsler (1958, pp. 171–172) diagnostic profiles scores for organics and mental defectives do not significantly vary from the subtest mean. For schizophrenics there may be no deviation, or deviation as great as 3 or more units below the mean subtest score, depending on the type of schizophrenia. In anxiety states the score is expected to deviate from 1.5 to 2.5 units below *S*'s mean subtest score, while adolescent sociopaths may or may not deviate 1.5 to 2.5 units above the mean subtest score. Ladd's (1964) samples of brain damaged and neurotic patients did show no deviation from their own mean on Picture Completion, which agrees with Wechsler's findings. Otherwise, to the authors' knowledge, none of the above hypotheses have been experimentally verified.

Wolfson and Weltman (1960) compared normal and hospitalized women suffering various kinds of psychiatric disorders and reported that the patient group made specific and unique errors that differentiated them from the normal group. According to Wiener (1957), high distrustful subjects, when compared to low distrustful individuals, differed significantly in their spontaneous comments of disbelief. For the PC these included expressions such as "Nothing is missing from this picture." "Is there always something missing?" etc. However, instructions designed to create a distrustful attitude did not produce significant impairment for either high distrustful or low distrustful groups or for both combined.

One other study, that of Bloom (1959), examined the "etological" factors on this subtest. Student nurses in St. Louis were compared to an equivalent group in Hawaii, none of whom had ever visited the mainland. Bloom concluded that the test may be less suitable for use in Hawaii than on the mainland. On the other hand, using psychiatric samples, Bloom and Goldman (1962), comparing Connecticut and Hawaiian psychotic patients, found no differences on this subtest.

ADVANTAGES OF THE SUBTEST

The PC is a rapidly administered and easily scored subtest. Although only moderately reliable, it correlates well with general intelligence. The range of items is wide, allowing the evaluation of subjects with a wide range of intellectual competencies. The task is nonverbal in that pointing is acceptable. Specific failures on certain items have proved to have diagnostic value.

LIMITATIONS OF THE SUBTEST

The test has two drawbacks. It is easier for men than women, a problem in selecting a brief test and some items require knowledge of environmental factors, which may favor those in one area over another. Also a test taking "set" such as denial of missing parts can conceivably distort results.

CONCLUSIONS

High scores on the PC may indicate good perception and concentration and interest in the environment. Those with a wide fund of general information tend to be successful here as well. Concentration somewhat parallel to that needed in the more verbal Arithmetic subtest is called upon, and the ability to identify essential from nonessential elements is involved. An obsessive attention to detail can be helpful, as can the overalertness associated with paranoia. The canny delinquent who "doesn't miss a thing" can do well here.

Poor scores might be due to such factors as the following: A focus on minutia without ability to differentiate can lower scores. Negativism and suspicion may lead to insistence that nothing is missing. The same insistence may also tap concern over injury and subsequent denial. Simply naming objects seen, rather than following instructions, is characteristic of subjects with a low mental age (6 or below). Specific failures can be diagnostically meaningful. Schizophrenics may insist that specific individuals are missing, for example, on #8 a fiddler, rather than the violin peg. Inability to attend to the picture may suggest anxiety leading to distractability. Erratic failures may indicate the same or suggest some interference with reality testing, while absurd answers are clear clues to problems in testing reality.

REFERENCES

Berger, L., Bernstein, A., Klein, E., Cohen, J., & Lucas, G. Effects of aging and pathology on the factorial structure of intelligence. *Journal of Consulting Psychology*, 1964, **28**, 199–207.

Bloom, B. L. Ecological factors in the WAIS Picture Completion test. *Journal of Consulting Psychology*, 1959, **23**, 375.

Bloom, B. L., & Goldman, R. K. Sensitivity of the WAIS to language handicap in a psychotic population. *Journal of Clinical Psychology*, 1962, **18**, 161–163.

Cohen, J. A factor-analytically based rationale for the WAIS. *Journal of Consulting Psychology*, 1957, **21**, 451–457. (a)

Cohen, J. The factorial structure of the WAIS between early adulthood and old age. *Journal of Consulting Psychology*, 1957, **21**, 283–290. (b)

Dennerll, R. D., Den Broeder, J., & Sokolov, S. L. WISC and WAIS factors in children and adults with epilepsy. *Journal of Clinical Psychology*, 1964, **20**, 236–240.

Ladd, C. E. WAIS performances of brain-damaged and neurotic patients. *Journal of Clinical Psychology*, 1964, **20**, 114–117.

Newland, T. E., & Smith, P. A. Statistically significant differences between subtest scaled scores on the WISC and the WAIS. *Journal of School Psychology*, 1967, **5**, 122–127.

Payne, D. A., & Lehmann, I. J. A brief WAIS item analysis. *Journal of Clinical Psychology*, 1966, **22**, 296–297.

Pintner, R., & Paterson, D. G. *A scale of performance tests.* New York: Appleton, 1917.

Quershi, M. Y. Optimum limits of testing on the Wechsler Intelligence scales. *Genetic Psychology Monograph*, 1968, **78**, 141–190.

Riegel, R. M. & Riegel, K. F. A comparison and reinterpretation of factor structures of the W-B, the WAIS, and the HAWIE on aged persons. *Journal of Consulting Psychology*, 1962, **26**, 31–37.

Russell, E. W. A WAIS factor analysis with brain-damaged subjects using criterion measures. *Journal of Consulting and Clinical Psychology*, 1972, **39**, 133–139.

Saunders, D. A. A factor analysis of the Picture Completion items on the WAIS. *Journal of Clinical Psychology*, 1960, **16**, 146–149.

Shaw, D. J. Factor analysis of the collegiate WAIS. *Journal of Consulting Psychology*, 1967, **31**, 217.

Sprague, R. L., & Quay, H. C. A factor analytic study of the responses of mental retardates on the WAIS. *American Journal of Mental Deficiency*, 1966, **70**, 595–600.

Taylor, J. B. The structure of ability in the lower intellectual range. *American Journal of Mental Deficiency*, 1964, **68**, 766–774.

Wechsler, D. *The measurement and appraisal of adult Intelligence.* Baltimore: Williams & Wilkins, 1958.

Wiener, G. The effect of distrust on some aspects of ingelligence test behavior. *Journal of Consulting Psychology*, 1957, **21**, 127–130.

Wolfson, W., & Weltman, R. E. Implications of specific WAIS Picture Completion errors. *Journal of Clinical Psychology*, 1960, **16**, 9–11.

Zimmerman, S. F., Whitmyre, J. W., & Fields, F. R. J. Factor analytic structure of the WAIS in patients with diffuse and lateralized cerebral dysfunction. *Journal of Clinical Psychology*, 1970, **26**, 462–465.

CHAPTER 11

BLOCK DESIGN

Kohs (1923) composed the first Block Design (BD) test, suggesting it as a comprehensive measure of nonverbal intelligence. Later, Arthur (1930) incorporated the Kohs designs in her Performance Scale. As used in the Wechsler Bellevue I, the original requirements were modified in terms of number and complexity of designs. In the WAIS there was a further modification; only two-color blocks were used. These changes reduced both the length of administration and the complexity of the task.

Orientation in space is one of the key elements governing the individual effectiveness of behavior in the environment. Spatial orientation can be measured in two general ways: the individual can orient himself within the environment, as in mazes, or he can orient objects within the environment into patterns or designs of his own choice. Block Design is an example of the latter. The subject must construct various geometric parts into meaningful and recognizable entities.

The ability to see meaningful spatial relationships, to analyze visually, and to synthesize abstract geometric designs provide clues to intelligence.

WHAT THE TEST MEASURES

Block Design is one of the few subtests in the WAIS in which reasoning rather than memory is the principal component involved. As is characteristic of all problem-solving tasks, the way a subject goes about finding a solution offers valuable clues to his intellectual functioning. In the Block Design tasks there is only one correct solution to each problem, thus ruling out creativity as a dimension, but at the highest levels analysis of spatial relations and the rigid application of logic can be discerned. Easier problems can of course, be solved in trial-and-error fashion.

The subtest is so constructed that visual-motor integration and speed of performance, particularly at the upper levels, are also measured; but, as compared to the earlier Wechsler Bellevue version, Block Design does not allow for inferences about disturbances in color perception, whatever the associated deficit, because of the limited number of colors present. However, concern over minor color variations are sometimes expressed.

Nonintellective factors, such as excessive cautiousness, impulsiveness, and distractability, can be observed under some conditions. Advancing age, with its concomittant slowing of motor speed, is reflected in lower test scores.

DESCRIPTION

The subtest consists of a series of ten designs that are to be constructed from patterns presented in a booklet. Although current designs borrow from those in the earlier Wechsler Bellevue I, certain changes should be noted. The multicolor blocks have given way to only red and white, and the total number of blocks used in any design is nine rather than 16. All designs are scored, even the two demonstrations. Unlike the WB version in which time bonuses were obtainable from the first design, bonuses are not allowed until design #7 in the WAIS. Time limits for the most difficult items have been reduced from the earlier 140 seconds to 120 seconds, and in the present version the test has been lengthened by three scorable items. Lastly, the basic score for each correctly executed design is now 4 points instead of the previous 3.

FACTOR ANALYSIS

In Cohen's (1957a) analysis of the standardization groups Block Design emerges as a fair measure of G. The correlation averages 0.70 for the younger through middle-age groups, dropping to 0.65 for the aged. Cohen also found that throughout the age levels BD is substantially correlated with the perceptual organization factor. When Berger, Bernstein, Klein, Cohen, and Lucas (1964) reanalyzed the standardization groups, BD again emerged as an indication of the perceptual organization factor, with no contamination. In the Birren analysis (quoted by Reigel & Riegel, 1962), however, freedom from distractability and verbal comprehension are major factors, while a negative loading occurs on perceptual organization.

For college students (Shaw, 1967), chronic schizophrenics (Berger et al., 1964) and chronic brain-damaged patients (Russell, 1972), epileptics (Dennerll, Den Broeder, & Sokolov, 1964), and any of the three differentiated brain-damaged groups (Zimmerman, Whitmyre, & Fields, 1970), the subtest is again a measure of perceptual organization. The picture is less clear for the dull and mentally retarded. Taylor (1964) noted that Block Design loads highly only on the factor similar to perceptual organization, but Sprague and Quay (1966) reported low positive correlations on both the verbal comprehension factor and freedom from distractability.

In short, this subtest, relative to the standardization sample, is a fair measure of those aspects of general intelligence that emphasize the ability to visualize and construct various geometric designs from component parts. Essentially, the same skills seem required on those tests of aptitude evaluating the capacity to perceive spatial relationships. With some populations the initial difficulty of the subtest might establish it as a measure of concentration and perseverence. Still others might conceive of the task in terms of verbally describable and specific designs rather than just abstract geometric shapes.

ADMINISTRATION

The Kohs blocks used in Block Design have been sold as toys for many years. Typically, subjects mention this test as something for their children; if vehemently stressed, this could indicate a defensive stance.

Sometimes, depending on the subject, a word as to the relationship of BD to engineering skills may make it more palatable for the *S*.

The first six items must be finished within a minute each, the last four within 2 minutes. Testing can usually be completed within 10 minutes since most subjects complete the initial items well below the 2-minute time limit.

The first design is demonstrated and left standing by the examiner for the subject to copy. If failed, the design is rebuilt from the subject's blocks, leaving the original model intact. (There are no demonstration cards and designs as in the Wechsler Bellevue.) The second design is demonstrated by the examiner, who presents the picture and puts the blocks together to duplicate it. If the subject fails on his first attempt, the design is again constructed for him, and a second trial is given. By the time design #3 is reached, the subject must work from the picture alone without further help. The blocks are always scrambled before the presentation of the next design. With item #7, the subject is instructed that nine instead of four blocks will be used.

The subject should be asked to say when he is finished. In case of a minute error, the examiner's silence can lead the subject to make spontaneous corrections. This may be scored plus if it is made within the time limit.

There is no time bonus until item #7; consequently, the construction is more emphasized than on the Wechsler Bellevue, and speed bonuses are not necessary for an average, or better than average, score.

This subtest is discontinued after three consecutive failures. However, failure on *both* trials on either design #1 or #2 are considered only one failure.

Elwood (1969) has suggested that automated administration slightly lowered scores on this subtest in comparison to the face-to-face situation.

TESTING THE LIMITS

Testing the limits can be particularly valuable with the BD. Pointing out an incorrect design and asking the subject to correct it can be considered if the failed item seems within the subject's ability. In addition, one can give the subject increments of help, noting how much aid is needed before completion (for instance, demonstrating the diagonal pattern by putting two diagonal blocks together). Sattler (1969) indicates that for the Wechsler Bellevue I version giving extra help (one cue) hardly affects the BD performance. However, when several cues are given, scores can be raised even on retest.

SCORING

Occasionally the rapid assessment of the accuracy of a design can be difficult for an examiner who himself has perceptual problems. In such a case it can be helpful to draw a full-size, block-by-block duplicate of the designs, inserting this in the manual to check against while scoring. This procedure also gives graphic evidence of bizarre designs. The extra answer sheet available through the Psychological Corporation provides blanks for entering actual constructions. The regular answer sheet simplifies both basic scoring and the time bonuses for the last four designs.

Table 11—1
ITEM PLACEMENT OF AVERAGE SCORES FOR FOUR AGE LEVELS

Age 16—17	(average raw score 29—32)	success through item #8
Age 25—34	(average raw score 31—33)	success through item #8
Age 45—54	(average raw score 27—28)	success through item #7
Age 65—69	(average raw score 24—27)	success through item #6

A raw score of 40 can be obtained without time bonuses.
Source: D. Wechsler, *Manual, Wechsler Adult Intelligence Scale* (New York: Psychological Corporation, 1955), p. 101—108.

ITEM PLACEMENT

BD reveals a constant decline in average raw scores past the young adult level (Table 11—1). At age 16 the average raw score is 29 to 32, usually reflecting success in copying the first eight designs. Scores rise slightly to 31 to 33 (again, success through item #8) for age 25 to 34. A decline is observed for the middle-age level, 45 to 54, with average raw scores of 27 to 28, or success through design #7. The decline is marked for the older age group, 65 to 69, with an average raw score of 24 to 27, or design #6 or better.

Time need not be a factor in success since a raw score of 40, or superior, is theoretically possible without any time bonuses being required. A limited upper range is suggested by the fact that 24 percent of the standardization sample were able to pass the more difficult items (Wechsler, 1958). Obviously, the use of time bonuses can be helpful in extending the upper range. However, the initial difficulty of items has yet to be corrected.

Table 11—2
DIFFERENCES BETWEEN BLOCK DESIGN AND ALL OTHER SCALED SCORES NECESSARY TO SATISFY THE 0.05 AND 0.01 CONFIDENCE LEVELS

CA	*Confidence levels*	*Subtests* *I*	*C*	*A*	*S*	*D*	*V*	*DS*	*PC*	*PA*	*OA*
18—19	0.05	3	4	4	3	4	3	3	3	4	4
	0.01	4	5	5	4	5	3	4	4	5	5
25—34	0.05	3	4	4	3	4	3	a	3	4	4
	0.01	4	5	5	4	6	4		4	6	5
45—54	0.05	3	4	3	3	4	3	a	3	4	4
	0.01	4	5	5	5	5	3		4	5	5

[a] DS omitted.
Source: From T. E. Newland and P. A. Smith, Statistically significant differences between subtest scaled scores on the WISC and the WAIS, *Journal of School Psychology,* 1967, 5, 126.

SIGNIFICANT DIFFERENCES BETWEEN THE BLOCK DESIGN AND OTHER SUBTESTS

Newland and Smith (1967) report that differences of three to four weighted score points between Block Design and any other subtests are required to reach the 0.05 level of significance, and a difference of three to six points when the 0.01 level is required. Information, Similarities, and Vocabulary require the least difference, when compared to Block Design, to reach significance, while Comprehension, Digit Span, Picture Arrangement, and Object Assembly do not reach significance until relatively large differences are obtained (See Table 11–2.)

ITEM COMPOSITION AND DIFFICULTY

The ten designs of this subtest allow the subject to copy the first two from actual block constructions and thus have some practice on what might be a new experience. However, even with this practice, the early items are too difficult for low functioning subjects.

The designs vary in difficulty for different subjects, depending upon their set to respond. For example, design #6, a chevron, may be solved with ease or completely bewilder subjects, according to their comprehension of the diagonal construction. The transition from four to nine blocks at design #7 is smooth for most subjects. However, the next design, #8, calling for diagonal lines, is unexpectedly difficult: the failure rate rises to 59 percent of the standardization sample as compared to 25 percent or less for the previous designs (Wechsler, 1958).

Payne and Lehmann (1966) have almost no disagreement with the item placement proposed by Wechsler. However, like Shaw (1965), they note sex differences favoring men, specifically designs #6, #8, and #9. Also, between items #7 and #8 there was a marked increase in difficulty for both men and women.

RESEARCH WITH THE BLOCK DESIGN SUBTEST

Saunders and Gittinger (undated) regard the Block Design subtest as measuring a "generalized 'perceptual threshold'." Witkin (1965) has reasoned that the Block Design along with the OA and PC subtests measures analytic thinking. He notes a positive relationship between this skill and field independence. In the Wechsler (1958) analysis of diagnostic groups organics, depending on the type of impairment, are expected to obtain scores deviating

3 or more units below the mean subtest score or to obtain scores within +1.5 to −1.5 units of the mean subtest score. When they do obtain deviant scores relative to the mean subtest score, schizophrenics tend to deviate 1.5 to 2.5 units above the mean. The same pattern as in schizophrenics is expected of the mental retardate, while for the sociopath the reverse pattern seems to be characteristic. In anxiety states the Block Design score is expected to remain within +1.5 to −1.5 units of *S*'s mean subtest score.

Ladd's findings (1964) agree with Wechsler's for a neurotic sample, who showed no deviation from their own mean. On the other hand, his brain-damaged sample also showed no deviation, while as noted, Wechsler's results varied, with some of his subjects scoring considerably below average. There was a significant difference (0.05 level) between Connecticut and Hawaiian psychotic patients, reflecting the latters' better performance on Block Design (Bloom & Goldman, 1962).

Although there have been several studies of the Block Design subtest as used in the entire Wechsler series (Ogdon, 1964), there have been relatively few in which the WAIS version has been used. Sarason and Minard (1962) report a significant negative relationship between the Test Anxiety Scale results and the BD score. Jurjevich (1963) similarly concluded that the Wechsler subtests (A, BD, DS) had little predictive validity for levels of conscious anxiety as measured on the MMPI.

Following the lead of Witkin (1965), Morgan (1966) used an "analytic index" (the summed scaled scores of PC, OA, and BD) as an indicator of rehospitalization of schizophrenic servicemen. The hypothesis that *S*s who were rehospitalized would show a lower mean "analytic index" was confirmed.

De Wolfe, Barrett, Becker, and Spaner (1971) compared older brain-damaged *S*s with older schizophrenic *S*s. Brain-damaged *S*s showed a greater deficit in the BD performance relative to mean performance level than did schizophrenics. However, Watson (1965) had previously reported that there was no WAIS pattern that could distinguish between schizophrenics and brain-damaged *S*s.

Hirt and Cook (1963) made use of multiple regression equations with subtests and applied the derived formula to known organic cases (the Grassi test as criterion). When BD was combined with DS, PC, and PA, the combination yielded a correlation of 0.77. The correlation between BD alone and the Grassi was reported as 0.66.

One other study, that of Shaw (1965), questioned whether sexual bias existed on BD. Using 50 male and 50 female college students matched on FIQ, he reported women to be superior only on Digit Symbol.

Noting minor geometric errors in the Wechsler versions of Koh's patterns, Berringer (1971) hypothesized that this could influence ability to copy the designs. However, for a college sample representing a range of spatial relations skills, the substitution of "correctly" drawn designs did not influence scores.

ADVANTAGES OF THE SUBTEST

The BD subtest is an excellent measure of nonverbal reasoning and analytic thinking and a reliable and meaningful measure of general intelligence. Block Design can detect perceptual problems since it is factorially specific for perceptual organization. The range of items at the upper level is good. Chance variations are minimal, and while timed, this does not seriously affect scores. Also, the test is relatively culture-fair. Block Design offers an opportunity to observe work habits. Although requiring some dexterity, it can be done with the nondominant hand.

LIMITATIONS OF THE SUBTEST

Early items tend to be difficult for dull subjects since there is a relatively high floor, and zero scores are, therefore, likely. Dexterity can influence scores positively, particularly for those using a trial-and-error approach. The administration time can be very lengthy for those able to do, or at least try, all designs. A learning set may be observed to influence scores, either by too rapid giving up or a sudden unexpected mastery.

CONCLUSIONS

This subtest is often high for the bright and gifted. It serves as a nonverbal measure of reasoning, and scores can be similar to verbal measures. Convergent skills (here, copying) are rewarded.

High scores may indicate a number of factors: experience with Kohs blocks as a child, analytic talent, and speed and accuracy in sizing up a problem. Success may reflect different approaches, for example, that achieved by an emphasis on detail, in block-by-block matching. Flexible thinking, as seen in rapid trial and error, can raise the score. Here coordination may be involved.

Low scores may reflect a speedy, careless approach or a lack of reflectiveness in performance. Those with a "failure" orientation may refuse to try or give up too readily (the point reached here is worth noting). A compulsive trend leading to slow and methodical checking and rechecking can penalize an otherwise bright and efficient worker. Anxiety may be suggested by planless fumbling or failing to check the production. A focus on unessential details (concern about differences between blocks) or a compulsive need for accuracy may be involved in low scores. Bizarre solutions (design constructed on top of the card, or made vertically) can indicate poor reality ties. Suspiciousness ("not enough blocks," "can't be done") might reflect a projection of failure onto the material. Inability to use the diagonal blocks in production can be checked to differentiate between the dull and a bizarre thinking process. Fumbling and failing to see the equivalence from one side or one block to another, may characterize the brain damaged.

REFERENCES

Arthur, G. *Arthur point scale of performance tests.* Chicago: Stoelting, 1930.

Berger, L., Bernstein, A., Klein, E., Cohen, J., & Lucas, G. Effects of aging and pathology on the factorial structure of intelligence. *Journal of Consulting Psychology*, 1964, **28**, 199–207.

Berringer, D. E. An examination of geometric errors in the WAIS Block Design and the effects upon performance as a function of spatial relations ability. *Dissertation Abstracts International*, 1971, **31**, 6313 B.

Bloom, B. L., & Goldman, R. K. Sensitivity of the WAIS to language handicap in a psychotic population. *Journal of Clinical Psychology*, 1962, **18**, 161–163.

Cohen, J. The factorial structure of the WAIS between early adulthood and old age. *Journal of Consulting Psychology*, 1957, **21**, 283–290.

DeWolfe, A. S., Barrett, R. P., Becker, B. C., & Spaner, F. C. Intellectual deficit in chronic schizophrenia and brain damage. *Journal of Consulting and Clinical Psychology*, 1971, **36**, 197–204.

Dennerll, R. D., Den Broeder, J., & Sokolov, S. L. WISC and WAIS factors in children and adults with epilepsy. *Journal of Clinical Psychology*, 1964, **20**, 236–240.

Elwood, D. L. Automation of psychological testing. *American Psychologist*, 1969, **24**, 287–289.

Elwood, D. L., & Griffin, H. R. Intellectual intelligence testing without the examiner: reliability of an antomated method. *Journal of Consulting and Clinical Psychology*, 1972, **38**, 9–14.

Hirt, M. L., & Cook, R. A. Use of a multiple regression equation to estimate organic impairment from Wechsler scale scores. *Journal of Clinical Psychology*, 1963, **16**, 80–81.

Jurjevich, R. M. Interrelationships of anxiety indicies of Wechsler intelligence scales and MMPI scales. *Journal of General Psychology*, 1963, **69**, 135–142.

Kohs, S. C. *Intelligence measurement: a psychological and statistical study based upon the Block-Design tests.* New York: Macmillan, 1923.

Ladd, C. E. WAIS performances of brain-damaged and neurotic patients. *Journal of Clinical Psychology*, 1964, **20**, 115–117.

Morgan, D. W. WAIS "analytic index" and rehospitalization of schizophrenic servicemen. *Journal of Consulting Psychology*, 1966, **30**, 267–269.

Ogdon, D. P. *Psychodiagnostic and personality assessment: a handbook.* Los Angeles: Western Psychological Services, 1967.

Payne, D. A., & Lehmann, I. J. A brief WAIS item analysis. *Journal of Clinical Psychology*, 1966, **22**, 296–297.

Riegel, R. M., & Riegel, K. F. A comparison and reinterpretation of factor structures of the W-B, the WAIS, and the HAWIE on aged persons. *Journal of Consulting Psychology*, 1962, **26**, 31–37.

Russell, E. W. A WAIS factor analysis with brain-damaged subjects using criterion measures. *Journal of Consulting and Clinical Psychology*, 1972, **39**, 133–139.

Sarason, I. G., & Minard, J. Test anxiety, experimental instructions, and the WAIS. *Journal of Educational Psychology*, 1962, **53**, 299–302.

Sattler, J. M. Effects of cues and examiner influence on two Wechsler subtests. *Journal of Consulting and Clinical Psychology*, 1969, **33**, 719–721.

Saunders, D. R., & Gittinger, W. Patterns of intellectual functioning and their implications for the dynamics of behavior. Reprinted from *The role and methodology of classification and psychopathology*. Washington, D.C. U.S. Department of Health, Education, and Welfare, Public Health Service, undated.

Shaw, D. J. Sexual bias in the WAIS. *Journal of Consulting Psychology*, 1965, **29**, 590–591.

Shaw, D. J. Factor analysis of the collegiate WAIS. *Journal of Consulting Psychology*, 1967, **31**, 217.

Sprague, R. L., Quay, H. C. A factor analytic study of the responses of mental retardates on the WAIS. *American Journal of Mental Deficiency*, 1966, **70**, 595–600.

Taylor, J. B. The structure of ability in the lower intellectual range. *American Journal of Mental Deficiency*, 1964, **68**, 766–774.

Watson, C. G. WAIS profile patterns of hospitalized brain-damaged and schizophrenic patients. *Journal of Clinical Psychology*, 1965, **21**, 294–295.

Wechsler, D. *The measurement and appraisal of adult intelligence.* Baltimore: Williams & Witkins, 1958.

Witkin, H. Psychological differentiation and form of pathology. *Journal of Abnormal Psychology*, 1965, **70**, 317–336.

Zimmerman, S. F., Whitmyre, J. W., & Fields, F. R. J. Factor analytic structure of the WAIS in patients with diffuse and lateralized cerebral dysfunction. *Journal of Clinical Psychology*, 1970, **26**, 462–465.

CHAPTER 12

PICTURE ARRANGEMENT

DeCroly (1914) is credited with the formulation of picture arrangement items as a measure of intelligence. By 1917 psychologists in America began to experiment with this format for group tests. Although the efforts were at first unsuccessful, the "Foxy Grandpa" series were incorporated into the Army Performance Scale (1921). Wechsler (1958) stated that difficulties encountered in scoring, and in obtaining good sequences, hindered early acceptance of such a measure in America. However, by 1934, Cornell and Cox has successfully adapted a picture arrangement format in their scale. Sequences used in the Wechsler Bellevue I were in part based on those from the Army Group Tests, but also included Soglow's "Little King" series which had appeared in the *New Yorker* magazine. The WAIS series is a slightly altered version of the Wechsler Bellevue I form.

Cartooning has long reflected the critical and sometimes amusing aspects of the cultural mores in succinct form. To understand the meaning implicit in cartoons, one must first have knowledge of the general aspects propogating such customs. The Picture Arrangement (PA) subtest attempts to tap a basic understanding of some of the more commonly accepted customs in today's culture. In the present format there are some additional requirements, namely, that a person not only understand the customs, but also can reconstruct the underlying theme when these customs are presented in pictorial but randomized form.

This test measures ability to comprehend or size up a total situation from deliberately scrambled clues. In the process, parts must be related to wholes and to each other in a logical manner, and sequential planning involved. The social knowledge and skill required are assumed to be related to intelligence.

WHAT THE TEST MEASURES

Visual perception, synthesis into wholes through planning, and ability to see cause-effect relationship are among the factors measured by the PA. Further, this test furnishes clues as to a person's interpersonal relationships as well as his ability to gauge social situations. Wechsler does not differentiate social intelligence from any other; he prefers to think of it as general intelligence applied to social situations.

As with all the subtests, cultural background is important in evaluating the results. In addition, the personal implications of some of the sequences give rise to interesting clinical material.

There are actually some experimental measures of social variables that have been found to relate to Picture Arrangement. These include introversion-extroversion and participation in extracurricular activities.

DESCRIPTION

The second picture test in the WAIS, Picture Arrangement consists of eight sequences that are presented in a predetermined scrambled order. The subject is asked to put the pictures in the proper sequence within a time limit. Six sequences have been retained from the Wechsler Bellevue I, but the introductory item, #1 (nest), is no longer a sample. Instead, initial success achieves full credit. If the subject fails this item, the correct solution is demonstrated, and a second trial is given. The same procedure is followed on the second item, but no further help is given. Less weight is given to speed on the WAIS version of Picture Arrangement, a maximum of 2 instead of 3 points is allowed per item.

FACTOR ANALYSIS

In the Cohen (1957) analysis the PA subtest ranks at about the median level as a measure of G, with a correlation of 0.70 through the middle-age level for the standardization group. For the aged, the correlation drops to

0.65. What Picture Arrangement measures beyond G is open to question in the Cohen analysis. It correlates very weakly with perceptual organization, accounting for about 4 percent of the variance at all age levels. For the aged, verbal comprehension accounts for about 9 percent of the variance. Berger, Bernstein, Klein, Cohen, and Lucas (1964) found Picture Arrangement a relatively pure moderate indicator of perceptual organization for ages 18 to 19, 25 to 34, and for those over 60, but for the 45 to 54 age group, there is an indication of an unspecified factor. In the Birren study (quoted in Riegel & Riegel, 1962) verbal comprehension was the primary factor with small positive loadings on freedom from distractability. Surprisingly, Picture Arrangement was negatively correlated with perceptual organization for this combined age group.

The main specific factor identified with college students (Shaw, 1967) is perceptual organization, although at a quite low level (4 percent of the variance). Chronic schizophrenics show positive, and again relatively low, loadings on both verbal comprehension and perceptual organization (Berger et al., 1964). However, for chronic organic patients, there is a relatively large loading on perceptual organization (Russell, 1972). That factor specificity varies with diagnostic categories is further illustrated by Dennerll, Den Broeder, and Sokolov (1964) in their study of epileptics. The major loading for this group occurs on an unspecified fifth factor. The highest loading is again found on the unspecified fifth factor for the Zimmerman, Whitmyre, and Fields (1970) differentiated organic groups, this time for the right side involved (RI) group. But there are also significant loadings for the diffused involved (DI) on both the fifth factor and perceptual organization and on freedom from distractability for the left side involved (LI) group. Perceptual organization appears to be the main factor represented by this subtest for the dull and mentally retarded (Sprague and Quay, 1966; Taylor, 1964). Taylor's study also gave some support to the widely held assumption that Picture Arrangement measures social competency. So far this finding has not been cross-validated factorially.

The research bears out that the PA subtest deals with those general aspects of intelligence that involve attending to, recognizing, and ordering sequences denoting probable life situations. At this point one really does not know the number of ways that subjects can solve the problems presented. As noted, the whole gamut of recognizable factors has been covered.

ADMINISTRATION

This "comic strip" task can be bothersome to some humorless or defensive individuals. On the other hand, to most people rearranging picture cards to make a proper sequence proves to be interesting and challenging.

When the first item is presented, the subject is told that it represents "a story of a bird building a nest." If the subject fails the first trial, the examiner constructs and explains the sequence and allows a second trial. On the second item there is no explanation unless the item is failed. In that case, the examiner again constructs the sequence and explains it and allows another trial. If failures occur on both trials of items #1 and #2, administration is discontinued. Otherwise all items are to be administered. However, Affleck and Frederickson (1966) note that this rule is broken relatively often (in 26% of a mentally retarded sample), usually because of patient resistance, bewilderment, or obvious confusion. Their findings suggest that after four successive failures termination might be considered if patient resistance is strong.

For items #1 through #6, 60 seconds each are allowed and 2 minutes for items #7 and #8. Partial credits are allowed only from item #6; bonuses for speedy solutions only on items #7 and #8.

The subject should be asked to let the examiner know when he is finished. Verbatim stories may be recorded whenever a question is raised by the placement. This modification in administration procedures can be challenged on the basis that it may increase scores, since the subject might use this request as a clue to reconsider his construction. However, Golland and Herrell (1970) suggest that even when a subject is asked to explain all, and not just the most difficult sequences, scores are not necessarily increased. The advantage of verbatim stories lies in its contribution to understanding of the subject. For instance, occasionally the sequence is correct without the subject seeing the point of the story, or the reverse: the sequence may be incorrect, but the point of the story is grasped. Examination of the thought processes involved in solving each item may reveal important aspects of the subject's cognition—precise or confused and tangential, socially oriented or self-oriented, realistic or bizarre, the ability or inability to relate verbal to visual-motor tasks. Failures may occur because of poor planning or because of false perceptions stimulated by emotionally charged ideas.

TESTING THE LIMITS

In testing the limits the subject can be asked to try again after failure, perhaps after receiving cues from the examiner as to what the story entails. Pointing out classic errors, for example, "He is carrying a dummy" or "It is the same person in each picture," and asking for another sequence may give valuable information regarding rigidity and reality testing. Addition of WISC items may indicate the degree of limitation involved in marked failure. Also a comparison with the Picture Completion score can clarify the role of visual acuity in failure.

SCORING

The well-designed answer sheet for the PA with all creditable sequences entered greatly simplifies the scoring. However, interpretation can be helped by comparing each response order to presentation order to see what changes were made. A maximum of 4 points each can be obtained for items #1 through #6. Needing two trials on the first two items reduces the score to 2 points each. Time bonuses totaling 2 points are possible for items #7 and #8. These are added to the 4 points for a correct solution. Partially correct solutions on the last three items limit the score to 2 points each.

ITEM PLACEMENT

Average scores on PA show the sharpest decline with age of any of the WAIS measures. At age 16 to 17 a raw score of 24 to 25 is average, usually consisting of success on the first six items. A decline to 23 to 24 occurs for the 25- to 34-year age group. However, by age 45 to 54 the decline is marked, with average scores of 17 to 19 (some success through item #5), and by age 65 to 69 the average score is reduced still further to 13 to 15, or some success through item #4 (Table 12–1).

Time need not be a factor in success on this subtest, since a raw score of 32, or superior, is theoretically possible without any time bonuses.

The limited upper range of this subtest is indicated in that only 35 percent of the standardization sample had passed the most difficult item (Wechsler, 1958).

Table 12–1
ITEM PLACEMENT OF AVERAGE SCORES FOR FOUR AGE LEVELS

Age 16–17	(average raw scores 24–25)	success through item #6
Age 25–34	(average raw score 23–24)	success through item #6
Age 45–54	(average raw score 17–19)	success through item #5
Age 65–69	(average raw score 13–15)	success through item #4

A raw score of 32 can be obtained without time bonuses.
Source: D. Wechsler, *Manual, Wechsler Adult Intelligence Scale* (New York: Psychological Corporation, 1955), p. 101–108.

Table 12–2
DIFFERENCES BETWEEN PICTURE ARRANGEMENT AND ALL OTHER SCALED SCORES NECESSARY TO SATISFY THE 0.05 AND 0.01 CONFIDENCE LEVELS

		Subtests									
CA	*Confidence level*	*I*	*C*	*A*	*S*	*D*	*V*	*DS*	*PC*	*BD*	*OA*
18–19	.05	4	4	4	3	5	4	4	4	4	5
	.01	5	6	6	5	6	5	5	5	5	6
25–34	.05	4	4	4	4	5	5	a	4	4	5
	.01	5	6	6	5	6	7		5	6	6
45–54	.05	3	4	4	4	4	3	a	3	4	4
	.01	4	5	5	5	6	4		4	5	5

[a]DS omitted.

Source: From T. E. Newland and P. A. Smith, Statistically significant differences between subtest scaled scores on the WISC and the WAIS, *Journal of School Psychology*, 1967, **5**, 126.

SIGNIFICANT DIFFERENCES BETWEEN THE PICTURE ARRANGEMENT AND OTHER SUBTESTS

Differences between PA weighted scores and scores on all other subtests must generally be four or more points to reach the 0.05 level of confidence, and five or six points, even as high as seven, to reach the 0.01 level. (See Table 12-2.) These are among the largest differences required between any subtests.

ITEM COMPOSITION AND DIFFICULTY

The Picture Arrangement subtest permits two "practice" items, giving the subject a chance to copy correct solutions if he has initial difficulty. This allows the subject to use "steps of learning that prepare and familiarize him with the test so that he is better prepared for the more difficult series at the end" (Barnes, 1969, p. 7).

While there is little that is upsetting about the items in this subtest, the more difficult usually elicit bizarre responses from seriously disturbed patients. The most frequent errors on the test are failures to understand sequences. Retarded or brain-injured individuals may simply reposition one card or perseverate in using the same moves (such as first card to last position) from item to item. Item #4 (Louie) can prove confusing to subjects because of the sudden increase in pieces and a relatively complicated theme; #8 (taxi) is frequently misinterpreted when the subject fails to perceive the dummy. Wechsler (1958) notes a cultural difference on #6 (flirt) from flirtation to chivalry in Japan.

Payne and Lehmann (1966) in a review of college records found the item placement slightly but not significantly out of line. Item #6 (flirt) was easier than #4 (Louie)—although this might be due to further practice. In contrast, #5 (enter) ranked seventh in difficulty. Since all items are administered, repositioning is not critical. No sex differences were noted.

RESEARCH WITH THE PICTURE ARRANGEMENT SUBTEST

In the Saunders and Gittinger report (undated) "conditionability" is the main dimension of this subtest. The organics and mental defectives in Wechsler's diagnostic groups (1958) proved to be similar in that a deviation ranging anywhere from +1.5 to −2.5 units below *S*'s mean subtest score could be expected. Schizophrenics also vary widely, obtaining scores ranging from 1.5 to 2.5 units below the mean subtest score to 1.5 to 2.5 units above the mean subtest score. For anxiety states, little or no deviation is expected. Adolescent sociopaths, on the other hand, generally do well on this test, with scores deviating 3 or more units above *S*'s mean subtest score.

Brain-damaged and neurotic samples in Ladd's (1964) analysis did not deviate from their own mean, while Wechsler's subjects tended to fall below their average. Thus, Wechsler's clinical hypotheses just cited above still await empirical validation.

Considering the value of Picture Arrangement in identifying organics, Fogel (1965) administered a partial WAIS. He reported PA to be a better discriminator than five other subtests, including BD and S, and considerably surpassing the Gorham Proverbs Test.

When Graham and Kamano (1958) compared delinquents with good and poor reading skills, they found the former to obtain higher PA scores.

The Connecticut and Hawaiian psychotic samples studied by Bloom and Goldman (1962) showed minor differences, the latter tending to score slightly higher on Picture Arrangement.

Current research has centered on the social significance of high and low PA scores and the relationship to the subject's ability to plan and anticipate. Social introverts and extroverts selected on the basis of the MMPI Social Isolation scale were compared on obtained scores on the PA test by Schill (1966). The introverts obtained significantly lower PA scores. However, Johnson (1969) failed to replicate these results with psychiatric patients and concluded "at least for psychiatric patients, PA subtest performance may not be directly related to the social introversion–extroversion continuum" (p. 182).

Schill, Kahn, and Meuhleman (1968a) further related high PA scores with participation in extracurricular activities both at the high school and college levels. Those students with high PA scores generally tended to report participation in a greater number of different extracurricular activities. Schill, Kahn, and Muehlman (1968b) then noted that high scoring *S*s tended to produce more plural nouns on the Greenspoon plural-nouns verbal conditioning task. They felt that the results confirmed the hypothesis that PA scores are positively associated with sensitivity to subtle social clues.

Blatt and associates have studied the hypothesis that PA scores measure anticipation. Dickstein and Blatt (1966) used PA to investigate the relationship between the degree of conscious concern and preoccupation with death and anticipation of the future. They assumed that a high concern with death would curtail interest in future temporal experience. In their study high death-concern *S*s obtained lower PA scores, and this was interpreted to reflect a restriction in their capacity for anticipation and planning (Dickstein & Blatt, 1967). They found a significant positive relationship between PA performance and future time perspective on TAT stories. Finally, Blatt and Quinlan (1967) repoted that punctual as compared to procrastinating students (in terms of meeting course requirements) obtained higher PA scores. Again, the higher PA scores were concluded to indicate a capacity for anticipation and planning.

The question as to whether or not *S*s should explain their Picture Arrangement stories was explored by Golland and Herrell (1970). Earlier, Herrell and Goland (1969) had found that this procedure applied to the WISC tended to increase the subject's obtained scores. However, for adults matched for age, full-scale IQ, and reason for referral, there were no significant differences between scores of *S*s who told PA stories and those who did not.

ADVANTAGES OF THE SUBTEST

The PA subtest is amusing and not objectionable to most subjects. It is a good measure of logical, sequential planning and appears to be relatively culture-fair. Scores can be compared to those of Picture Completion to rule out visual or perceptual defects as a cause of failure.

Picture Arrangement can illuminate emotional problems, and by having the subject tell the story of his construction, a thematic apperception measure can be elicited.

Two beginning items allow some degree of practice for those unaccustomed to this sort of task.

LIMITATIONS OF THE SUBTEST

Visual acuity is essential for success on the PA and thus poses a problem for the partially sighted. Necessary life experiences can also be considered a prerequisite as well as a degree of humor, or at least of flexibility. Since a mental age of about 8 is necessary before sequences are readily understood, this limits application to those who are no more than mildly retarded.

CONCLUSIONS

Success on Picture Arrangement requires the individual to perceive the details of pictures, to detect sequences, and to assemble pictures in an order to tell a story.

Those who do well must have the ability to delay a solution until all the components are perceived and their possible implications understood. The successful individual is alert to details and capable of logical, sequential thought. Various studies indicate that interest in others, foresight, planning, social skills, and social awareness are all related to success.

Low scores may indicate transient attention or impulsiveness and failure to monitor one's own behavior. Bizarre thinking may be revealed. Asking the subject to describe his sequence may clarify the meaning of an error. A random shuffling of pictures may indicate incapacitating anxiety. Mental deterioration may be indicated by a tendency to see the elements as unrelated (mental age below 8), or trying to match the edges rather than observe the sequence. Poor scores have been attributed to depressed psychotics and chronic schizophrenics, among others.

REFERENCES

Affleck, D. C., & Frederickson, W. K. Testing limits of WAIS Picture Arrangement tests. *American Journal of Mental Deficiency*, 1966, **70**, 605–606.

Barnes, C. Trends in the adult Wechsler individual intelligence scales from the 1939 WB I to the new 1968 Spanish EIWA. Paper given at California State Psychological Association Convention, January 1969.

Berger, L., Bernstein, A., Klein, E., Cohen, J., & Lucas, G. Effects of aging and pathology on the factorial structure of intelligence. *Journal of Consulting Psychology*, 1964, **28**, 199–207.

Blatt, S. J., & Quinlan, P. Punctual and procrastinating students, a study of temporal parameters. *Journal of Consulting Psychology*, 1967, **31**, 170–174.

Bloom, B. L., & Goldman, R. K. Sensitivity of the WAIS to language handicap in a psychotic population. *Journal of Clinical Psychology*, 1962, **18**, 161–163.

Cohen, J. The factorial structure of the WAIS between early adulthood and old age. *Journal of Consulting Psychology*, 1957, **21**, 283–290.

DeCroly, I. Epreuve nouvelle pour l'examination mental. *Annual Psychologie* 1914, **20**, 140–159.

Dennerll, R. D., Den Broeder, J. & Sokolov, S. L. WISC and WAIS factors in children and adults with epilepsy. *Journal of Clinical Psychology*, 1964, **20**, 236–240.

Dickstein, L. S. & Blatt, S. J. Death concern, futurity, and anticipation. *Journal of Consulting Psychology*, 1966, **30**, 11–17.

Dickstein, L. S., & Blatt, S. J. The WAIS Picture Arrangement subtest as a measure of anticipation. *Journal of Projective Techniques and Personality Assessment*, 1967, **31**, 32–38.

Fogel, M. L. The Proverbs Test in the appraisal of cerebral diseases. *Journal of General Psychology*, 1965, **72**, 269–275.

Golland, J. H., & Herrell, J. M. Should WAIS subjects explain Picture Arrangement stories? *Journal of Consulting and Clinical Psychology,* 1970, 35, 157-158.

Graham, E. E., & Kamano, D. Reading failure as a factor in the WAIS subtest patterns of youthful offenders. *Journal of Clinical Psychology,* 1958, 14, 302-305.

Herrell, J. H., & Golland, J. M. Should WISC subjects explain Picture Arrangement stories? *Journal of Consulting and Clinical Psychology*, 1969, **33**, 761–762.

Johnson, D. T. Introversion, extroversion, and social intelligence: a replication. *Journal of Consulting and Clinical Psychology*, 1969, **25**, 181–183.

Ladd, C. E. WAIS performances of brain-damaged and neurotic patients. *Journal of Clinical Psychology*, 1964, **20**, 115–117.

Payne, D. A., & Lehmann, I. J. A brief WAIS item analysis. *Journal of Clinical Psychology*, 1966, **22**, 296–297.

Riegel, R. M., & Riegel, K. F. A comparison and reinterpretation of factor structures of the W-B, the WAIS, and the HAWIE on aged persons. *Journal of Consulting Psychology*, 1962, **26**, 31–37.

Russell, E. W. A WAIS factor analysis with brain-damaged subjects using criterion measures. *Journal of Consulting and Clinical Psychology*, 1972, **39**, 133–139.

Saunders, R., & Gittinger, W. Patterns of intellectual functioning and their implications for the dynamics of behavior. Reprinted from *The role and methodology of classification and psychopathology.* Washington, D. C.: U. S. Department of Health, Education, and Welfare, Public Health Service, undated.

Sattler, J. M. Effects of cues and examiner influence on two Wechsler subtests. *Journal of Consulting and Clinical Psychology*, 1969, **33**, 719–721.

Schill, T. The effect of MMPI social introversion on the WAIS PA performance. *Journal of Clinical Psychology*, 1966, **22**, 72–74.

Schill, T., Kahn, M., & Muehleman, T. WAIS PA performance and participation in extracurricular activities. *Journal of Clinical Psychology*, 1968, **24**, 95–96(a).

Schill, T., Kahn, M., & Muehleman, T. Verbal conditionability and Wechsler Picture Arrangement scores. *Journal of Consulting and Clinical Psychology.* 1968, **32**, 718–721.(b)

Shaw, D. J. Factor analysis of the collegiate WAIS. *Journal of Consulting Psychology*, 1967, **31**, 217.

Sprague, R. L., & Quay, H. C. A factor analytic study of the responses of mental retardates on the WAIS. *American Journal of Mental Deficiency*, 1966, **70**, 595–600.

Taylor, J. B. The structure of ability in the lower intellectual range. *American Journal of Mental Deficiency*, 1964, **68**, 766–774.

Wechsler, D. *The measurement and appraisal of adult intelligence.* Baltimore: Williams & Witkins, 1958.

Zimmerman, S. F., Whitmyre, J. W., & Fields, F. R. J. Factor analytic structure of the WAIS in patients with diffuse and lateralized cerebral dysfunction. *Journal of Clinical Psychology*, 1970, **26**, 462–465.

CHAPTER 13

OBJECT ASSEMBLY

The manipulation of parts to make familiar whole configurations has been the basis for countless puzzles. Although Pinter and Paterson (1917) designed the forms later used in the Wechsler series, the use of form boards as a measure of general intelligence date to the pioneering work of Seguin in the nineteenth century. Variations of the assembly theme are seen in the picture puzzles incorporated in the Merrill-Palmer Scale and the "patience" pictures of the Stanford Binet. The distinctive feature of the Wechsler variations is the extension of the ceiling to make this test applicable to an adult population. The initial item, the manikin, is essentially the same as that used on the original Pintner-Paterson scale and can also be found in the Merrill-Palmer scale.

While in Picture Arrangement analysis and reconstruction of scrambled clues involving social situations is demanded, in Object Assembly (OA) the reconstruction centers on simple everyday objects. To this extent, less sophisticated knowledge of society is required. Instead, an elementary aesthetic sense of composition is called upon. The synthesis of parts into wholes as an outcome of visual and motor manipulation is considered a valid criterion of intelligence. Speed is a factor in OA, as in Block Design, but the whole must be conceptualized by the subject rather than copied. Therefore, a lack of imagination can be a problem. Also, unlike blocks, units are not interchangeable; rather, each unit has a specific shape and meaning. The items chosen are commonplace stimulus objects in the environment. Recognition of them from their constituent parts is a sign of mental alertness and, hence, intelligence.

WHAT THE TEST MEASURES

Object Assembly involves visual analysis and its coordination with simple assembly skills. The test measures how efficiently the subject can make meaningful juxtapositions of parts.

Modes of thinking may be clearly revealed here. At one extreme there is the individual with a clear understanding of the relationship of parts to each other and to the whole. At the other is the individual who may demonstrate a complete lack of understanding of the concept. In between are those who see the whole but cannot quite fit the parts in and those who by stumbling trial and error belatedly find the object. A side light of the test is that here one can see attempted solutions, whereas in Arithmetic, for example, such attempts are usually not verbalized and thus are generally hidden from the observer. Such nonintellective factors as persistence and carefulness versus carelessness may also be observed.

DESCRIPTION

Four cut-up figures, essentially simple jigsaw puzzles, make up the OA subtest. Three of the four items used are identical to those used in the Wechsler Bellevue I and are presented in the same manner and sequence as that test. The fourth item is new to the WAIS and is presumably added to increase the test ceiling. The major differences between the Wechsler Bellevue I and WAIS versions lie in the scoring system. All items on the WAIS are scored for both time and accuracy; only two in the Wechsler Bellevue are scored for both. Time limits on the profile of the WAIS have been reduced to 120 seconds from 180 seconds, but credits without time bonuses are increased from 6 to 9 points. The basic score on the third item (hand) has been increased from 6 to 7 points, but on the manikin, it has been reduced from the former 6 points to 5.

FACTOR ANALYSIS

Cohen (1957) ranks the OA next to the lowest (Digit Span) in its correlation with G. It drops from an average of 0.64 for the young through middle age to 0.58 for the aged. However, it was termed a relatively fair measure of perceptual organization, slightly superior to Block Design in the three younger age groups. In the Berger, Bernstein, Klein, Cohen, and Lucas (1964) reanalysis, OA continues to be a measure of perceptual organization. However, the Birren results (in Riegel & Riegel, 1962) indicate a substantial correlation with verbal comprehension and a substantial negative correlation with perceptual organization. There was also a significant correlation on freedom from distractability. For college students (Shaw, 1967), chronic schizophrenics (Berger et al., 1964), chronic brain-damaged subjects (Russell, 1972), epileptics (Dennerll, Den Broeder, & Sokolov, 1964), and any of differentiated organic groups (Zimmerman, Whitmyre, & Fields, 1970), the significant loading is on the perceptual organization factor. For retardates, the findings are not conclusive: Sprague and Quay (1966) were unable to find significant loadings on any of the three factors (verbal, perceptual, and freedom from distraction), but Taylor (1964) noted a significant correlation with a factor similar to perceptual organization and minor positive loading on a verbal-numerical-educational factor.

Thus, with respect to the standardization group, college students, chronic schizophrenics, epileptics, and the brain-damaged, this subtest measures those aspects of general intelligence dealing with visual organization and motor execution of parts into identifiable wholes. Although the skills reflected in Object Assembly are similar and complementary to those used in the Block Design subtest, there is an important difference. In Block Design the essential task is that of copying a preassembled design. In Object Assembly the nature of the object to be constructed is not revealed and must be adduced without any formal help.

ADMINISTRATION

The last subtest in the WAIS, Object Assembly is readily accepted by most subjects as an inherently interesting and pleasant task. Nevertheless, some can be frustrated by the apparent absence of clues on the more difficult items.

After the parts have been prearranged behind a screen, each item is presented, with the simple instruction "Put this together as quickly as you can." Unlike the WISC, no verbal labels are given as clues to the identity of the object to be constructed. The subject is timed from the moment the screening device is removed. Timing continues until the subject indicates that he has constructed the object, or until the time limits have run out. In the latter case, partial credits are assigned for those pieces in correct juxtapositions. To avoid problems that might arise from spontaneous corrections, it may be helpful to add "Please tell me when you are finished." However, since further corrections may be made, it can help to record the time on the stop watch but to continue timing for the brief period between apparent completion and repacking the item in the box.

Busy clinicians in search of ways to shorten administration time can borrow from the suggestions of Shannon and Rossi (1952) and Taylor (1970). The former advocate the construction of stencils with insets for each of the pieces. The pieces for each item can be permanently prearranged and covered, ready to be set out in the presentation position. Taylor recommends placing each design in separate manila folders, with outlines of the pieces as guide to their placement. A reduction of administration time by as much as 50 percent is claimed.

Whatever the mode of presentation, the examiner should observe the subject's working procedure at all times. Notes can be made of such points as the use of trial and error, perseveration tendencies (such as rigidity in trying to position a piece in an incorrect location) ability to capitalize on accidental cues, and insight. It may also be useful to ascertain whether and how the subject "discovered" the identity of the object and to ask about previous experience with similar materials. Noting the rate of progress at different time intervals can be helpful. Such points may aid in understanding those cases where the Object Assembly performance appears out of line with the general pattern. As in all form-board tasks, there is a good deal of practice effect and carryover in this subtest.

The supplementary answer sheet with the objects pictured, which is available through the Psychological Corporation, allows the extent of assembly to be recorded easily.

TESTING THE LIMITS

In testing the limits overtime solutions can be encouraged. Specific urging can be utilized to see how much help is needed to reach the solution. Such help invalidates the increased score, but it can be useful in understanding the subject's approach to problem solving. As in Block Design, the assistance can be given in increments to check how much aid is needed.

Addition of simple puzzles such as the Binet form board to supplement the OA allows the examiner to assess the meaning of an unexpectedly low score.

SCORING

For rapid scoring, item parts can be numbered in the manual and on the back of each piece to indicate their position in the presentation. When scoring partial successes, the examiner should note the juxtaposition of specific numbers. This is particularly helpful for the third item (the four fingers of the hand). Even experienced examiners may find it difficult to separate correct placements from reversals.

ITEM PLACEMENT

While Object Assembly in the WAIS has been improved considerably from its earlier form in the Wechsler Bellevue, an examination of the average raw scores indicate some limitations. At age 16 to 17 an average raw score of 30 to 32 is expected, indicating success on all four items and a slight time bonus as well. By age 25 to 34 the average raw score rises minimally to 31 to 33, requiring similar item success. By middle age (45 to 54) an average score has declined to 27 to 29, or success on all items without time bonuses, while the older age group, (65 to 69) an average score to 25 to 27 is expected, indicating partial successes on all four items without time bonuses. (See Table 13–1.)

Object Assembly is the only subtest (apart from the totally timed Digit Symbol) in which time bonuses play a critical role even at the average level. The import of this can be seen by the fact that 67 percent of the standardization sample passed all four items (Wechsler, 1958).

Table 13–1

ITEM PLACEMENT OF AVERAGE SCORES FOR FOUR AGE LEVELS

Age 16–17	(average raw score 30–32)	success on all 4 objects plus minor time bonuses
Age 25–34	(average raw score 31–33)	success on all 4 objects plus minor time bonuses
Age 45–54	(average raw score 27–29)	some success on all 4 objects
Age 65–69	(average raw score 25–27)	some success on all 4 objects

A raw score of 29 can be obtained without time bonuses.

Source: D. Wechsler, *Manual, Wechsler Adult Intelligence Scale* (New York: Psychological Corporation, 1955), p. 101–108.

Table 13–2
DIFFERENCES BETWEEN OBJECT ASSEMBLY AND ALL OTHER SCALED SCORES NECESSARY TO SATISFY THE 0.05 and 0.01 CONFIDENCE LEVELS

		Subtests									
CA	*Confidence level*	*I*	*C*	*A*	*S*	*D*	*V*	*DS*	*PC*	*BD*	*PA*
18–19	0.05	4	4	4	4	4	4	4	4	4	5
	0.01	5	6	6	5	6	5	5	5	5	6
25–34	0.05	4	4	4	4	5	4	[a]	4	4	5
	0.01	5	6	6	5	6	5		5	5	6
45–54	0.05	4	4	4	4	4	3	[a]	4	4	4
	0.01	5	6	5	5	6	4		5	5	5

[a]DS omitted.

Source: From T. E. Newland and P. A. Smith, Statistically significant differences between subtest scaled scores on the WISC and the WAIS, *Journal of School Psychology*, 1967, 5, 126.

SIGNIFICANT DIFFERENCES BETWEEN THE OBJECT ASSEMBLY AND OTHER SUBTESTS

When Object Assembly weighted scores are compared with other subtest weighted scores, Newland and Smith (1967) note that differences ranging from three to five points, but centering almost wholely at four points, are necessary to reach the 0.05 level of significance, and these differences must increase to five or six points to reach the 0.01 level. These are among the largest differences between scaled scores required on the WAIS. (See Table 13–2.)

ITEM COMPOSITION AND DIFFICULTY

The four objects to be assembled in the OA differ considerably in difficulty, from the simple manikin, an item easy enough to begin the WISC series as well, through the many pieces of the profile, the confusing and often misinterpreted hand, and the suddenly more difficult elephant. In Payne and Lehmann's (1966) analysis of college records the item placement seemed appropriate. However, the last object was significantly easier for women than for men.

RESEARCH WITH OBJECT ASSEMBLY

The Object Assembly test has been hypothesized by Witkin (1965) as an indicator of field independence. Landfield and Saunders (1961) regard it as a measure of the "effect of uncertainty." Wechsler (1958) associates rise and fall of performance with various clinical groups. Depending upon the type of impairment, organics may obtain scores within their mean subtest score or deviate as much as 3 or more units below it. Schizophrenics and anxiety state *S*s are expected to deviate 1.5 to 2.5 units below their mean score. Delinquents and mental defectives are thought to obtain scores generally higher than the mean subtest score, as much as 3 units above it.

The brain-damaged sample of Ladd (1964) had Object Assembly scores 1.5 or more units below their mean, compared to Wechsler's wider ranging sample. His neurotic subjects showed no deviation, in contrast to Wechsler's.

Research with the WAIS version of the Object Assembly subtest has been limited, although the Object Assembly format in the Wechsler Bellevue and WISC has been used as an indicator of anxiety, organicity, depression, schizophrenia, good creative ability, and delinquency (see reviews by Blatt & Allison, Ogdon, 1967).

One interesting hypothesis proposed by Blatt, Allison, and Baker (1966) is that scores on the Object Assembly subtest can be disrupted by intense bodily concern. The criterion was the percentage of Rorschach responses denoting bodily concerns (anatomical, blood, sex, x-ray). Results were in the expected direction. A replication by Blatt, Baker, and Weiss (1970) confirmed earlier findings. They point out, however, that results with the WISC OA have been inconsistent.

Siegman's (1956) study revealed no significant relationship between OA or any other WAIS subtest and the Taylor Manifest Anxiety Scale. However, *S*s obtaining higher Taylor scores did score lower on what are called anxiety-sensitive subtests (OA combined with A, DS, D, and BD). Goldstein and Lundy (1967) found a combination of OA, S, DS, and PA the best predictor of grade-point average for low average high school students.

Hershenson (1967) singled out college student records that had Arithmetic as the highest subtest. Although these students drew the most accurate and detailed hands in a figure-drawing test, they failed to show superiority on OA or greater accuracy on the hand item of Object Assembly.

A lower OA relative to S scores was proposed by Parsons, Vega, and Burn (1969) as indicative of right-hemisphere damage. Woo-Sam's (1971) previously mentioned criticism of the use of age-corrected scores throws some doubt on their findings.

In a comparison of Connecticut and Hawaiian psychotic patients Bloom and Goldman (1962) found Object Assembly to favor the latter at the 0.05 level.

ADVANTAGES OF THE SUBTEST

A simple task, intrinsically interesting and challenging to most subjects, Object Assembly is a welcome break for many. Terminating the WAIS with this task generally leaves the subject with a feeling of accomplishment. As such, it complements the mood engendered by the initial subtest, Information. A combination of perceptual and visual motor skills, Object Assembly can be compared to Block Design, which has some of the same requirements but measures different facets of these skills. Both measure perceptual organization.

This subtest can reveal coping styles of the subject as demonstrated by his work habits. It can be done successfully with the nondominant hand.

LIMITATIONS OF THE SUBTEST

The OA subtest is the least reliable and lowest measure of general intelligence in the WAIS, and a poor measure of ability at the college level. It has numerous other limitations too. Administration and presentation time are somewhat lengthy, and it is readily affected by practice. If there is difficulty in gestalting the figures, the subtest can be extremely frustrating. Some subjects may object to the "childish" tasks. Pure trial and error can result in chance success. In addition, there appears to be a cultural bias, favoring the less verbal individual.

CONCLUSIONS

This subtest calls for mental organization and planning, in which the parts must be organized into wholes without clues concerning the goal. The freedom to explore new solutions or new directions and a flexibility of approach may be reflected in success. Yet a concrete, action-oriented individual may also succeed here, and individuals with below average ability do relatively well, as do those from a relatively low socioeconomic background. Bland schizophrenics can at times do well by sheer trial and error. With some subjects, the desire to succeed even to the extent of trying to peek across the screen, and thus "jump the gun," may be diagnostic of insecurity. The OA in combination with some other subtest measured high school grades.

Low scores may reflect aimless assembly due to anxiety. Rigidity and/or perseveration can penalize performance. Some individuals find it difficult to tolerate being observed, a clue to response to pressure.

"Losing" pieces by ignoring those to the side might indicate a reduced visual field. Failure to gestalt the presented figure after a period of trial and error may indicate low intelligence or, perhaps, perceptual problems. Brain damage can be detected on the OA when used in combination with other subtests. Placing pieces around the periphery of the profile and the hand suggests severe visual disorganization. When the subject piles pieces one on top of another, reality ties can be questioned. Emotional loading on the OA has been related to concerns about mutilation and body integrity, which is triggered by the cut-up figures. Also chronic anxiety in general tends to lower the scores not only on the OA but also on a combination of other subtests.

REFERENCES

Berger, L., Bernstein, A., Klein, E., Cohen, J., & Lucas, G. Effects of aging and pathology on the factorial structure of intelligence. *Journal of Consulting Psychology*, 1964, **28**, 199–207.

Blatt, S. J., & Allison, J. The intelligence test in personality assessment. In A. Rabin (Ed.), *Projective techniques in personality assessment.* New York: Springer, 1968. Pp.421–460.

Blatt, S. J., Allison, J., & Baker, B. L. The Wechsler Object Assembly subtest and bodily concerns. *Journal of Consulting Psychology*, 1967, **31** 169–174.

Blatt, S. J., Baker, B. L., & Weiss, J. Wechsler Object Assembly subtest and bodily concern: a review and replication. *Journal of Consulting and Clinical Psychology*, 1970, **34**, 269–274.

Bloom, B. L., & Goldman, R. K. Sensitivity of the WAIS to language handicap in a psychotic population. *Journal of Clinical Psychology*, 1962, **18**, 161–163.

Cohen, J. The factorial structure of the WAIS between early adulthood and old age. *Journal of Consulting Psychology*, 1957, **21**, 283–290.

Dennerll, R. D., Den Broeder, J. & Sokolov, S. L. WISC and WAIS factors in children and adults with epilepsy. *Journal of Clinical Psychology*, 1964, **20**, 236–240.

Goldstein, S. G., & Lundy, C. T. Utilization of the WAIS in predicting success with low average high school students. *Educational and Psychological Measurement*, 1967, **27**, 457–461.

Hershenson, D. B. Body image (hand) and arithmetic ability. *Perceptual and Motor Skills*, 1967, **25**, 967–968.

Ladd, C. E. WAIS performances of brain-damaged and neurotic patients. *Journal of Clinical Psychology*, 1964, **20**, 115–117.

Landfield, E. S., & Saunders, D. R. Anxiety as "effect of uncertainty": an experiment examining the OA subtest on the WAIS. *Journal of Clinical Psychology*, 1961, **17**, 238–241.

Newland, T. E., & Smith, P. A. Statistically significent differences between subtest scaled scores on the WISC and the WAIS. *Journal of School Psychology*, 1967, **5**, 122–127.

Ogdon, D. P. *Psychodiagnostic and personality assessment: a handbook.* Los Angeles; Western Psychological Services, 1967.

Parsons, O. A., Vega, A., Jr., & Burn, J. Different psychological effects of laterialized brain damage. *Journal of Consulting and Clinical Psychology*, 1969, **33**, 551–557.

Payne, D. A., & Lehmann, I. J. A brief WAIS item analysis. *Journal of Clinical Psychology*, 1966, **22**, 296–297.

Pintner, R., & Paterson, D. G. *A scale of performance tests.* New York: Appleton, 1917.

Riegel, R. M., & Riegel, K. F. A Comparison and reinterpretation of factor structures of the W-B, the WAIS, and the HAWIE on aged persons. *Journal of Consulting Psychology*, 1962, **26**, 31–37.

Russell, E. W. A WAIS factor analysis with brain damaged subjects using criterion measures. *Journal of Consulting and Clinical Psychology*, 1972, **39**, 133–139.

Shannon, W., & Rossi, P. D. Suggestions for efficient presentation of the Wechsler Bellevue Object Assembly subtest. *Journal of Clinical Psychology*, 1952, **8**, 413–415.

Shaw, D. J. Factor analysis of the collegiate WAIS. *Journal of Consulting Psychology*, 1967, **31**, 217.

Siegman, A. W. Cognitive, affective and psychopathological correlates of the Taylor Manifest Anxiety Scale. *Journal of Consulting Psychology*, 1956, **20**, 137–141.

Sprague, R. L. & Quay, H. C. A factor analytic study of the responses of mental retardates on the WAIS. *American Journal of Mental Deficiency*, 1966, **70**, 595–600.

Taylor, J. B. The structure of ability in the lower intellectual range. *American Journal of Mental Deficiency*, 1964, **68**, 766–774.

Taylor, J. F. Brief note on a simplified administration of Object Assembly subtest. *Journal of Clinical Psychology*, 1970, **26**, 182.

Wechsler, D. *The measurement and appraisal of adult intelligence.* Baltimore: Williams & Wilkins, 1958.

Witkin, H. A. Psychological differentiation and forms of pathology. *Journal of Abnormal Psychology*, 1965, **70**, 317–336.

Woo-Sam, J. Lateralized brain damage and differential psychological effects: Parsons, et al., re-examined. *Perceptual and Motor Skills*, 1971, **33**, 259–262.

Zimmerman, S. F., Whitmyre, J. W., & Fields, F. R. J. Factor analytic structure of the WAIS in patients with diffuse and lateralized cerebral dysfunction. *Journal of Clinical Psychology*, 1970, **26**, 462–465.

CHAPTER 14

ADAPTATIONS AND BRIEF FORMS OF THE WAIS

Since each of the eleven subtests are separately standardized, the WAIS has been a ready source of material for adaptations and brief form tests. The following sections describe type, composition and rationale for the most important of these.

ADAPTATIONS

Probably the most common adaptation of the WAIS is the procedure allowing the testee to continue past posted time limits or cut-off points. Of course, the former is applicable, with the exception of the Arithmetic subtest, only to the performance section. Giving items beyond the "discontinue" point is appropriate for both verbal and performance sections. The exceptions are DS, PC, and OA, which are administered in full. Quershi (1961) has demonstrated that for normal subjects extending the present cut-off points would not markedly improve the obtained scores.

Other variations from standard administration procedures consist of rewording items for simplicity, providing additional explanations and demonstrations, and translating items into the native language of the foreign-born. Taylor (1959) suggests that the clinician can additionally extend the base line on some difficult items by administering similar but easier items from other tests.

All the above approaches emphasize the general rationale of what is termed "testing the limits" or "extended testing." The clinician, confronted by what he perceives to be inconsistency in a particular subject's performance, liberalizes the rules in order to obtain clues to the inconsistency. Changes in performance resulting from such procedures must not be incorporated in the obtained test scores; they should be discussed in the report, thereby enriching the findings. Sometimes it may be necessary to adapt the test to special situations. "Selective-partial" WAISs are administered to subjects with various physical or cultural impairments (Allen & Jefferson, 1962). Common practice, for example, is to administer only the verbal section to blind subjects and only the performance section to the bilingual or non-English-speaking, the inarticulate, the speech handicapped, and the deaf. A particular advantage of the WAIS is that the more appropriate section of the test can be used as a measure or estimate of the subject's normal functioning skills, while the other section provides an indication of the degree of handicap. Myklebust (1960) suggests that by comparing the verbal and performance scores of the hard-of-hearing or deaf individual, one can obtain a rough estimate of the degree to which such an individual has mastered verbal concepts. On the other hand, for the subject with motor handicaps, the degree of verbal superiority might give a rough estimate of the degree of motor impairment.

Variations in administrative procedures may be used to compensate for known impairments. A verbal Digit Symbol has been suggested by Kaufman (1966). Ross (1967) provides instructions for pantomime presentation of the performance section to the deaf and foreign-language-speaking subject. McCarthy (1961) and others noted that left-handed subjects frequently cover the symbols of the Digit Symbol subtest in their ordinary writing position and advised that a second and visible record form be provided. A written presentation of certain subtests allows for group testing (Eme & Walker, 1969). Finally, a programmed presentation of subtests (Elwood, 1972) can reduce the effects of examiner variables and perhaps automate the WAIS.

In the above variations the results obtained are generally scored and included with those obtained from standard administration. However, specific changes must be well labeled so the IQs obtained will be understood for what they are.

BRIEF TESTS

A common approach to the WAIS is to select a number of subtests or even of individual items to be administered as a short or brief WAIS that can be used to estimate the full-scale IQ of the subject. Since a standard WAIS is estimated to take 60 to 90 minutes to administer (Barnes, 1969; Cronbach, 1960), a brief test generally cuts administration time by 50 percent. If all examinations that do not include the eleven subtests upon which the WAIS standardization is based are put in this designation, the percentage of brief forms of the WAIS administered probably far surpasses the number of complete tests given. L'Abate (1964), in a review of files for research purposes, found only 11 out of 55 brain-damaged patients had been given a complete Wechsler scale, making a total of 80 percent brief tests for that sample. Holmes, Armstrong, Johnson, and Ries (1965) estimate that 90 percent of all WAISs are given in abbreviated form.

Advantages

The WAIS has particular advantages when used in brief forms, especially when a rapid screening device is needed or perhaps when intellectual factors per se are not assumed to be the major question. Large institutions, such as mental hospitals, prisons, or clinics, may want to have avaiable some estimate of mental ability for all subjects, and yet they may not have adequate staff to administer and interpret the full-length WAIS scale. Certainly a major justification for this approach is that a brief test, by showing wide variation or markedly low scores, can indicate which cases demand the standard test. If following further evaluation, such as a staffing at a hospital or clinic, the partial results warrant it, a brief WAIS can always be completed and the subject tested in full.

Generally, brief forms allow for a rapid estimate of intelligence when finer delineation is not needed. For example, when previous testing is available, current status can be checked by a brief form. Brief forms are often of value when the subject being evaluated is an individual with such high achievement (college graduate, high level manager) that his intellectual functioning is not seriously questioned. For such an individual, a full test might add very little, since it must be pointed out that superior intelligence is not adequately measured by the WAIS or, for that matter, by the Stanford Binet L—M (Kennedy, Willcutt, & Smith, 1963).

A useful approach with the brief WAIS is to choose a form that will answer specific questions, such as scholastic achievement or orientation—(I, A—(Kennedy et al., 1963), verbal problem solving-C, S—or visual-motor skills—BD, OA—(Cohen, 1957). A brief form allowing for some estimate of both verbal and performance skills presents a better rounded picture of the individual.

Objections

Before discussing brief form combinations, the many objections to the brief form can be summarized along with suggested answers.

Wechsler himself (1958) presented one of the most cogent criticisms of brief forms when he asserted that the WAIS is a clinical, projective tool that should present more than just a numerical score. Administering the full WAIS allows an examiner a unique insight into the work habits and characteristic coping approaches of a subject. The individual reliabilities of some subtests are low so that reliance on half the items or only a few subtests to draw conclusions is inadvisable.

L'Abate (1964) summarizes other points in Wechsler's argument, noting the loss of such features as verbal-performance differences, indexes of inner and intratest variability, the extra-intelligence areas of functioning, the masculinity-feminity index, and the internal content of responses. Anastasi (1961) points out that a brief test is at best a rough screening device. Not only are qualitative observations lost, but the full-scale norms are being applied to prorated scores. Kramer and Francis (1966) point out the chance of serious error in calculating an IQ from a brief form, in that 71 percent of their sample of psychiatric patients were misclassified by a three-subtest brief form. Even though this seems extreme, such differences are a serious source of concern when classification is used as a basis of action (Luszki, Schultz, Laywell, & Dawes, 1970).

L'Abate (1964) further makes an issue of the long-standing role of the test of intelligence as the special tool of the psychologist. He feels one should "maximize the advantage of such tests, rather than minimize them" (p.186).

There might be added to these objections another critical point: once a brief form of the WAIS is given, the results are usually entered somewhere *as* a WAIS, rarely as a "brief-WAIS" score. Later, some critical decision might be made using this score with the same assurance as if it were based upon a carefully and fully administered individual test of intelligence. Where in the full administration there is almost always a detailed summary of results, including valuable material as to the ability of the subject to respond adequately to the various aspects of the examination, the brief WAIS is often rather slap-dash and fails to note the absense of critical information.

Two suggestions are offered as alternatives to brief WAISs. The first is to follow Ross (1959), who has pointed out that the best brief test is either the entire verbal or entire performance scale, since both correlate extremely well with the full scale, and such an administration does not violate any aspect of standardization.

The second is to use one of a number of screening tests available for adults when screening is required. In this way the WAIS remains inviolate for use as a clinical instrument. Earlier in this book, various screening tests were compared to the WAIS in terms of adequacy of measurement.

BACKGROUND FOR BRIEF FORMS

Current studies of brief forms of the WAIS uniformly emphasize one thing, namely, the correlation of the various combinations of subtests or selected items with the total number of subtests or items. Such an approach seems to be a carryover from the Stanford Binet brief forms, where the omission of items is based purely on their lesser discrimination value in predicting the total score. However, for adults there are an enormous number of subtest combinations and item combinations that adequately predict the full-scale IQ. A stress only on the highest possible correlation was criticized by Guertin, Ladd, Frank, Rabin, and Hiester in the 1966 review of the WAIS, when they wondered

> whether much is to be gained by further juggling of different subtests in varied combinations in order to increase somewhat the second decimals of the coefficients of correlations between the IQs (p. 389).

The potential value of serial subtests is to provide valuable information about the subject's approach to certain intellectual tasks. That certain subtests rather than others be omitted merely to obtain a tiny and inconsequential increase in accuracy of measurement is to be deplored.

Brief forms are of most value when chosen to suit a particular purpose. Although brief tests are rarely reported in the literature from a clinical viewpoint, there are numerous studies where one subtest, often Vocabulary (since it correlates so very well with the total test), is used as a base line or for matching subjects, while other subtests are used for their specific contribution to understanding the subject. An example of the latter is the research employing Picture Arrangement as a measure of social introversion or extroversion. The subtest analysis chapters should provide clues for specific subtest selection.

SELECTING A BRIEF FORM

Since so many combinations are reported in the literature, no one brief form can be considered in preference to any other. However, there is one rule of thumb to keep in mind. Schwartz and Levitt (1960) reporting on the WISC note that a correlation of 0.90 between the brief form and the full scale would result in an estimated error of 8.6 scale score units. In other words, the IQ calculated from the brief test would be no more than nine IQ points above or below the full scale IQ for two-thirds of the cases.

On this basis, a correlation in the lower 0.90s for the population being assessed should be an absolute base line of allowable error in prediction. This might be considered, furthermore, in terms of what the measure is to assess. If explusion fróm a training program were set at an 80 IQ, for example, the examiner might consider than one-sixth (16 percent) of his sample scoring between 70 and 80 on the brief form were rejected because of inadequacies of measurement. That is, of the one-third who were more than nine IQ points from their "true" IQ (here, the full-scale WAIS, which was not administered), theoretically, half might be above, half below the "true" IQ; hence, one out of six would be incorrectly rejected, and an equal number incorrectly selected. Obviously, the problem is how serious a decision is to be made on the basis of a brief test.

McNemar in 1950 set the format for brief Wechsler tests by basing his investigation on the standardization sample. His formula for determining the validity of all possible short forms was employed by Maxwell (1957) to establish the best of all possible combinations of subtests from two through five. These findings were later criticized by Levy (1968) and others as supuriously high in failing to account for the extent of overlap being measured when the brief test is correlated with the full scale, which includes the brief test. Silverstein (1970) also noted the failure to allow for the unreliability of specific subtests. He recalculated all combinations and reported results that varied considerably from Maxwell's findings, although the best forms were only 0.02 points lower than the earlier results. Nevertheless, the ten best combinations differ markedly when more than two subtests are used. (See Tables 14–1 through 14–4 below.)

In selecting a brief form of the WAIS the chosen combination of subtests can be compared to Tables 14–1–14–4, where Maxwell and Silverstein selections, based on the standardization data, are listed. Obviously, at the adult level, many brief forms meet the criterion of predicting the full-scale IQ at a high level, typically in the 0.90s.

Table 14—1
CORRELATION COEFFICIENTS BETWEEN THE ELEVEN BEST DYADS OF WAIS SUBTESTS AND FULL-SCALE SCORE

Maxwell (1957)		*Silverstein (1970)*	
Dyads	r	*Dyads*	r
V BD	0.924	V BD	0.908
I BD	0.917	V PC	0.907
I PA	0.917	I V	0.900
V PC	0.914	I BD	0.900
I V	0.912	I PC	0.899
V PA	0.909	I S	0.890
I PC	0.906	I DS	0.887
I S	0.903	V OA	0.885
I OA	0.900	A V	0.885
V OA	0.898	I PA	0.884
S PA	0.898		

Source: Adapted from: Maxwell, E. Validities of abbreviated WAIS scales. *Journal of Consulting Psychology,* 1957, 21, 121—126, p. 122; and Silverstein, A. B. Reappraisal of the validity of WAIS, WISC, and WPPSI short forms. *Journal of Consulting and Clinical Psychology,* 1970, 34, 13.

Pairs (Dyads)

When two subtests are combined, correlations with the WAIS IQ are 0.90 or better for the first nine selected by Maxwell and the first four in Silverstein's corrected, more stringent list (Table 14—1). However, differences between the various combinations are minimal. Both authors consider the combination Vocabulary-Block Design to be the best, and there is considerable similarity in their other choices. Silverstein (1970) has prepared a table for converting the sum of scaled scores on V-BD directly to an estimate of full-scale IQ, with an automatic age correction.

Triads

When three subtests are chosen, the correlations with the full WAIS are all above 0.90 for both lists. Those of Maxwell range from 0.94 to 0.95, and Silverstein's are only slightly lower (Table 14—2). Generally, the best combinations are composed of the best pairs plus one. Thus, both authors head their lists with Information added to Vocabulary and Block Design.

Table 14–2
CORRELATION COEFFICIENTS BETWEEN THE TEN BEST TRIADS OF WAIS BUSTESTS AND FULL-SCALE SCORES

Maxwell (1957) Triads	r	*Silverstein (1970)* Triads	r
I V BD	0.952	I V BD	0.936
I V OA	0.947	I V PC	0.929
I S PA	0.944	S V BD	0.927
I S BD	0.942	A V PC	0.927
I S OA	0.942	I S BD	0.926
I V PA	0.942	I V OA	0.925
V PC PA	0.941	V DS PC	0.924
V BD PA	0.941	V PC BD	0.923
V PC BD	0.940	I DS BD	0.922
I BD PA	0.940		

Source: Maxwell, E. Validities of abbreviated WAIS Scales. *Journal of Consulting Psychology*, 1957, 21, 121–126, p. 122; Silverstein, A. B. Reappraisal of the validity of WAIS, WISC, and WPPSI short forms. *Journal of Consulting and Clinical Psychology*, 1970, 34, 13.

Table 14–3
CORRELATION COEFFICIENTS BETWEEN THE TWELVE BEST TETRADS OF WAIS SUBTESTS AND FULL-SCALE SCORE

Maxwell (1957) Tetrads				r	*Silverstein (1970)* Tetrads				r
I	V	BD	PA	0.964	I	V	DS	BD	0.945
I	S	BD	PA	0.963	I	V	PC	BD	0.944
I	S	PA	OA	0.961	I	S	V	BD	0.943
S	V	PC	BD	0.960	I	V	DS	PC	0.942
I	V	PA	OA	0.960	A	V	DS	PC	0.942
I	C	DS	BD	0.959	I	S	DS	BD	0.940
I	S	PC	PA	0.959	I	A	DS	PC	0.940
I	V	PC	BD	0.959	I	A	V	BD	0.940
A	V	PC	PA	0.959	I	C	DS	BD	0.940
A	V	BD	PA	0.959	I	V	BD	PA	0.940
S	V	BD	PA	0.959					
D	V	PC	PA	0.959					

Source: Maxwell, E. Validities of abbreviated WAIS scales. *Journal of Consulting Psychology*, 1957, **21**, 121–126, p. 123; Silverstein, A. B. Reappraisal of the validity of WAIS, WISC, and WPPSI short forms. *Journal of Consulting and Clinical Psychology*, 1970, **34**, 13.

Quartets

The combinations for four subtests are uniformly high, correlating 0.94 or better with the full WAIS IQ. One of the most frequently studied combinations, the Doppelt (Arithmetic, Vocabulary, Picture Arrangement, and Block Design), is midway in the Maxwell list but not included by Silverstein. A review of the literature on this combination for all sorts of pathological groups indicates that correlations almost never fell below 0.93 (Guertin, Ladd, Frank, Rabin, & Hiester, 1966, 1971).

Table 14–4
CORRELATION COEFFICIENTS BETWEEN THE TEN BEST PENTADS OF WAIS SUBTESTS AND FULL-SCALE SCORE

Maxwell (1957)						*Silverstein (1970)*					
Pentads					r	*Pentads*					r
I	S	V	PA	OA	0.972	I	V	DS	PC	BD	0.955
I	S	V	BD	PA	0.972	I	A	V	DS	PC	0.952
A	S	V	PA	OA	0.971	I	S	V	DS	BD	0.952
I	S	V	PC	BD	0.971	A	V	DS	PC	BD	0.951
I	A	S	PA	OA	0.971	I	A	V	DS	BD	0.951
I	D	V	PC	BD	0.970	I	A	V	PC	BD	0.951
I	D	V	BD	OA	0.970	I	S	V	PC	BD	0.951
I	V	DS	BD	PA	0.970	S	V	DS	PC	BD	0.950
I	V	PC	BD	PA	0.970	I	C	V	DS	BD	0.950
I	S	DS	BD	PA	0.970	C	V	DS	PC	BD	0.950

Source: Maxwell, E. Validities of abbreviated WAIS scales. *Journal of Consulting Psychology*, 1957, 21, 121–126, p. 123; Silverstein, A. B. Reappraisal of the validity of WAIS, WISC, and WPPSI short forms. *Journal of Consulting and Clinical Psychology*, 1970, **34**, 13.

Quintets (Pentads)

Correlations for the best of the five subtest brief forms never fall below 0.95. Therefore, the point of selecting one over another must be based on far more than the ability to predict the full IQ alone. Certainly here, at least, choice will reflect clinical needs or intuitions of the examiner.

THE SPLIT-HALF APPROACH

Abbreviated forms of the WAIS were given new impetus by the publication of a brief verbal WAIS that included all subtests but reduced the number of items administered (Wolfson & Bachelis, 1960). Using every third item of the I and V subtests and odd items of C, A, and S (with D given intact), the raw scores were multiplied by the appropriate factor of two or three, depending upon the item reduction process. Satz and Mogel (1962) extended this approach to include the performance scale, taking every third PC item and every odd item of other subtests (with all of DS intact). This made about 46 percent of the total item pool available for scoring. Correlations between the partial and total verbal, performance, and full-scale IQ ranged from 0.97 to 0.99. For their sample, 91 percent of the cases scored within four points of the full IQ. However, correlations between the partial and total subtests were naturally lower, ranging from 0.77 for OA to 0.97 for V.

Mogel and Satz (1963) further validated their brief form in a study that answered the objection made to brief tests extracted from a standard administration. When they compared a WAIS test-retest control group with a WAIS versus abbreviated-scale retest experimental group, the results were comparable enough to serve as further evidence of the Satz-Mogel validity.

Pauker (1963) added a true split-half brief form to the literature by drawing items at random from successive pairs of items (except for D and DS). However, results were no better than for the Satz and Mogel approach.

A variety of further studies served as cross-validations of the Satz and Mogel brief form. Holmes, Armstrong, Johnson, and Ries (1965) felt this form to be preferable in a clinical setting to other short forms. In a 1966 study the same group reported their results fell almost invariably within six points of the FIQ. Estes (1963) found the Saltz-Mogel brief test of value for high ability subjects as well as psychiatric patients. However, Zytowski and Hudson (1965) noted that the verbal scale could be more easily shortened than the performance scale, with its lower reliability. They suggested caution in interpreting profiles based on this short form. Silverstein (1968) turned to the standardization data to calculate reliabilities. He noted that the uncorrected figures were uniformly higher than the reliabilities of the original full scales (split–half), hardly a logical outcome. His corrected figures were 0.94 VIQ, 0.90 PIQ, and 0.96 FIQ.

The major objection to the Satz and Mogel brief form is that it provides a "profile" of the most doubtful reliability. It certainly is an approach to be questioned in view of the never ending evidence of the reliability problems for the full-scale profile (see Chapter 1). Luszki and associates (1970) observe that the subtest reliability of this approach would be reduced by 50 percent. Thus, for example, if a difference between two subtests of at least five points is required for significance, this would increase to a minimum of 7.5 points for the short form. Watkins and Kinzie (1970) further stress the exaggerated scatter and less reliable profiles of this brief form.

A BRIEF VOCABULARY SUBSCALE

One of the best validated item selection approaches to a brief WAIS is that employed by Jastak and Jastak (1964). Utilizing the Vocabulary subtest—always the most reliable and valid single Wechsler subtest and traditionally the best brief measure of intelligence—the authors reduced the item pool by half. The 20 words were then repositioned on the basis of further standardization, and a detailed scoring guide prepared. Unfortunately, not too many studies are available utilizing the Jastak Vocabulary. In an English psychiatric sample Burton (1968) noted a correlation of 0.92 between the Jastak and original Wechsler form, but the former tended to overestimate the latter by one scale score unit. Burton questioned using it alone because of this. Brown (1968), utilizing a large American psychiatric patient population, reported the same underestimation, in spite of unusually high correlations between the Jastak and the original WAIS Vocabulary (0.94 for males, 0.99 for females). Silverstein has not yet applied his correction formula to bring such findings closer to reality.

REFERENCES

Allen, R. M., & Jefferson, T. W. *Psychological evaluation of the cerebral palsied person.* Springfield: Thomas, 1962.

Anastasi, A. *Psychological testing.* New York: Macmillan, 1969.

Barnes, C. Trends in the adult Wechsler individual intelligence scales from the 1939 WB I to the new 1968 Spanish EIWA. Paper given at the California State Psychological Association Convention, January 1969.

Brown, F. Applicability of the Jastak short form revision of the WAIS Vocabulary subtest to psychiatric patients. *Journal of Clinical Psychology*, 1968, **24**, 454–455.

Burton, D. A. The Jastak short form WAIS Vocabulary applied to a British psychiatric population. *Journal of Clinical Psychology*, 1968, **24**, 345–347.

Cronbach, L. J. *Essentials of psychological testing.* New York: Harper & Row, 1960.

Cohen, J. The factorial structure of the WAIS between early adulthood and old age. *Journal of Consulting Psychology*, 1957, **21**, 283–290.

Elwood, D. L., & Griffin, H. R. Testing without the examiner. *Journal of Consulting and Clinical Psychology*, 1972, **38**, 9–14.

Eme, R. F., & Walker, R. E. The WAIS as a group test of intelligence. *Journal of Clinical Psychology*, 1969, **25**, 277–278.

Estes, B. W. A note on the Satz-Mogel abbreviation of the WAIS. *Clinical Psychology Monographs*, 1963, **19**, 103.

Guertin, W. H., Ladd, C. E., Frank, G. H., Rabin, A. I., & Hiester, D. Research with the WAIS, 1960–1965. *Psychological Bulletin*, 1966, **66**, 385–409.

Guertin, W. H., Ladd, C. E., Frank, G. H., Rabin, A. I., & Hiester, D. Research with the WAIS: 1965–1970. *Psychological Record*, 1971, 21, 289–339.

Holmes, D. S. Armstrong, H. E., Johnson, M. H., & Ries, H. A. Further evaluation of an abbreviated form of the WAIS. *Psychological Reports*, 1965, 16, 1163–1164.

Holmes, D. S., Armstrong, H. E., Johnson, M. H., & Ries, H. A. Validity and clinical utility of the Satz and Mogel abbreviated form of the WAIS. *Psychological Reports*, 1966, **18**, 992–994.

Jastak, J. F., & Jastak, S. R. Short forms of the WAIS and WISC Vocabulary subtest. *Journal of Clinical Psychology*, 1964, Monograph Supplement 18, 1-35.

Kaufman, A. An oral Digit Symbol test. *Journal of Clinical Psychology*, 1966, **22** 180.

Kennedy, W. A., Willcutt, H., & Smith, A. Wechsler profiles of mathematically gifted adolescents. *Psychological Reports*, 1963, **12**, 259–267.

Kramer, E., & Francis, P. S. Errors in intelligence estimation with short forms of the WAIS. *Mental Retardation Abstracts*, 1966, **3**, 431.

L'Abate, L. *Principles of clinical psychology.* New York: Grune & Stratton, 1964.

Levy, P. Short form tests: a methodological review. *Psychological Bulletin*, 1968, **69**, 410–416.

Luszki, M. R., Schultz, W., Laywell, H. R., & Dawes, R. M. Long search for a short WAIS: stop looking. *Journal of Consulting and Clinical Psychology*, 1970, **34**, 425–431.

Maxwell, E. Validities of abbreviated WAIS scales. *Journal of Consulting Psychology*, 1957, **21**, 121–126.

McCarthy, D. Administration of Digit Symbol and Comprehension subtests of the WAIS and WISC to left-handed subjects. *Psychological Reports*, 1961, **8**, 407–408.

McNemar, Q. On abbreviated Wechsler Bellevue subtests. *Journal of Consulting Psychology*, 1950, **14**, 79–81.

Mogel, S., & Satz, P. Abbreviation of the WAIS for clinical use: an attempt at validation. *Journal of Clinical Psychology*, 1963, **19**, 298–300.

Myklebust, H. *The psychology of deafness.* New York: Grune & Stratton, 1960.

Pauker, J. D. A split half abbreviation of the WAIS. *Journal of Clinical Psychology*, 1963, **19**, 98–100.

Quershi, M. Y. Effects of various scoring cut offs on reliability estimates. *American Journal of Mental Deficiency*, 1961, **65**, 753–760.

Ross, A. *The practice of clinical child psychology.* New York, Grune & Stratton, 1959.

Ross, D. R. Test performance of deaf adults under two modes of test administration. *Dissertation Abstracts*, 1968, **28**, 2992A.

Satz, P., & Mogel, S. An abbreviation of the WAIS for clinical use. *Journal of Clinical Psychology*, 1962, **18**, 77–79.

Schwartz, L., & Levitt, E. E. Short forms of the WISC for children in the educable, non-institutionalized mentally retarded. *Journal of Educational Psychology*, 1960, **51**, 187–190.

Silverstein, A. B. Validity of a new approach to the design of WAIS, WISC, and WPPSI short forms. *Journal of Consulting and Clinical Psychology*, 1968, **32**, 478–479.

Silverstein, A. B. Reappraisal of the validity of a short form of Wechsler's scales. *Psychological Reports*, 1970, **26**, 559–56l. (a)

Silverstein, A. B. Reappraisal of the validity of WAIS, WISC, and WPPSI short forms. *Journal of Consulting and Clinical Psychology*, 1970, **34**, 12–14. (b)

Taylor, E. M. *Psychological appraisal of children with cerebral defects.* Cambridge: Harvard University Press, 1959.

Watkins, J. T., & Kinzie, W. B. Exaggerated scatter and less reliable profiles produced by the Satz-Mogel abbreviation of the WAIS. *Journal of Clinical Psychology*, 1970, **26**, 343–345.

Wechsler, D. *The measurement and appraisal of adult intelligence.* Baltimore: Williams & Wilkins, 1958.

Wolfson, W., & Bachelis, L. An abbreviated form of the WAIS verbal scale. *Journal of Clinical Psychology*, 1960, **16**, 421.

Zytowski, D. G., & Hudson, J. The validity of split-half abbreviations of the WAIS. *Journal of Clinical Psychology*, 1965, **21**, 292–295.

CHAPTER 15

REPORTING RESULTS

The end point of the evaluation process is the submission of a report, written or oral. The report is the principal and often the only means by which the examiner can communicate his findings. Hartlage and Merck (1971) correctly point out that: "It is perhaps a truism that the most valid and reliable test instruments are of limited value unless interpreted to a potential user in some usable form" (p. 459). It is obvious that if the report is to provide information that will influence the decisions and actions of those requesting the information, there are certain conditions to which the writer of the report must adhere.

GENERAL RULES

The following general rules have been found useful:

1. *Information should be stated as simply and concisely as possible.* Verbosity bores the perennially harassed practitioner. It is commonplace

knowledge that longer reports in most instances are simply skimmed, interest centering on the summary.

2. *Writing style should reflect the human elements inherent in the report.* The pursuit of scientific objectivity should not displace human warmth and understanding.

3. *The report should be adapted to the specific purpose and requirement of the reader or readers.* Hartlage and Merck (1971) suggested that psychologists tend to write reports with good theoretical consistency but with little decisional value. Reports must conform to the requirements of the specific setting. Following a survey, Hartlage, Freeman, Horine, and Walton (1968) claimed that psychological reports were of "little value in contributing toward treatment decisions" (p. 483). If such suggests a disenchantment with testing and the interpretations of the test results, as presented, the following study may prove encouraging. Affleck and Strider (1971) report that in a medical setting the psychological report does contribute new and significant or corroborating information and thus patient management and disposition are affected by the findings and recommendations contained in the reports.

The corrollary to the above points is obviously that those requesting a report should be as explicit as possible regarding what they wish. "John X is head injured. Psychometrics needed" is a request so broad as to be meaningless. On the other hand, "John X is retarded. Administer the WAIS" is not only too narrow, but also infringes on the testor's prerogatives. Rapprochement between examiner and referring source should be established to the point that the examiner can answer the following questions as he writes: (a) Who will read the report? (b) What questions does he need answered? (c) How much and what kind of information does he require? (d) What purpose or purposes will the report serve?

4. *Technical jargon should be minimized.* The knowledgeable writer should be able to communicate even the most difficult concept in simple and understandable language. Jargon is too often used to mask incomplete understanding or ignorance. Over two decades ago Grayson and Tolman (1950) observed that the concepts used by psychologists and psychiatrists were "loose and ambiguous" and filled with "theoretical confusion."

5. *Reports should be organized in a manner that makes it easy for the reader to follow the ideas presented.* Highlight the main ideas or chief points. Allow the reader to see their development and the logic of the conclusions.

6. *If an authority is cited, make sure (a) that he is qualified* by education, experience, and knowledge of the specific situation to give a qualified opinion, *(b) that he is not prejudicial* or has reason to be so in his opinion, *(c) that the readers will accept him as an authority.*

7. *Do not make sweeping generalizations or overstate your case.* The Barnum phenomen (Meehl, 1956), types of comments apparently applicable to almost everybody, has no place in an objective endeavor. On the other hand, do not hedge with the overuse of "apparently," "indicative of," "likely," and the like, so as to make conclusions at best meaningless.

8. *Before adducing any cause and effect relationship, consider the possibility of alternatives, the strength of the relationship,* and *whether the link can be logically and directly established.* Current fads and trends should be identified as such. Generalized, vague "personality" descriptions when presented as interpretations based on psychological tests have repeatedly been shown to be accepted by the recipients, even when the same description was given to everyone in a class (Forer, 1949; Merrens & Richards, 1970; Sundberg, 1955; and Ulrich, Stachnik, and Stainton, 1963). Furthermore, Ulrich et al. (1963) claimed that it made no difference whether the "personality" interpretations were made by a professional psychologist or an inexperienced student.

THE RULES APPLIED TO THE WAIS SITUATION

The essential task in the report is the verbal portrayal of the subject at the time of the evaluation—his appearance, his manner, his fears, his joys, his attitude toward the examiner and the various tasks required in the examination, and the probable significance that these have relative to the referral.

It is common practice to organize the report in the following manner.

1. Identification
   a. Subject's name, sex, age, date of birth, religious affiliation, race (if appropriate), occupation, and identification number, if any
   b. Examiner's name, place of examination, date of examination
2. Reason for referral
   a. Source of referral
   b. Specific question to be answered
3. Tests given
   (During the present evaluation as well as any previous evaluations)
4. Relevant history
   (Specific to the questions being asked in the present evaluation)
5. Testing behavior
   a. Physical description, attire, anything unusual about gait
   b. Manual skills

c. Relevant verbalizations made prior, during, and post evaluations
d. Inferred attitudes toward the evaluation in general, specific sections of the evaluation, the examiner.

6. Test results and interpretation
   a. Intellectual functioning: how reliable and valid, how it has been affected by situational variables, does it typify everyday behavior
   b. Positive or strong factors (assets), weak or negative factors (liabilities).
   c. Evaluation of the socioemotional aspects of the personality and relationship to intellectual function
7. Summary
   a. Conclusions and recommendations
   b. Brief summary of overall findings
   c. What conclusions can be drawn relative to questions asked in the referral
   d. What recommendation can be made relative to the questions asked in the referral

The general overall organization of the report need seldom be of concern. If necessary, an agreed-upon format can be standardized for any particular situation. Problems arise when the organizational structure is rigid. The first concern is the amount of and what information is to be given in the report. Generally, information divulged should be enough to answer all questions raised by the referral source. If not enough data can be gathered to answer the questions raised, as occasionally occurs with an overly negativistic subject or one so threatened by the test situation that the adequacy of performance is seriously impaired, this fact should be stated. In such instances recommendations should be made of possible corrective measures necessary in order to comply with referral requests.

Having decided upon the kind and amount of information to be relayed and the broad outline to be followed, the reporter must consider the techniques to be used in the presentation. This task can be simplified if it is remembered that the WAIS, or any psychological test, for that matter, is but an instrument, albeit highly specialized and refined. The use of such an instrument is predicated on the belief that information otherwise unavailable or difficult to obtain by other means becomes readily available through the application of this tool. However, instruments provide only raw data, meaningful only to those capable of understanding the significance.

In the case of the WAIS, scaled scores are given on each of 11 subtests as well as Verbal, Performance, and Full-Scale IQs. Without interpretations these scores convey little. The problem (the assumption being that the test has been properly administered) is how to interpret and convey test results. We shall illustrate the point with the case of John Doe. John Doe, an industrial worker 20 years old, with a twelfth-grade education, recently laid off from his job, obtained a verbal score of 92, a performance score of 100, and a full-scale score of 95 on the WAIS. All scores are within the normal intellectual range and consistent with expectations regarding the intellectual functioning of the subject. The interpretation on the basis of these three scores will stress the normalcy of functioning. However, suppose the same Jack Doe had obtained the identical full-scale score of 95, but with verbal and performance scores of 111 and 74, respectively. The clinician will immediately note this as an abnormal pattern, since by virtue of his clinical expertise he knows that a difference of such magnitude between Verbal and Performance IQ does not ordinarily occur under normal circumstances and that, when such is the case, studies have indicated probable diagnostic significance.

But no clinician can merely report that the difference between the two scores is unusually large. He should try to explain the significance. It is at this point that he must be careful in drawing a testable hypothesis. A desire to explore alternatives is of paramount importance since, as L'Abate (1964) has noted, the stronger the examiner holds to a preconceived hypothesis, the greater the likelihood that he will be able to elicit it from test material. The observation that the stronger the preconceived hypothesis, the greater the need for contradictory data to annul it must be kept firmly in mind. The presence of preconceived ideas may be due to specious confirmation in the past, a paucity of alternatives, the fact that it superficially fits into a pattern which allows the examiner to deal with familiar material. Examination of the case history, the reason for referral, the type of behavior encountered during testing as well as specific test results should be used in adducing viable alternative hypotheses. Fashionable trends in interpretation must yield to sober appraisal.

Let us return to our case. The 27-point difference between verbal and performance scores can be interpreted as indicative of organicity. However, before this interpretation is made, it behooves the clinician to consider other cases with this pattern and then show that organicity is the best diagnosis among the various considerations. Verbal skills higher than performance skills, per se, can also be found in schizophrenics and subjects with anxiety states. Wechsler himself (1958, p. 169) acknowledges that there is a great deal of overlap in psychometric signs for schizophrenics and organics. Obviously, in this instance, background data denoting adequate adjustment prior to referral shifts the alternatives away from a hypothesis of schizophrenia or anxiety state. Further, additional data stating that unemployment coincided with a recent head injury felt at the time of the accident to be minor greatly enhances a hypothesis of organicity. Research findings, as reviewed, for example, by Guertin et al. (1971) to the effect that recent trauma to the right hemisphere of the brain is associated with a lowering of the performance score, definitely favor the organicity hypothesis, as does test behavior marked by low frustration tolerance, deficient planning, and rigidity.

Even at this point the examiner should not conclude on a hypothesis of organicity. Following Wechsler's (1958) method of successive sieves, he should then examine for differences between subtest scores to see if they fit an organic pattern. If other tests were also administered at the time, their results should be discussed as they are relevant. If other tests were not administered, recommendations should be made as to what other tests are needed. A conclusion as pointedly far reaching as organicity should not be based on the clinical findings of only one test. Finally, it should also be recommended that psychological findings be supported or questioned by a thorough neurological examination. Obviously, in the long run, a psychological test will never diagnose a medical condition (nor should a medical examination diagnose a psychological condition), but the test may describe a state like that seen in individuals with proven organic (brain damage) difficulties.

Astute readers at this point may contend that we have overdone our illustration by considering only organicity and the relationship to intellectual skills. Perhaps this opinion will be modified by the next consideration. Lubin and Lubin (1972) in a survey of the pattern of psychological services in the United States from 1959 to 1969 point out that when psychologists are asked to provide diagnostic services, 83 percent of the referral questions can be contained under the following categories: "questions of organicity, intellectual evaluation, evaluation of personality and emotional controls, and diagnosis" (p. 64).

The portrayal of the functioning person considers not only the way he resembles others (diagnostic category), but also those skills, strengths, and weaknesses uniquely his own. Does he express himself well, or is his vocabulary limited? Is he plagued with anxiety, and does this affect his performance? How does he do on tests of visual motor perception? How do these traits combine to set him apart from another person similarly diagnosed, or with the same IQ score?

There is one important caveat. The portrayal represents the testing situation. Statements about behavior in general are inferential. However, the clinician as an expert in the use of his tests and in knowledge of the human condition to which the tools are applicable should be able to draw meaningful conclusions regarding everyday behavior. To claim, as does Bersoff (1971), that intersituational variables have differing effects on behavior and, therefore, what are needed are "psychosituational assessments" seems to be a case of reducio ad absurdum. Do not intrasituational variables exert differential effect? Why should we stop only at intersituational variables? While Bersoff argues that testing, particularly intellectual evaluations in which the examiner is eager to achieve and maintain rapport, may represent an optimal rather than an average or actual situation, clinicians can cite countless other examples where no amount of coaxing, reassurance, and the like will alleviate the fears and apprehensions generated by a testing situation.

The report is concluded with a summary statement of the data presented and the conclusions drawn. Recommendations are made relative to the problem or problem areas considered in the referral and the relative priorities of each of the recommendations. In preparing the report, do avoid such jargon as the standardization sample, standard deviation, standard error of estimate, and the like. The purpose of a report is to communicate findings, not obfuscate. Understanding is enhanced by the presentation in language and style familiar to the user.

In the following sections three reports from actual evaluations are presented. They do not by any means stand as models of the principles we have been advocating, but rather as examples of the ways in which one sets about to organize and write reports in everyday practice. Two reports have been foreshortened, since the concern here is to present relevant data drawn principally from the WAIS.

In addition to the reports, two profiles available to WAIS users are presented as additions to the protocols.

Psychological Examination—Mental Retardation

Dear Sirs: CONFIDENTIAL!

Re: James Brown, CA 17-11
BD 7/17/5—

Here is a summary of the psychological examination of young James Brown, seen July 1, 197— at my office to check on his eligibility for aid for the totally disabled. Jim has always been enrolled in special classes at school. He has a history of grand mal epileptic seizures, which further limit his educational and vocational progress. After the examination it was possible to obtain previous test data, which is included for comparison:

CA 10—8 WISC 58/61/56; CA 13—3 WISC 53/65/55; CA 17—2 WAIS 64/75/67

A thin, boyish looking youngster, Jim entered the office readily, and appeared at ease. At difficult items he shrugged and tossed off a flat "Who knows?" His attention wandered to objects on the desk ("What you got this for?"), but he returned to the questions as directed.

Intellectually, Jim is functioning at the retarded level, with performance skills surpassing the verbal (WAIS VIQ 63; PIQ 78; FIQ 68). In the latter area he is penalized by unreflective responses and instant associations without real understanding. For example, asked why we should keep away from bad company he replied "Stinks! 'Cause it stinks! (Q)— ". He defined a thermometer as "temperature" and could not expand further. In contrast, he could assemble items readily at the average level, and he showed some ability on all performance tasks.

The opportunity to compare Jim's responses over a 7-year period provides an indication of the reliability of the present IQs. Results for the two WAIS administrations are remarkably similar. However, there is a ten-point change over the WISC scores, an increase that is an overestimate of ability typically seen in examining retarded individuals.

In summary, Jim is functioning at the retarded level (WAIS IQ 68, corrected to 58 for overestimation). He is capable of mastering certain work tasks, such as those available in a sheltered workshop setting. However, this young man will require lifelong support and supervision.

Case Report Protocol

James Brown

Birth Date: 7/17/5— Age: 17 Sex: M Marital Status: S Nationality: U.S.
Color: white Tested by: Place of Examination: office Date: 7/1/7—

Occupation: student Education: special classes for 12 years

WAIS

Information

(1) 1. red—white, blue
(1) 2. round
(0) 3. —Q—
(0) 4. temperature! Q d.k. Q
(0) 5. —tire—Q d.k.—junk pile
(0) 6. —nope. Q Johnson. Q First was Washington, sixteenth was Lincoln. Q—
(0) 7. Who's he?

Sum 2

Comprehension

(2) 1. They're dirty.
(2) 2. to go

(2) 3. —Q d.k. Q Mail it.
(0) 4. Stinks! Cause it stinks! Q
(1) 5. —Call Fire Department.
(0) 6. It's the law.
(0) 7. Huh? Q Unuh!
(0) 8. Don't know that one either.
(0) 9. Mark 'em. Q the trees. Q d.k. Q—

Sum 7

Arithmetic

(1) 1. +
(1) 2. +

(1) 3. + (counts laboriously)
(0) 4. one penny
(0) 5. —d.k. Q
(0) 6. —d.k. Q
(0) 7. —no Q

Sum 3

Similarities
inattentive, looking around

(2) 1. to eat, fruit
(0) 2. Whatcha got this for? (desk object) Q d.k. Q—Is that a painting?
(0) 3. axe, chop, saw, cut. Q not (alike)
(0) 4. Don't know. Did you write my name down? Q Lion roars and dog barks. Q
(0) 5. North has north; west has west. Q

Sum 2

Digit Span

Forward 3+
Backward 2+
Sum 5

Vocabulary

(2) 1. sleep on
(2) 2. sail on
(2) 3. money

(1) 4. snow. Q no
(2) 5. fix
(1) 6. —food. Q eating
(0) 7. —Q—no
(1) 8. cut
(0) 9. Who knows? Q no
(0) 10. nope. Q
(0) 11. d.k. Q
(0) 12. (shrugs) Q no
(0) 13. who knows? Q

Sum 11

Digit Symbol

Sum 31 (skips second line, has to be told to return to it)

Picture Completion

(1) 1. +
(1) 2. teeth! Q +
(1) 3. +
(0) 4. hinges
(1) 5. +
(1) 6. (points +)
(1) 7. +
(0) 8. bow
(0) 9. man
(0) 10. plugs
(0) 11. pole
(0) 12. steps. Q feet steps (point to man)
(0) 13. colors of U.S.
(1) 14. smoke stacks
(1) 15. foot
(0) 16. make-up
(0) 17. sweater
(0) 18. overcoat
(0) 19. man
(0) 20. animals
(0) 21. d.k. Q

Sum 8

Block Design

(2) 1. (1) no concept (2) 10" +
(4) 2. 20" +
(4) 3. 10" +
(4) 4. 13" +
(4) 5. 15" +
(0) 6. 60" – Sgt! Can't get it.
(0) 7. 90" – (solves with only one corner error)
(0) 8. 50" –

Sum 18

Picture Arrangement

(4) 1. 10" +
(4) 2. 8" +
(4) 3. 15" +
(0) 4. 35" – atocim (no change, reversed)
(0) 5. 40" – (reverses presentation)
(0) 6. 45" – jneta
(0) 7. 50" – (shuffles only)
(0) 8. 35" – (shuffles aimlessly)

Sum 12

Object Assembly

(5) M. 30" "easy!" +
(9) P 67" +
(7) H 60" +
(8) E 58" +

Sum 29

Psychological Report—Mental Deterioration

Name: Mrs. Mary Smith
Date of Birth: 5/11/1—
Age: 56 years
Education: 12 years

Occupation: retired, shop manager

Date of Examination: 2/6/7—; 2/13/7—
Examiner:
Place of Examination: (office)
Tests Administered: WAIS, Rorschach, Bender, MMPI, DAP
Previous testing: none

Reason for referral:
Mrs. Smith was referred by her husband, John Smith, for psychological evaluation following a progressive and insidious decline in memory over a 2-year period. She had held a responsible job as manager of a chain of shops until 2 years ago, when she retired. At that time she was only a little "forgetful," but her condition has worsened steadily until at the present time she cannot handle simple household chores (forgetting, for example, how to turn off the stove, or removing the silverware immediately after setting the table). Even the notes she makes for herself to jog her memory she later finds incomprehensible. The problem is to assess the degree of mental deterioration, to differentiate between actual loss and (malingering, hysterical?) exaggeration, and to make recommendations as to remediation.

Description:
This pretty, white-haired, well-groomed woman struggled to respond to the examination. She was poignantly aware of her limitations ("It makes me so mad!") and told of her former good memory. Questions had to be repeated frequently, and at one point she responded to an earlier question instead of the one asked. An occasional "clang" association intruded (assemble: "a musical cymbal"). On certain tasks, she perseverated the same response without awareness (i.e., Digit Symbol).

Test results:[1]
Intellectually, Mrs. Smith is functioning at the low average level on verbal tasks but is held to the borderline level on performance tasks (WAIS Verbal IQ 90, Performance IQ 70). The difference between the two areas of functioning is larger than would be expected by chance alone, and in itself suggests deterioration. However, an examination of the actual responses and intratest scatter adds a great deal to the picture. On the test of general information, for example, she reveals a scattering of failures even at the easiest levels, a loss of "overlearned" material (president of the United States, weeks in a year) of

[1] This report focuses on the WAIS, although the other tests noted above were part of the overall report.

WAIS TEST PROFILE

WECHSLER ADULT INTELLIGENCE SCALE

NAME Mary Smith — DATE 2/6/7–

ADDRESS – — AGE 56 — SEX F

BIRTH DATE 5/11/1–

SCHOOL OR OCCUPATION retired — GRADE OR EDUCATION H. S.

REASON FOR TESTING Memory loss

SCALED SCORES FROM AGE GROUP TABLES – Page 101-110 WAIS MANUAL*

Circle Appropriate Scaled Score

VERBAL

	0	1	2	3	4	5	6	7	8	9	10	11	12	13	14	15	16	17	18	19
INFORMATION General Knowledge – Long Term Memory from Experience – Education	0	1	2	3	4	5	6	7	8	9	10	11	12	13	14	15	16	17	18	19
COMPREHENSION Practical Knowledge and Social Judgment – Reasoning – Logical Solutions	0	1	2	3	4	5	6	7	8	9	10	11	12	13	14	15	16	17	18	19
ARITHMETIC Concentration, Enumerating – Arithmetic Reasoning – Sequencing	0	1	2	3	4	5	6	7	8	9	10	11	12	13	14	15	16	17	18	19
SIMILARITIES Relationship & Abstract Thinking – Association of Abstract Ideas	0	1	2	3	4	5	6	7	8	9	10	11	12	13	14	15	16	17	18	19
DIGIT SPAN Attention, Concentration, Rote & Immediate Memory – Sequencing	0	1	2	3	4	5	6	7	8	9	10	11	12	13	14	15	16	17	18	19
VOCABULARY Word Knowledge – Verbal Fluency – Expressive Vocabulary	0	1	2	3	4	5	6	7	8	9	10	11	12	13	14	15	16	17	18	19

PERFORMANCE

	0	1	2	3	4	5	6	7	8	9	10	11	12	13	14	15	16	17	18	19
DIGIT SYMBOL Speed and Accuracy of Learning Meaningless Symbols – Immediate Visual Memory – Motor Control	0	1	2	3	4	5	6	7	8	9	10	11	12	13	14	15	16	17	18	19
PICTURE COMPLETION Visual Memory & Alertness to Details	0	1	2	3	4	5	6	7	8	9	10	11	12	13	14	15	16	17	18	19
BLOCK DESIGN Reproduce Abstract Design from Pattern – Visual Perception	0	1	2	3	4	5	6	7	8	9	10	11	12	13	14	15	16	17	18	19
PICTURE ARRANGEMENT Interpretation of Social Situation – Sequencing – Visual Alertness	0	1	2	3	4	5	6	7	8	9	10	11	12	13	14	15	16	17	18	19
OBJECT ASSEMBLY Reproduce Familiar Forms from Memory – Visual Retention	0	1	2	3	4	5	6	7	8	9	10	11	12	13	14	15	16	17	18	19

VERBAL I.Q.	≤41	52	60	68	75	84	90	100	110	116	125	132	140	148	167+
PERFORMANCE I.Q.	≤35	52	60	68 70	75	84	90	100	110	116	125	132	140	148	185+
FULL SCALE I.Q.	≤41	52	60	68	75	84	90	100	110	116	125	132	140	148	179+
PERCENTILE RANK			<1%	2%	5%	16%	25%	50%	75%	84%	95%	98%	99%+		
	RETARDED			BORDER-LINE		LOW	AVERAGE			HIGH	SUPERIOR	VERY SUPERIOR			

BACKGROUND INFORMATION & IDENTIFYING DATA

Consulting Psychologists Press

577 College Avenue, Palo Alto, California 94306

Fig. 1. Sample WAIS profile. Reproduced, with special permission, from *WAIS Test Profile*, by James Massey. Copyright 1968, Consulting Psychologist Press, Inc.

DEVIATION QUOTIENTS FOR WAIS FACTOR MEASURES

Instructions Copy age-scaled scores from reverse side or pp. 101-110 of WAIS Manual.

1. Add age scale scores required for each deviation quotient.
2. Find subject's "(a) weight" and "(b) weight," using his age in the tables at right.
3. Multiply total of age-scaled scores by (a), then add (b) to obtain deviation quotient.
4. See instruction sheet for discussion of factor scales and deviation quotients.

Subject's Age 56

Verbal Comprehension

Subtest	Score
Information	6
Comprehension	9
Similarities	9
Vocabulary	9
Total	33

Total	33
(a)	× 1.4
	46
(b)	+ 44
D.Q.	90

Age	(a)	(b)
18-19	1.4	44
25-34	1.4	44
45-54	1.4	44
60-64	1.4	44
65-69	1.5	40
70-74	1.5	40
75	1.5	40

Memory & Freedom from Distractibility

Subtest	Score
Arithmetic	8
Digit Span	9
Total	17

Total	17
(a)	× 2.8
	48
(b)	+ 44
D.Q.	92

Age	(a)	(b)
18-19	2.9	42
25-34	2.9	42
45-54	2.8	44
60-64	2.9	42
65-69	2.9	42
70-74	2.8	44
75	2.7	46

Perceptual Organization

Subtest	Score
Block Design	0
Object Assembly	7
Total	7

Total	7
(a)	× 2.8
	19.6
(b)	+ 45
D.Q.	65

Age	(a)	(b)
18-19	2.7	46
25-34	2.8	44
45-54	2.8	44
60-64	2.7	46
65-69	2.7	46
70-74	2.8	44
75	2.7	46

EXAMINER

Fig. 1. Sample WAIS profile. Reproduced, with special permission, from *WAIS Test Profile*, by James Massey. Copyright 1968, Consulting Psychologist Press, Inc.

which she is poignantly aware ("I used to have such a memory! It takes the incentative (sic) out of you."). Not only did she fail easy questions, but at times she would forget the question before she could answer. Repeatedly her responses combined high level answers with failures reflecting memory loss or slowed mentation (she could repeat six digits forward and only three backward, and answered three arithmetic questions correctly but over the time limit).

On the performance tasks Mrs. Smith revealed confusion and impotence, particularly impairing her ability to adapt to new situations. On the Block Design, for example, she copied the first red and white design with all-white blocks. On item #2, she attempted to place the blocks on top of the small picture of the design, then perseveratively returned to the all-white construction.[2]

In summary, Mrs. Smith is performing intellectually at a level that confirms the seriousness and pervasiveness of the memory loss reported by her husband and herself. The test battery confirms the wide spread effect of the deterioration, which has invaded almost every area of thinking. This rules out any suspicion of her difficulties representing malingering or hysteria.

At this point, Mrs. Smith must be considered to have a serious medical problem, and only following a thorough neurological examination should further planning be considered.

Follow up:

An EEG indicated mild diffuse slowing. Her behavior worsened, if anything, following initial medication. The neurological examination utilized brain scan and skull x-rays to differentiate between frontal lobe brain tumor and cerebral atrophy. The latter proved to be the final diagnosis, and plans for home care were made.

Case Report Protocol

Mrs. Mary Smith BD 5/11/1–:
CA 56 years
Occupation: shop manager until 2 years ago
Referral Problem: Progressive memory loss

Date of Testing: 2/6/7–
Education: 12

WAIS

Information

(1) 1. +
(1) 2. +
(1) 3. 12
(1) 4. temperature

(1) 5. tree
(0) 6. Eisenhower, Johnson, an ah–makes me so mad–Kennedy. Q–Used to have such a memory. Takes the incentative (sic) out of you.
(1) 7. wrote poems

[2] Other test data discussed in the full report omitted.

(0) 8. 4 x 12 = 48–49?
(1) 9. south
(0) 10. In ah, ah, M', ah near Mexico, isn't it?
(0) 11. say 5'2".
(0) 12. –Q–
(0) 13. dye? coloring?
(0) 14. 22nd of–here I go!

(from this item on, testing the limits, not scorable)

(1) 15. Shakespeare?
(0) 16. in Rome. What is the Vatican? Church, something to do with Church.
(0) 17. guess 10,000
(0) 18. Egyptians–what is that last thing we talked about? In the old country.
(0) 19. heat. Q rises. Q Mother baked bread. Levening. Q rises. Q the yeast. Q with heat. Q–
(0) 20. Have to laugh. 10,000
(0) 21. Don't know. Q 13
(1) 22. along with Bible, beginning of life
(0) 23. fahrenheit–Q–
(0) 24. –Don't know.
(0) 25. –Lost me.
(0) 26. –no
(0) 27. –no
(0) 28.
(0) 29.

Sum 7

Comprehension

(4) 1. & 2. (assumed credit)
(2) 3. put in mail box.
(1) 4. Well, in first place it leads to trouble–, – Q–
(1) 5. Probably run. Q Turn in an alarm.
(2) 6. Have to have a government, feed the needy. Q feed to our government
(1) 7. Do it right now.
(1) 8. Protects them–read it again? Q keep. Let young kids work. I don't know how, want to tell you.
(1) 9. sunshine. Q Shows on side of trees. Q direction Q south, north Q Sunshine, tell direction. Q Good question. Q Don't know.
(1) 10. Because he doesn't hear anything. Q Must, huh? Q Hearing is one thing if can't hear, can see–Q Maybe *because* deaf.
(0) 11. umm. Q Go back over last little bit? Q more money in the city. Q expenses. Q of living. Q Don't know.
(1) 12. (shakes head) Don't know. (laughs) A lot doesn't have.–Keep track of everything and everybody.
(0) 13. water flows–, –Q Q Q–
(0) 14. never heard. Q no

Sum 15

Arithmetic

(3) 3.
(1) 4. (15") (repeated)
(1) 5. (1")
(1) 6. (1")
(1) 7. (1")
(0) 8. (repeated)—20? 24? 3 into 24—not right? (laugh) 3 into 24, 3 into 27 (overtime)
(0) 9. (repeated) 14—(overtime)
(0) 10. (repeated) 14—(overtime)
(0) 11. Lost!

Sum 7

Similarities

(1) 1. have to be peeled. Q Q
(2) 2. clothing
(2) 3. building. Q tools
(1) 4. four legs (laughs)
(0) 5. well one is—Q no, not same Q Is it! Are they? (laugh) Q South? I don't know.
(1) 6. in your—head—both may not take it as that type.
(0) 7. go together. Q some—evaporate
(2) 8. One stands, one sits. Q furniture
(0) 9. they. Hen had to lay an egg to get a chicken.
(0) 10. Oh, gosh, don't have *any* idea.
(0) 11. Drink it or rub on (laughs). Q Q Preservative?
(0) 12. —, —Praise and punishment?
(0) 13. —fly and tree—huh—make liquor. Q Oh no, must have missed something. (*given to test limits*)

Sum 9

Digit Span

Forward
(3) +
(4) +
(5) –; +
(6) +
(7) –; –

Backward
(2) (forward) Q don't know first –; +
(3) –; +
(4) –; –

Sum 9

Vocabulary

(2) 1. to lie on
(2) 2. Know what I want to say. Q big boat
(2) 3. Penny? Q money

(1) 4. cold. Q cold, snow. Q Q
(0) 5. —work Q Q
(1) 6. meal. Q let's see. Q Coffee, stuff like that there? Q bacon and eggs
(1) 7. material
(1) 8. cut. Q Q to cut. Q scissors
(2) 9. a musical something symbol (misheard) Q (*given word list*) together Q gather
(2) 10. hide
(1) 11. large
(1) 12. fast
(1) 13. Don't know how to explain. Q Q—to be sentence? Q Write a sentence. Q Could be a sentence in a line of, ah, writing. Q Also intermediate sentence to prison
(0) 14. Regulate your time. Q Q Q (laughs)
(2) 15. to start
(0) 16. slow
(2) 17. a cavelike affair
(0) 18. —Q Q
(1) 19. at home
(2) 20. could be eating
(1) 21. to be not there any more
(2) 22. ah, in the way
(1) 23. sadness
(1) 24. a church
(0) 25. had none
(2) 26. not want to do it
(1) 27. very sad situation
(0) 28. determined
(2) 29. quiet
(0) 30. outside of building (thought "facade"?)
(0) 31. love and—love
(2) 32. anything you can touch
(0) 33. round
(0) 34. no
(0) 35. no
(0) 36. no
(0) 37. no

Sum 36

Digit Symbol

2 correct

Picture Completion

(1) 1. +
(1) 2. pig Q +
(1) 3. lady Q +
(0) 4. no driver Q head lights –
(1) 5. +
(0) 6. —nothing –
(1) 7. +
(0) 8. bow –

(0) 9. rower –
(0) 10. no bulb –
(0) 11. –flag pole –
(0) 12. One leg? –
(0) 13. – –
(0) 14. nobody –
(0) 15. On crab? Head? –
(0) 16. chair –
(0) 17. –ear –
(0) 18. –moon? –

Sum 5

Block Design

(0) 1. (1) (overtime; all whites)
(0) (2) (overtime; no concept)

(0) 2. (1) (overtime; places on top of card; uses all white blocks.)
(0) (2) (uses all white blocks)

Sum 0

Picture Arrangement

(0) 1. (1) (no concept)
(2) (2) "this is—no eggs first!"
(4) 2. +
(4) 3. +
(0) 4. "simple, crazy!" MIC
(unchanged) OAT
(0) 5. OESNP 90"
(0) 6. ATJNE (65")
(0) 7. (stares at pictures, fails to rearrange. Q Q)
(0) 8. (same)

Sum 10

Object Assembly

(5) M 47"
(8) P 2' (ear reversed)
(1) H 3' (poor T&E. Fits fingers end on end, thumb, places wrist twice reversed, places vertically!)
(0) E 3' (no concept)

Sum 14

Psychological Report—Vocational Rehabilitation

Name: John Doe Sex: M Age: 28 Born: 6/11/4— Marital Status: S Occupation: unemployed (formerly general laborer) Education: 13 years Place of Testing: clinic Date: 6/21/7— Examiner:

Reason for referral:

Mr. Doe has applied for vocational rehabilitation, specifically for financial aid in order to pursue a training program in auto repair. His listed disability is "mental illness" and he has been hospitalized on a number of occasions in the last 7 years. A diagnosis of paranoid schizophrenia was once considered.

The rehabilitation counselor needs an estimate of the tolerance and capacity for stress, general functional intelligence, aptitude, and manual dexterity.

Procedures used:

WAIS, Rorschach, Draw-a-Person, Purdue Pegboard, Bennett Mechanical Comprehension (AA)

Previous testing:

GATB

Observations:

A sallow-faced, lanky man, neatly dressed in work clothes, Mr. Doe arrived punctually and explained his need for training: "This way if I ever get sick again, I can always have something I can go back to—hopefully." He questioned the purpose of testing, wondering whether he could be rehospitalized as a result. "This could throw me back in the hospital, as far as I know." Reassured that the examination was an assessment of his ability to pursue a training program, he relaxed and cooperated throughout the testing period.

During the evaluation, Mr. Doe noted a similarity between himself and the examiner: "The way you write is the way I write—very stingy with the pencil." Spontaneous comments describing difficulties or inadequacies were expressed throughout: "I can't draw, Sir. I don't know how to make anything beautiful." "I draw just like a child." "Not too well coordinated, my brains and my hand." "I think I really goofed up this one." Despite such expressions of discomfort, he continued working on all assigned tasks.

Results:

Intellectually, the general functional level is normal. (WAIS Full-Scale, Verbal, and Performance IQs are respectively 97, 97, and 97.) However, examination of the individual verbal subtest responses suggest that everyday behavior is much more erratic and unpredictable than would be expected from the obtained general functioning level. At times he appears learned and sophisticated despite average formal education, at other times inordinately naive and ignorant. Let us examine his fund of general information. He correctly identified the author of the *Iliad* as Homer and the Koran as the bible of the Moslems, but he was unable to give the average height of the American woman or the date of Washington's birthday. The same phenomenon occurs on associative reasoning tasks. The fact that a fly and a tree are both living things is readily perceived, but note his inability to generalize on the similarity between a dog and a lion: "They both use their teeth, well, they eat meat. They both eat bones."

An indication of the effectiveness of everyday behavior as inferred from responses on the Comprehension subtest is illustrated in the following examples. Given a hypothetical situation of being lost in the forest in the daytime, he was then asked to indicate a way out:

> "Well, if the sun rises in the east, I, either follow the moon; no, how could I do that? I look at the moon or if I can find the north side, if I can see it, and then I can determine north and west from that point."

Asked to explain "Shallow brooks are noisy" he concluded:

> "Well it can hurt. (Q) When you throw a rock in, into it you can hear it hit. Shallow emotions, shallow person easily hurt or easily sensitive by what goes round about him."

A deterioration of an otherwise admirable compulsive attention to detail is evident. (The attached protocol gives several other examples of breakdown.)

In contrast, on those tasks requiring motor skills, Mr. Doe does not demonstrate the type of thinking disorder that characterizes his verbalization. This is potentially an area of strength. Since his interest is in auto repair, the fact that he perceives spatial relationships conventionally and at a level commensurate with proposed training requirements is a factor in favor of his qualifying for vocational training.

However, the real issue is whether this man is able to adjust adequately in society, rather than in isolation on a specific task. For this reason personality characteristics were further evaluated on other tasks.[1]

In summary, this presently unemployed laborer with a history of psychiatric breakdown has applied for vocational rehabilitation. The general intelligence level, aptitude, and manual dexterity are commensurate with the type of training desired. However, when one looks at the many evidences of disorganized thinking under stress and limited stress tolerance (details in omitted parts of the report), the conclusion is that he would be unable to complete a training program at this time. Mr. Doe is not ill enough to be hospitalized, but outpatient treatment and evaluation based on prògress are recommended. Should the evaluation then indicate that his overall status is less tenuous, he should certainly be reconsidered for job training.

Case Report Protocol

Mr. John Doe Born: 6/11/4–; CA 28 years Date of Testing: 6/21/7–
Occupation: unemployed; previous psychiatric hospitalizations
Education: 13 Referral Problem: estimate of capacity to tolerate stress and general functional level

WAIS

Information

(4) 1–4 (assumed creditable)

(1) 5. A plant in Indonesia, Indochina, or in South America, it's a plant or tree.
(1) 6. Grant (Q since 1900), T. Roosevelt, D. Roosevelt, Kennedy, Eisenhower, Johnson
(1) 7. writer
(1) 8. 52
(1) 9. south
(1) 10. South America

[1] For the purposes of this volume, only the WAIS results are reported.

(0) 11. 5'7"
(1) 12. Capital income about 200. (Q capital) Rome
(0) 13. Ah, well, material is thicker; material tends to be thicker; less air can transfer through.
(0) 14. February—close as I can get.
(1) 15. Shakespeare
(1) 16. Is that the physical center of Roman Catholicism where the pope lives? (some stuttering and eye blinking)
(1) 17. about 3,000 miles
(1) 18. Ah, in, ah, ah, north, northeast Africa.
(0) 19. Ah, I don't know.
(1) 20. 170 million

(0) 21. The beginning of ah, ah, the universe or the beginning of individuals, the earth, more specific, and life after that. (Q explain more) Well, you know, the beginning of earth, the universe, the moon and stars, all that is; it explains it in a poetical means, how life started.
(0) 23. I don't know.
(1) 24. Homer
(0) 25. veins (S looks puzzled, and continues), is smaller article of vesicle
(1) 26. similar to our Bible for Moslems, North African people
(0) 27. I don't know.
(0) 28. I don't know.
(0) 29. I don't know.

Sum 18

(S made the following observation during this part of the testing: "The way you write is the way I write, very stingy with the pencil.")

Comprehension

(4) 1. & 2. (assumed creditable)
(2) 3. Put it in the mail box.
(2) 4. Well, they tend to influence one's behavior, just to social, you might do something unsocial society-wise.
(2) 5. (smiles) Run to the manager, that's what I should do. (smiles) No, I say "fire" if it's really there. Q Tell the manager.
(1) 6. To support, first for the defense of the country and second to have service; the nation as a whole to have a social standard, it provides services for the people.
(1) 7. It seems to me it just means iron could be bent at that point. (nervous laugh) That a saying? I don't know what it means.
(0) 8. For one thing, in the interest of the child and, ah, that's about it. Q
(0) 9. Well, if the sun rises in the east, I either follow the moon; no, how could I do that? I look at the moon or if I can find the north side, if I can see it, and then I can determine north and west from that point.
(2) 10. Oh, because they are unable to hear so they can't copy the person they're hearing from. Have no means to imitate.

RHODES WAIS SCATTER PROFILE

by Fen Rhodes, Ph. D.

NAME John Doe AGE 28 DATE TESTED 6/21/7- EXAMINER ——

INSTRUCTIONS:

1. Record subtest scores in the "Scaled Score" column. Scaled scores adjusted for the subject's age must be used for accurate profile results. Age-adjusted scaled scores are tabled in the WAIS manual, pp. 99-110. **Do not copy the scaled scores from the test record form.**

2. Compute IQs following normal WAIS procedure. Convert Full Scale JQ into an equivalent scaled score using the table below. Record this value in the blank labeled "Converted FSIQ."

3. Subtract converted IQ from each subtest score and record these differences (+ or –) in the second column.

4. Plot each difference with an **X** on the "Profile of Deviations." A score outside the shaded area of the profile represents a significant difference ($p < .05$) from over-all test performance. Deviations within the shaded area must be attributed to error of measurement. Scatter within the Verbal and Performance Scales may be evaluated separately by using the profiles provided on the reverse side. The same conversion table employed for Full Scale IQs should be used to convert Verbal and Performance IQs.

FULL SCALE SCATTER

SUBTEST	SCALED SCORE	DIFF. FROM CONV. FSIQ	PROFILE OF DEVIATIONS FROM FULL SCALE IQ
Information	11	+2	X at +2
Comprehension	10	+1	X at +1
Arithmetic	9	0	X at 0
Similarities	10	+1	X at +1
Digit Span	6	−3	X at −3
Vocabulary	11	+2	X at +2
Digit Symbol	7	−2	X at −2
Picture Completion	9	0	
Block Design	11	+2	X at +2
Picture Arrangement	11	+2	X at +2
Object Assembly	9	0	

Full Scale IQ 97

Converted FSIQ 9

-9 -8 -7 -6 -5 -4 -3 -2 -1 0 1 2 3 4 5 6 7 8 9

Points Above or Below Converted Full Scale IQ

CONVERSION TABLE

WAIS IQ	Scaled Score
62 down	2
63-67	3
68-72	4
73-77	5
78-82	6
83-87	7
88-92	8
93-97	9
98-102	10
103-107	11
108-112	12
113-117	13
118-122	14
123-127	15
128-132	16
133-137	17
138 up	18

Note: Any subtest difference large enough to fall outside the shaded area of the profile should be regarded as statistically significant at the .05 level. This means that it is more than 95 percent certain that a true performance difference of some size greater than zero does in fact exist. It does *not* mean that the true difference is probably equal in magnitude to the difference plotted on the profile. The true deviation may be larger or smaller than the deviation plotted from testing, but it is more likely (especially with extreme deviations) that the true value is smaller rather than larger.

Fig. 2. Rhodes WAIS Scatter Profile.

VERBAL SCALE SCATTER

SUBTEST	SCALED SCORE	DIFF. FROM CONV. VIQ	-9	-8	-7	-6	-5	-4	-3	-2	-1	0	1	2	3	4	5	6	7	8	9
			PROFILE OF DEVIATIONS FROM VERBAL IQ																		
Information	11	+2												X							
Comprehension	10	+1											X								
Arithmetic	9	0																			
Similarities	10	+1											X								
Digit Span	6	-3							X												
Vocabulary	11	+2												X							

Verbal IQ 97

Converted VIQ 9

Points Above or Below Converted Verbal IQ

PERFORMANCE SCALE SCATTER

SUBTEST	SCALED SCORE	DIFF. FROM CONV. PIQ	-9	-8	-7	-6	-5	-4	-3	-2	-1	0	1	2	3	4	5	6	7	8	9
			PROFILE OF DEVIATIONS FROM PERFORMANCE IQ																		
Digit Symbol	7	-2								X											
Picture Completion	9	0																			
Block Design	11	+2												X							
Picture Arrangement	11	+2												X							
Object Assembly	9	0																			

Performance IQ 97

Converted PIQ 9

Points Above or Below Converted Performance IQ

SUBTEST PERCENTILE EQUIVALENTS

Scaled Score	%ile Rank
17 up	99
16	98
15	95
14	91
13	84
12	75
11	63
10	50
9	37
8	24
7	16
6	9
5	5
4	2
3 down	1

IQ PERCENTILE EQUIVALENTS

WAIS IQ	%ile Rank	WAIS IQ	%ile Rank	WAIS IQ	%ile Rank
133 up	99	111	77	89	23
132	98	110	75	88	21
131	98	109	73	87	19
130	98	108	70	86	17
129	97	107	68	85	16
128	97	106	66	84	14
127	96	105	63	83	13
126	96	104	60	82	12
125	95	103	58	81	10
124	95	102	55	80	9
123	94	101	53	79	8
122	93	100	50	78	7
121	92	99	47	77	6
120	91	98	45	76	5
119	90	97	42	75	5
118	88	96	40	74	4
117	87	95	37	73	4
116	86	94	34	72	3
115	84	93	32	71	3
114	83	92	30	70	2
113	81	91	27	69	2
112	79	90	25	68	2
				67 down	1

Fig. 2. Rhodes WAIS Scatter Profile.

(2) 11. Well, city because there is a population density and because it's the amount of supply.

(1) 12. Ah. Well, so that, that, ahm to uphold our morality so that you won't be married to more than one woman at a time, also for health reasons too.

(0) 13. Well, it can hurt. (Q) When you throw a rock in, into it you can hear it hit. Shallow emotions, shallow person easily hurt or easily sensitive by what goes round about him.

(1) 14. I been told this by a psychologist before, and it means that if a man hit me once, it doesn't mean that every man I see will hit me all the time.

Sum 18

Arithmetic

(2) 1. & 2. (assumed creditable)
(1) 3. R (4")
(1) 4. R (1")
(1) 5. R (3")
(1) 6. R (14")
(1) 7. R (2")
(1) 8. R (2")
(0) 9. W (8") (Q repeated) (S continues 2 x 36 but gives correct answer anyway)
(0) 10. W (21")
(0) 11. W (18")
(2) 12. R (9")
(0) 13. (30") I don't know. Q no
(0) 14. (35") I don't know. Q no

Sum 10

Similarities

(2) 1. Both fruit.
(1) 2. They cover people, keep them warm.
(1) 3. They cut wood, they cut.
(0) 4. They both use their teeth. (Q explain more) Well they eat meat; they both eat bones.
(0) 5. Ah, they both, they go from center, from a center point. It means leaving the direction you're in. You're moving from one direction to another, from one point to another distance, or they're both directions.
(2) 6. Both ah, ah. They're two of our five senses.
(1) 7. They're both elements.
(2) 8. Both f' furniture.
(2) 9. Well, they both, beginning of life or the first step in the beginning of life into a life form.
(2) 10. Well, they both have an esthetic value; both have an esthetic value.
(0) 11. They're not (smiles). Q (no elaboration)
(0) 12. Ah praise and punishment; Well, they're not alike, but they are alike in that they're both human behavior.
(2) 13. A fly and a tree? Well, they're both alive; well, even a tree is alive, they're both alive.

Sum 15

Digit Span

Forward
3 +
4 – ; –
5 + (testing limits)
6 – ; –
Backward
3 +
4 +
5 – ; +
6 – ; –

Sum 8

Vocabulary

(6) 1. – 3. (assumed creditable)
(2) 4. It means ah, ah. . . it means it's cold, it's a season.
(2) 5. Put something, make something work, work again as it did before it was broken.
(2) 6. It's eating in the morning.
(2) 7. cloth
(1) 8. What does it mean? Slice of meat, slice of bread, it could be a piece of something, part of something or else food.
(2) 9. Put something together.
(2) 10. Conceal means to hide something
(2) 11. something very large
(2) 12. to, ah, to hurry up.
(1) 13. It's part of our–part of a paragraph, part of a structure in a paragraph, or a statement, one complete statement.
(2) 14. to control
(2) 15. to begin
(2) 16. to think with
(0) 17. I don't know. Q
(2) 18. to, ah, appoint responsibility as a master or authority.
(0) 19. something within, within, ah, example, a home, domestic within.
(2) 20. to eat or to use.
(2) 21. to ah, stop.
(2) 22. to get in the way of
(1) 23. sad
(1) 24. ah, recluse, a place of recluse
(2) 25. No equal.
(2) 26. hesitant
(2) 27. catastrophy
(1) 28. virtue. (Q explain more) Doesn't stop easily. (S looks about the room) Like see person continues his goal with little interruption, little hesitancy.
(2) 29. peaceful
(0) 30. ah, ornament
(0) 31. feelings. (Q explain more) Feeling one has for another.
(2) 32. Something you can touch. (S is scratching left elbow)

(0) 33. the circle, outer circle. (Q explain more) circle.
(0) 34. I'd be guessing. Q
(0) 35. I don't know. Q
(0) 36. an emotion—outrage
(0) 37. I don't know.
(1) 38. to copy. (Q explain more) To copy without authorization.
(0) 39. to interfere.
(0) 40. something very small, but not too important.

Sum 52

Digit Symbol

39 correct—no errors

Picture Completion

(9) 1.—9. +
(0) 10. Don't know. Q
(0) 11. Hm, one thicker than other.
(0) 12. (20," overtime) Man's foot not showing.
(0) 13. Alaska and Hawaii
(0) 14. Don't know. Q
(3) 15. —17. +
(0) 18. Hand not showing.
(0) 19. rider
(0) 20.—21. nothing

Sum 12

Block Design

(4) 1. +
(2) 2. – ; +
(4) 3. + (initially at a loss, suddenly gets right: "Oh gee!")
(25) 4.—9. + with time bonus on 8.
(0) 10. – —(can't seem to place blocks in the right justapositions)

Sum 35

Picture Arrangement

(4) 1. wxy 3"
(4) 2. pat 4"
(4) 3. abcd 5"
(4) 4. atomic 21"
(4) 5. opens 35"
(2) 6. jnaet 30"
(4) 7. efghij 76"
(0) 8. saelum 99"

Sum 26

Object Assembly

(6) 1. (17") +
(9) 2. (55") + (some difficulty placing ear pieces)
(7) 3. (90") + (recognized object to be constructed after 30")
(8) 4. (117") + (almost immediately recognized object to be constructed, but encountered difficulty making placements initially)

Sum 30

REFERENCES

Affleck, D. C., & Strider, F. D. Constribution of psychological reports to patient management. *Journal of Consulting and Clinical Psychology*, 1971, **37**, 177–179.

Bersoff, D. "Current functioning" myth: an overlooked fallacy in psychological assessment. *Journal of Consulting and Clinical Psychology*, 1971, **37**, 391–393.

Forer, B. The fallacy of personal validation: a classroom demonstration of gullibility. *Journal of Abnormal and Social Psychology*, 1949, **44**, 118–123.

Grayson, H. M., & Tolman, R. S. A semantic study of concepts of clinical psychologists and psychiatrists. *Journal of Abnormal and Social Psychology*, 1950, **15**, 215–231.

Guertin, W. H., Ladd, C. E., Frank, C. H., Rabin, A. I., & Hiester, D. Research with the WAIS: 1965–1970. *Psychological Record*, 1971, **21**, 289–339.

Hartlage, L. C., Freeman, W., Horine, L., & Walton, C. Decisional utility of psychological reports. *Journal of Clinical Psychology*, 1968, **24**, 481–483.

Hartlage, L. C., & Merck, K. H. Increasing the relevance of psychological reports. *Journal of Clinical Psychology*, 1971, **27**, 459–460.

L'Abate, L. *Principles of clinical psychology.* New York: Grune & Stratton, 1964.

Lubin, B., & Lubin, A. W. Patterns of psychological services in the U. S.: 1959–1969. *Professional Psychology*, 1972, **3**, 63–65.

Meehl, P. E. Wanted—a good cookbook. *American Psychologist*, 1956, **11**, 263–272.

Merrens, M., & Richards, W. Acceptance of generalized versus "bona fide" personality interpretations. *Psychological Reports*, 1970, **27**, 691–694.

Sundberg, N. The acceptability of "fake" versus "bona fide" personality test interpretations. *Journal of Abnormal and Social Psychology*, 1955, **50**, 145–147.

Ulrich, R., Stachnik, T., & Stainton, R. Student acceptance of generalized personality interpretations. *Psychological Reports*, 1963, **13**, 831–834.

Wechsler, D. *The measurement and appraisal of adult intelligence.* Baltimore, Williams & Witkins, 1958.

Index

4 b
5 c
6 d
7 e
8 f
9 g
0 h
1 i
8 2 j